A gift for winter fireside
reading .

With my love,

Mary xxxx

NOTES FROM THE GARDEN

EDITED BY RUTH PETRIE

guardianbooks

Published by Guardian Books 2009

2 4 6 8 10 9 7 5 3 1

Copyright © Guardian News and Media Ltd 2009

Every effort has been made to contact copyright holders.
The publishers will be pleased to make good any omissions or rectify
any mistakes brought to their attention at the earliest opportunity.

First published in Great Britain in 2009 by
Guardian Books
Kings Place, 90 York Way
London N1 9GU

www.guardianbooks.co.uk

A CIP catalogue record for this book
is available from the British Library

ISBN 978-0-85265-127-8

Typeset by seagulls.net

Printed and bound in Great Britain by Clays Ltd, St Ives PLC

Contents

Introduction

Among the *Manchester Guardian*'s earliest archived mentions of 'the pleasures of gardening' is a worthily earnest article of August 1837, reprinted from *Loudon's Suburban Gardener*: 'To labour for the sake of arriving at a result, and to be successful in attaining it, are, as cause and effect, attended by a certain degree of satisfaction to the mind, however rude and simple the labour may be, and however unimportant the result obtained … A man who plants a hedge, or sows a grass-plot in his garden, lays a more certain foundation for enjoyment than he who builds a wall or lays down a gravel walk …' The sober tone, the enlistment to hard work and the satisfactions gained went on for many thousands of words and typified much of the journalistic writing of those early days.

This collection is not at all a 'how-to-garden' (although the paper did provide its readers with a constant flow of advice), but rather a potted history read through the feature writing across the decades. I have played fast and loose with the parameters of 'gardening' to include any cultivation of the soil, and any activities on that soil – from rights of access to Richmond Park in the 1840s to a garden gnome with itchy feet in 2008. This selection of writings from the *Guardian*'s archives reflects significant cultural changes and demographic shifts, growing urban and suburban concerns. Witty send-ups of horticultural enthusiasms. The newspaper covered every aspect of gardening of local and national interest, either through its correspondents, or by reprinting articles from other sources: the opening of the new botanical gardens around the country, suffragette law-breaking at Kew, reviews of new gardening books and manuals, observations on the changing fashions in planting, the Great Exhibition of 1851, the opening of royal parks to the public, the first of the gardening magazines, and much comment on women gardeners – all were the stuff of column inches.

Throughout the 19th century these pieces were delivered in writing that was precise and minutely detailed, with a reverence for the new, and for the great and the good. The 'working man' continued to be addressed as a figure requiring moral guidance and morale boosting; the smoke-filled cities where city parks provided 'green lungs' and the bedding-out of plants were heatedly discussed, as were the competitions for most colourful window box.

Both wars produced a spate of writing on vegetable growing and the necessity to transform public spaces into allotments. With the 'Dig for Victory' came a more demotic voice – inclusive, relaxed, chatty even. And in the spirit of 'we're all in this together' Churchill was pictured in 1928 building his garden wall at Chartwell, hat on head and cigar between the teeth. Among the feature articles, the suburban garden was given more attention, and in the public sphere, readers were urged by the National Garden Scheme's *Yellow Book* to visit private gardens opened for a day.

The gardening columnists were either unnamed, or credited just with their initials. In 1957, the paper's 'Gardening Correspondent', identified simply as 'DS', reviewed Christopher Lloyd's *The Mixed Border*: 'Here is good writing of another kind – forthright, irreverently critical, giving reasoned advice based solely on first-hand experience. The summer foliage of bearded irises … is to Mr Lloyd "blatantly disgusting"; once again, it is a matter of taste.'

As austerity lessened, the number of allotment holders fell from a wartime high of one and a half million down to 950,000 by the late 50s – due to full employment, no food shortages and the purchase of television sets. In 1960, Dr Hessayon published the first in his series of 'Expert' books, *The House Plant Expert*. By the 1970s the nation flocked to the new garden centres for plants and barbecues. At the *Guardian*, Derek Senior became the paper's gardening editor and continued to provide his judicious, knowledgeable columns and book reviews until the mid-80s. In 1977, he announced that he was adding to his gardening fraternity: Christopher Lloyd was to write on flowers and foliage, George Seddon on indoor plants, Alan Mitchell on trees, and Michael Hyde on allotments – and this impressive group kept readers informed and entertained for years to come. Christopher Lloyd's first column was published in October 1977 and his last, printed in January 2006, the week after his death.*

In the 1980s Geoff Hamilton made TV history with his Barnsdale Gardens. From the 90s through to the millennium, the *Guardian*'s increased coverage mirrored its readers growing obsession with gardens and all things green – as well as anything made of decking/metal/rock/bamboo/other exotica. Our spending reached astronomical proportions and our seeming addiction to TV gardening make-over programmes had us couch-potatoed indoors rather than outdoors with our rakes and hoes.

In these post-millennium years, we have begun to face the stark evidence of climate change and environmental disasters. The newspaper's urgent address of these issues, taking in global as well as local perspectives, has meant that gardening concerns have widened to include a rejection of 'quick fix' garden transformations, changes in planting, the preservation of almost-lost fruits and vegetable seeds through heritage seed exchanges, supporting wild life, challenging the loss of green-belt land, going organic, growing your own. And now, as Kew celebrates its 250th anniversary year, we continue to turn to gardens, public and private, for sanctuary, rejuvenation and sheer pleasure, growing for an unknown future, but growing all the same.

A bouquet to Helen Brooks at Guardian Books for all her good work in producing this book.

* See *Cuttings: A Year in the Garden with Christopher Lloyd,* Guardian Books/ Pimlico

Prospects of Pleasure: 1830s–1899

John Claudius Loudon's *Encyclopedia of Gardening*, 1822 * Edward Budding invents the lawnmower, 1831 * The Great Exhibition, 1851 * The Royal National Rose Society established, 1876

The Manchester Zoological Gardens
June 2 1838

These gardens – of the site, nature, and disposal of which we gave so full an account in the *Guardian* of June 7 1837 as to render it needless now to repeat it – were opened to the public on Thursday last. The occasion was celebrated by a public breakfast, or cold collation, in a large marquee, 120 feet in length and 40 feet wide, erected for the purpose by Mr B Edginton, of London. But, before noticing the proceedings of the day, some description of the attractions which the gardens now present to the visitor may not be unacceptable to our readers. The gardens cover about 15 acres.

The state of the grounds, under the able direction of the garden curator, Mr John Mearns, late head gardener to the Duke of Portland, at Wellbeck (the grounds at which seat he designed and laid out), have assumed an appearance which could hardly have been anticipated for a year or two to come. The general planting was only commenced last autumn; and the plants, as everywhere else, have suffered considerably from the severe winter, and the protracted cold weather of the spring. From the liberality of a number of noblemen and gentlemen (amongst whom it would be invidious to particularise any), and the circumstance of Mr Mearns being a well-know periodical botanical writer, and much respected, he was enabled to obtain as donations for the gardens a great variety of trees, &c. far more advanced in growth than are usually obtained by purchase; so that the grounds have already, in some parts, the appearance of having been planted four or five years. We believe that the gardens already contain the largest collection of hardy shrubs and plants, to be met with in any zoological gardens in the kingdom. To this class of plants, and to that called the half-hardy, the botanical collection in the gardens must of necessity be confined, as all are to be grown in the open air. We perceive that a great number of the trees, shrubs, and plants, have already their botanical names attached; and we learn that it is the intention of Mr Mearns, when he has a little more leisure, to add to these the English or common names, so as to form a botanical dictionary and directory of the most popular kind, for visitors.

But to return to the fete of Thursday. The morning was lowering; but it cleared up, and a great number of tickets were sold previous to eleven o'clock, the hour of opening. From that time to one o'clock, the visitors continued to arrive, and there were probably at one time about 750 ladies and gentlemen in the grounds. The day continued fine (with the exception of a thunder shower in the afternoon), the sun shone, and the scene was a very lively and animating one. Groups of ladies and gentlemen promenaded the grounds, or congregated in the various buildings to observe whatever was curious or rare; while the fine band of the Royal Irish Dragoons, stationed in the refreshment saloon, and the brass band of the gardens (which consists of a number of musicians, employed in various capacities, as carpenters, keepers, &c.), played a variety of popular and favourite pieces.

Manchester Botanic Gardens
July 21 1838

Last Wednesday evening was the finest promenade evening of the season. Tempted by the clear sky and bright weather, the attendance of subscribers and other visitors was very numerous, and very general admiration was expressed at the excellent condition of the gardens, considering the severe weather of the last winter, and the continued cold, wet, and ungenial state of the atmosphere through the spring and early summer. In a walk round the gardens, we saw many proofs of the severity of the weather, especially amongst the evergreens, which were much cut up, several fine specimens of laurustinus and cistus having greatly suffered. The rhodedendrons, which it might be supposed would be less able to withstand the force and rigour of the elements, have generally proved more hardy: they have flowered with their usual profusion, but, of course, their glories are now over. We must not omit to notice, that fine ornamental yet hardy plant, the Arauearia imbricala, or Chilian pine; its lower leaves have been a good deal browned by the inclemency of the season, but it is now looking healthy, and putting forth with vigour. This pine, we are told, forms one of the most noble ornaments of the Chilian forest; the natives call it Araucanos. It was introduced into this country by Sir Joseph Banks, in 1796.

Proceeding to the conservatories we were stopped at the entrance by a sight reflecting no small disgrace on some parties, and those, we fear, rather numerous, frequenting these gardens; a fine large aloe (Agaree Americana), not one of whose leaves has escaped being covered with incisions, in the form of initials of names; and even in some cases Christian and surnames at full length have been cut through the outer membrane into the substance of the leaf. This practice was commenced some twelve months ago; but has of late prevailed to so considerable extent, that the council have found it necessary to suspend to this barbarously injured and mutilated plant a printed notice, in the following terms: 'Visitors are strictly prohibited from writing on the aloes, on pain of expulsion from the garden.' When it is recollected that no gentleman, a resident of Manchester, and not a subscriber, can obtain admission to the gardens, except perhaps two or three times a year, at the public botanical and horticultural exhibitions of the society, and that, of course, the working classes are wholly excluded, the imputations of these wanton outrages cannot attach to any but visitors from a distance, or subscribers. Notwithstanding the notice, we believe, another name, or the initials of one, were cut into a leaf so recently as Tuesday last.

Amongst the plants, in another compartment of the conservatories, containing chiefly those from the Cape and from New Holland, we noticed a fine Burchellila Carpensis, which has recently flowered; a Psoralea pamatu, also from the Cape, with its delicate lavender coloured flowers and pinnated foliage; a Semperrium arboreum or tree houseleek (from the Levant), in blossom; a Calanthe reratrifolia (from the East Indies), in flower; a singular plant named the Sarracenia purpurea, or side-saddle plant (from America): its small pitchers half filled with the bodies of flies, and with water; a Zamia horrida, (from the Cape) its foliage having a singular Glaueus-like appearance, or peach bloom; a Pholidota imbruata (from Nepal); an Epidendrum ellapticum (from Rio de Janeiro), with its long slender white roots depending from every branch, as if seeking the soil; an Epulendrum elongatum (from the West Indies), distilled honey clothing the foot of its purplish flowers; an Oncidium flexuosa (from Brazil) and various other orchidaceous plants. Amongst other fine plants in flower were the Crinum seabrum (from the Azores), with its crest of blush-pink flowers; and the plant figured in the *Botanical Register* as the Irus bicolor, but by botanists generally called the Diates bicolor, whose flowers present the striking contrast of a bright yellow and deep blue or purple, observable in the pansy, and some Irises. We had nearly omitted to notice another fine plant, in the centre conservatory, the Erythrina glauca, one of the coral trees (from the Caraccas), which, on the erection of the conservatory, was removed thither from a pot, and during the present season has grown between five and six feet, being now a fine towering plant, of between 11 and 12 feet in height, and forming another striking instance of the rapid progress of tropical vegetation.

But our notices of these inhabitants of tropical and other climes have extended to greater length than we purposed, and we must conclude. The company promenaded the garden, enjoying the fine evening and the fragrance around, and enlivened by the performance of the band of the Third Dragoon Guards, stationed on the lawn, till, shortly before eight o'clock, a few drops of rain fell, which seemed to be the signal for a general departure; and most of the visitors departed about eight o'clock, at which hour the band concluded their performances with the national anthem.

Cottage Gardening
September 12 1838

It is hardly possible to conceive, that any one can travel through this country, without observing the number of gardens by the roadside, cultivated by the extra industry of the humble tenants of the road-side cottages. The increase of these little allotments, considerable of late, can scarcely have failed to impress on any one the important additions these small plots give to the beauty of the scene. In a rich and populous country like England, it is in vain to look for the grander beauties of rugged and untamed nature. A traveller, amidst the scenes of English wealth, must rather expect to see moral beauty derived from proofs of order and industry, and from the evidence which these offer, of the comfort and the well doing of the numerous human beings that meet his view, even in the most sequestered hamlets of this island.

If a traveller, as he passes along, is delighted with the appearance of a well-trimmed hedge, small crops of vegetables regularly planted, well and cleanly kept, if he sees in them a promise of many a comfortable and wholesome meal to reward the care and industry of the humble owner of these riches, he will no less enjoy, likewise, the small plot of flowers, for simple ornament. The pendant honeysuckle with its fragrant flowers, or the rosebud with its tufted blossoms, will delight, not his senses of sight or smell alone, but must carry him on to reflections still more gratifying then those mere senses can afford. It is impossible not to draw from sights like these, a conviction of the comforts of his poorer brethren, of the pleasure which the simplest and most innocent sources of enjoyment are yielding them. These crops of useful and ornamental vegetation declare that the owners, however humble their lot, are not struggling through ill-requited toil, in the midst of penury, distress, and starvation, without enjoyments which they share with their wealthier neighbours.

If cottage gardens administer pleasure to travellers, or country residents, do those whom inclination or necessity lead to the more crowded haunts of the metropolis, or of our manufacturing or commercial towns, derive less gratification from the view of the pots of beautiful and gaudy flowers with which, in many instances, the humblest dwellings are ornamented? Let any one who really feels an interest in the welfare of a human being, however lowly may be his condition, step in to such a dwelling: let even a lady do so, she may do it confidently. In such a dwelling, she will find nothing to shock or to alarm the most sensitive delicacy, the most refined sensibility; but she will be most unfortunate, indeed, if, upon the testimony of these silent witnesses, she does not find that neatness, order, cleanliness, comfort, and civility, too, are the inmates of such dwellings. If, then, such be the almost insensible but certain effects of these harmless engagements, why does not everyone encourage them? Why does not every one labour to promote so cheap, so innocent, so beneficial a pleasure? And every one, at the expense of a very little trouble, can do so. The modes in which each may do so are various. One may grant land; and let it be remembered, that the most sterile bit of soil, in careful hands, will soon lose its barren character, and the great object in view will probably have been attained by the occupier in the course of that change.

In farms or gardens which are to furnish a livelihood for the occupier, the goodness of the soil, which will influence the price of the product, must be considered; in the present case we look for another kind of product, we look for health, for recreation, for innocent employment after the weightier occupations of daily toil. The production, then, of the soil is here only a secondary matter. But even the barren spot does not belong to all persons; yet such as cannot add to the number of small gardens may contribute from their own, or their friends' gardens, something towards improving the beauty or the value of those that belong to their poor neighbours. A few seeds, or a cutting of a plant, a few grafts of a valuable fruit tree, or some buds, cost the possessor nothing; but, in truth, extend the gratification of his taste for the beauties of nature, by enabling him to see to the right and left those splendid productions of the vegetable world, which, but for such cheap though real kindness, must continue to be confined to his own domain.

Still if this is beyond the power of any individual, there are other means of advancing this good work, by the encouragement to be held out to small gardening efforts, by supporting horticultural societies and exhibitions. These have become very numerous; and many, if not most of them, offer prizes to cottage productions – vegetables, fruit, and flowers; several add prizes for instances of combined skill and industry in the cottages and gardens themselves. It is greatly to be wished, that these societies were spread all over the country. No one who has not witnessed it could guess the important influence which these societies exert upon the condition of the labouring poor; and he has only patiently to continue his exertions for a few years, and we are much mistaken if he will not begin to see his care and labour well recompensed by the silent, though sure, advancement of industry and comfort, and their certain attendants, sobriety and contentment.

Spitalfields and its Weavers
May 20 1840

The district of Spitalfields now included within the north-eastern boundaries of the metropolis, is the older seat of the silk manufacture in England, and, though in a greatly fallen-off condition, still employs several thousand looms. Anciently, the district was an open space of ground without the city walls, belonging to the Hospital or 'Spital of St. Austin – hence its present name – and it was not till about the beginning of the last century that it became fully covered with houses, or was made the seat of the silk manufacture. The immediate cause of this change in its condition, was the revocation of the edict of Nantes in 1685, when at least 50,000 refugees, most of them weavers and other craftsmen, arrived from France, and threw themselves upon the charity of the English nation. In consequence of previous religious persecutions on the continent, many thousands of silk weavers had arrived in England, and been permitted to reside and carry on their trade at Canterbury; the new host of refugees, having spread to the metropolis, were permitted to settle in Spitalfields, and relieved from immediate starvation by a parliamentary vote of £15,000 per annum. We should suppose this munificent donation did not require to be long continued; for the weavers of Spitalfields quickly became very flourishing, and, in 1713, the silk trade had attained such importance, that upwards of 300,000 persons were maintained by it in England.

There is still a remnant of the love of gardening among the Spitalfields weavers. On the east of Bethnal Green is situated an enclosure of about six acres of ground, called Sanderson's Gardens. This space is divided into 170 small gardens, some larger than others, and each separated by palings from the others, as well as from the intersecting pathways. In almost every garden is a neat summer-house, where the weaver and his family may enjoy themselves on Sundays and holidays, and where they usually dine and take tea. Much care is bestowed on the cultivation of these spots. When visited in June 1838, some of the gardens had cabbages, lettuces, and peas; but most of the cultivators had a far loftier ambition. Many had tulip beds, in which the proprietors not a little gloried, and over which they had screens which protected them from the sun and from the storm. There had been a contest for a silver medal amongst the tulip proprietors. There were many other flowers of a high order; and it was expected that the show of dahlias for that season would not fail to bring glory to Spitalfields.

Richmond Park
October 20 1841

For some years past, steps have been taken silently to deprive the public of the right of admission to Richmond Park – the largest of the royal parks in the neighbourhood of London. The poor of Richmond formerly enjoyed the privilege of picking mushrooms in the park: this is now disallowed. No objection used to be made to walking on the grass; but this is now formally forbidden. Keepers are employed to warn passengers against trespassing on the turf; and on Sundays especially, when a greater number of persons are likely to desire a stroll among the trees, extra keepers, sometimes on horseback, are engaged to prevent the enjoyment of this innocent and rational means of relaxation. The following notice appears on a board placed at the entrance of the park: 'VR No persons in carriages or on horseback to be admitted in this park without having a proper order. All persons having leave for admission through Richmond Park are very particularly desired to keep to the gravel roads, whether in carriages or on horseback. Persons on foot are desired to keep on the public footpaths, and to take notice that the keepers, in shooting deer, only pay attention to the direction of the public footpaths. No dogs can be admitted unless they are led; and all dogs found straggling or hunting in this park will be shot.' This is undoubtedly the most extraordinary notice to which the letters 'VR' have ever been appended; and we are quite certain her majesty is not aware, that any such proclamation has been issued in her name – a proclamation in which she is made to tell her subjects, that a keeper is at liberty to shoot them if walking upon the grass, because, in aiming at the deer, he is not bound to use any precaution against taking away the life of a fellow-creature. The reader will observe what is distinctly implied by the notice – that the present public thoroughfare through the park will be a public thoroughfare no longer than till a safe opportunity occurs for entirely closing the gates against all comers. The reason of this is not regard for the deer, but for the birds. Richmond Park (containing upwards of 1,000 acres) is now being turned into a game preserve, and a patch of ground in the park has even been ploughed up to supply the birds with grain. We have always considered it in extremely bad taste on the part of any private gentleman having a large park, which perhaps he never visits but once or twice in the year, to shut it up from his poor neighbours. That he has a legal right to do so is undoubted; but it is equally clear that, in exercising it, he puts himself morally in the wrong. It is something, however, much worse than bad taste to shut up a royal park, maintained at the public cost, and to which the public has had access from time immemorial.

Gardens of the Working Class at Nottingham
March 23 1842

There are (says William Howitt, in his *Rural Life in England*) in the outskirts of Nottingham upwards of 5,000 gardens, the bulk of which are occupied by the working class. A good many there are belonging to the substantial tradesman and wealthier inhabitants; but the great mass are those of the mechanics. These be on various sides of the town, in expanses of many acres in one place, and many of them as much as a mile and a half distant from the centre of the town. In the winter they have rather a desolate aspect, with their naked trees and hedges, and all their little summer houses exposed, damp-looking, and forlorn; but in spring and summer, they look exceedingly well, in spring all starred with blossoms, all thick with leaves; and their summer-houses peeping pleasantly from among them. The advantage of these gardens to the working class of a great manufacturing town is beyond calculation, and I believe no town in the kingdom has so many of them in proportion to its population. It were to be desired, that the example of the Nottingham artisans was imitated by those of other great towns; or rather, that the taste for them was encouraged, and in fact, created, by the example of the middle classes, and by patriotic persons laying out fields for this purpose, and letting them at a reasonable rate. A wide difference in the capability of indulging in this healthful species of recreation must, of course, depend on the species of manufacture carried on. Where steam-engines abound, and are at the foundation of all the labours of a place, as in Manchester for instance, there you will find few gardens in the possession of the mechanics.

Early in spring – as soon, in fact, as the days begin to lengthen, and the shrewd air to dry up the wintry moisture – you see them getting into their gardens, clearing away the dead stalks of last year's growth, and digging up the soil; but especially on fine days in February and March are they busy. Trees are pruned, beds are dug, walks cleaned, and all the refuse and decayed vegetation piled up in heaps; and the smoke of the fires in which it is burnt, rolling up from many a garden, and sending its pungent odour to meet you afar off. It is pleasant to see, as the season advances, how busy their occupants become; bustling there with their tools on their shoulders; wheeling in manure, and clearing out their summer houses; and what an air of daily increasing neatness they assume, till they are one wide expanse of blossomed fruit-trees and flowering fragrance. Every garden has its summer-house; and these are of all scales and grades, from the erection of a few tub staves, with an attempt to train a pumpkin or a wild hop over the tub, to substantial brick houses with glass windows, good cellars for a deposit of choice wines, a kitchen, and all the necessary apparatus, and a good pump to supply them with water. Many are very picturesque rustic huts, built with great taste, and hidden by tall hedges, in a perfect little paradise of lawn and shrubbery – most delightful spots to go and read in of a summer day, or to take a dinner or tea in with a pleasant party of friends. Some of

these places, which belong to the substantial tradespeople, have cost
their occupiers from £1,000 to £5,000; and the pleasure they take in
them may be thence imagined. But many of the mechanics have very
excellent summer-houses; and there they delight to go, and smoke
a solitary pipe, as they look over the smiling face of their garden,
or take a quiet stroll amongst their flowers; or to take a pipe with a
friend; or to spend a Sunday afternoon, or a summer evening, with
their families. The amount of enjoyment which these gardens afford
to a great number of families is not easily to be calculated – and then
the health and the improved taste! You meet them coming home,
having been busy for hours in the freshness of the summer morning
in them, and now are carrying home a basket brimful of vegetables
to the house. In the evening thitherward you see groups and families
going; the key which admits to the common paths that lead between
them is produced; a door is opened and closed; and you feel that they
are vanished into a pure and sacred retirement, such as the mechanic
of a large town could not possess without these suburban gardens.
And then to think of the alehouse, the drinking, noisy, politics-
bawling alehouse, where a great many of these very men would most
probably be, if they had not this attraction, to think of this, and then
to see the variety of sources of a beautiful and healthful interest
which they create for themselves here: what a contrast! What a most
gratifying contrast! There are the worthy couple, sitting in the open
summer-house of one garden, quietly enjoying themselves, and
watching their children romping on the grass plot, or playing about
the walks; in another, a social group of friends round the tea table, or
enjoying the reward of all their spring labours, picking strawberries
fresh from the bed, or raspberries, gooseberries and currants from
the bush. In one you find a grower of fine apples, pears, or plums, or
of large gooseberries; in another, a florist, with his show of tulips,
hyacinths, carnations, or other choice flowers, that claim all his
leisure moments, and are a source of a thousand cares and interests.
And of these cares and interests, the neat awning of white canvas,
raised on its light frame of wood; the glasses, and screens of board
and matting, to defend those precious objects from the rude attack of

sun, wind, or rain – all these are sufficient testimonies, and tell of hours early and late, in the dawn of morning and the dusk of evening, when the happy man has been entranced in his zealous labours, and absorbed in a thousand delicious fancies, and speculations of perfection. Of late, the splendid dahlia and the pansy have become objects of attention; and I believe of the latter flower, till recently derided and overlooked, except in the old English cottage garden, there are now more than a hundred varieties, of such brilliance and richness of hue, and many of them of such superb expanse of corolla, as merits the value set upon them.

Parks and Gardens of London
April 2 1842

Fresh air is a luxury of the Londoner. He drinks it up when he can get it, as a coalwhipper imbibes strong beer. The air of the densely populated parts of London – and what part of London is not densely populated? – surcharged with smoke and dust, and vomited forth once and again from a million and a half pairs of human bellows, becomes substantial vapour, gross and palatable. Sometimes you can smell it, oftener you taste it, and at intervals you may cut it with a knife. When you get into the parks, clear of the dusty town, your lungs at once inform you of the obligation you have conferred upon them by changing their diet; your muscular fibre, braved by the current of pure air, becomes endued with unwonted activity; your brain is exhilarated, and a pleasing intoxication stimulates every nerve; your impulse is to run until you are tired, and then to repose at length on the green grass, inhaling at every breath, with supplemental sniffs, the inventor of ventilation systems Dr Reid only knows how many cubic feet of the limpid atmosphere. Therefore is the mere sight of open spaces and greenswards a recreation to the townsman, and much more to the town's wife and town-bred children; and if all quarters of London were as nobly provided with 'respirators' as the West End, there would be no reason to complain of want of opportunity to indulge in this cheap, innocent, body-and-mind recruiting luxury. People have queer notions of property at times; we hear of people talk of royal parks, and royal rangers, and commissioners of woods and forests: be it known, then, by all to whom these presents shall come, greeting, that *we* are the proprietor of all the parks – St James's, Green, Hyde, Regent's, Primrose Hill, Kensington Gardens, with all pastimes, recreations, disports, thereunto appertaining; together will all that and those, the fresh air, bright sun, and rippling waters, greensward, gravelled walks, sweet breath of milking cow, savour of new-made hay, chirruping of cock sparrow, whistle of blackbird, song of nightingale; moreover, all blossoming of trees, berries green and red for gratification of sight only, bough of fragrant hawthorn for entertainment of mine nose, all vernal and autumnal hues of leaf on shrub or tree, are ours; held by us of her gracious majesty and her royal predecessors in perpetuity.

Mr Loudon, the Horticultural Writer
March 13 1844

Mr Loudon was born on April 8 1783, at Cambuslang, in Lanarkshire. He was brought up as a landscape gardener, and began to practice in 1803, when he came to England with numerous letters of introduction to some of the first landed proprietors in the kingdom. Mr Loudon's career as an author began in 1803, when he was only 20 years old, and it continued with very little interruption during the space of 40 years, being only concluded by his death. In 1822 appeared the first edition of the *Encyclopaedia of Gardening*, a work remarkable for the immense mass of useful matter which it contained, and for the then unusual circumstance of a great quantity of woodcuts being mingled with the text: this book obtained an extraordinary sale, and fully established his fame as an author. In 1824, a second edition of the *Encyclopaedia of Gardening* was published, with very great alterations and improvements; and the following year appeared the first edition of the *Encyclopaedia of Agriculture*. In 1826 the

Gardener's Magazine was commenced, being the first periodical ever devoted exclusively to horticultural subjects. The *Magazine of Natural History*, also the first of its kind, was begun in 1828. Mr Loudon was now occupied in the preparation of the *Encyclopaedia of Plants*, which was published early in 1829, and was speedily followed by the *Hortus Britannicus*. In 1830 appeared the *Encyclopaedia of Cottage, Farm and Villa Architecture*. This work was one of the most successful, because it was one of the most useful he ever wrote; and it is likely long to continue a standard book on the subject of which it treats. Mr Loudon now began to prepare his great and ruinous work, the *Arboretum Britannicum*, the anxieties attendant on which were, undoubtedly, the primary cause of that decay of constitution which terminated in his death. This work was not, however, completed till 1838, and in the meantime he began the *Architectural Magazine*, the first periodical devoted exclusively to architecture. The labour he underwent at this time was almost incredible. He had four periodicals, viz. the *Gardener's*, *Natural History*, and *Architectural Magazines*, and the *Arboretum Britannicum*, which was published in monthly numbers, going on at the same time; and to produce these at the proper times, he literally worked night and day. Immediately on the conclusion of the *Arboretum Britannicum*, he began the *Suburban Gardener*, which was also published in 1830, as was the *Hortus Lignosus Londinensis*; and in 1839 appeared his edition of Repton's *Landscape Gardening*. In 1840, he accepted the editorship of the *Gardener's Gazette*, which he retained till November 1841; and in 1842 he published his *Encyclopaedia of Trees and Shrubs*. In the same year he completed his *Suburban Horticulturalist*; and finally, in 1843, he published his work on *Cemeteries*; the last separate work he ever wrote. In this list, many minor productions of Mr Loudon's pen have necessarily been omitted; but it may be mentioned, that he contributed to the *Encyclopaedia Britannies*, and Brande's *Dictionary of Science*; and that he published numerous supplements, from time to time, to his various works. No man, perhaps, has ever written so much, under such adverse circumstances, as Mr Loudon. Many years ago, when he first came to England (in 1803), he had a severe attack of inflammatory rheumatism, which disabled him for two years, and ended in an anchylosed knee, and a contracted left arm. In the year 1820, while compiling *The Encyclopaedia of Gardening*, he had another severe attack of rheumatism; and, the following year, being recommended to go to Brighton to get shampooed in Mahomet's baths, his right arm was there broken near the shoulder, and it never properly united. Notwithstanding this, he continued to write with his right hand till 1825, when the arm was broken a second time, and he was then obliged to have it amputated; but not before a general breaking up of the frame had commenced, and the thumb and two fingers of the left hand had been rendered useless. He afterwards suffered frequently from ill health, till his constitution was finally undermined by the anxiety attending on that most costly and laborious of all his works, the *Arboretum Britannicum*, which has, unfortunately, not yet paid itself. He died at last of disease of the lungs, after suffering severely for about three months; and he retained all the clearness and energy of his mind to the last. His labours as a landscape gardener are too numerous to be detailed here; but that which he always considered as his most important was the laying out of the arboretum so nobly presented by Joseph Strutt, Esq, to the town of Derby. Never, perhaps, did any man possess more energy and determination than Mr Loudon: whatever he began he pursued with enthusiasm, and carried out, notwithstanding obstacles that would have discouraged any ordinary person. He was a warm friend, and most kind and affectionate in all his relations of son, husband, father, and brother; and he never hesitated to sacrifice pecuniary considerations to what he considered his duty. That he was always most anxious to promote the welfare of gardeners, the volumes of this magazine bear ample witness; and he laboured not only to improve their professional knowledge, and to increase their temporal comforts, but to raise their moral and intellectual character.

Devonshire Cottage Scenery
May 29 1844

The love of gardens and of gardening appears to be almost exclusively confined to the English, and is partaken of by the poor as well as by the rich. Nothing can be prettier than the gardens attached to the thatched cottages in Devonshire. They are frequently to be seen on the side, and oftener at the bottom of a hill, down which a narrow road leads to a rude single-arched bridge. Here a shallow stream may be seen flowing rapidly, and which now and then *slichles*, to use a Devonshire phrase, over a pavement of either pebbles or ragstone. A little rill descends by the side of the lane, and close to the hedge of the cottage, which is approached by a broad stepping stone over the rill, and beyond it is a gate made of rough sticks, which leads to the cottage. At a short distance an excavation has been cut out of the bank, and paved round with rough stones, into which the water finds, and then again makes it way, clear and sparkling. This is the cottager's well. His garden is gay with flowers. His bees are placed on each side of a window surrounded with honeysuckles, jesamine, or a flourishing vine, and the rustic porch is covered with these or other creepers. Here, also, the gorgeous hollyhock may be seen in perfection, for it delights in the rich red soil of Devonshire. Giant stocks, carnations, and china asters flourish from the same cause, and make the garden appear as though it belonged to Flora herself. Nor must the little orchard be forgotten. The apple trees slope down the hill, and in spring are covered with a profusion of the most beautiful blossom, and in the autumn are generally weighed down with their load of red fruit. Under them may be seen a crop of potatoes, and in another part of the garden those fine Paignton cabbages, one of the best vegetables of the county. In a sheltered nook is the thatched pigsty, partly concealed by the round yellow-faced sunflower, which serves both as a screen and as an ornament. The mud or *cob* walls of the cottage add to its picturesque appearance, when partly covered with creepers, and surrounded with flowers. Such is an accurate description of one of the many cottages I have seen in the beautiful and hospitable county of Devon, so celebrated for its illustrious men, and the beauty of its women. Those who, like myself, have wandered amongst its delightful lanes, will not think my picture overcharged.

The Arboretum at Derby
June 1 1844

Amidst the benefactors of the human race, none stand more conspicuous than the late Joseph Strutt, Esq; who, with an effective liberality and determined kindness, was spared to commence, carry on, and complete, the (emphatically speaking) garden of the poor. I visited this place on Sunday evening, April 21 last. The gardens open only in the afternoon. I observed a happy seriousness on the countenances of the visitors – a subdued enjoyment, which spoke volumes in favour of the judgment of the noble-minded man who had thus provided the means of bringing the works of the Almighty under the eye of those who, all the week, are busily engaged in earning their daily bread. Parents, with their children of various ges, might be seen quietly sitting on many of the substantial seats provided for them under the shade of trees, or strolling on the walks, admiring the early flowers on the shrubs. All the shrubs have a name attached to them, very conspicuous, yet not so as to be offensive to the fastidious eye. Bricks are made for the purpose: they are set on end, the upper angles being levelled off. The name is painted on the angle, and covered with glass, which keeps off the wet effectually. I only observed two in all the garden but what were as legible as the first day they were put down. It was amusing to see the children of ten years trying to read, no doubt to them hard names, and puzzling their little heads to make them out. I remarked the good behaviour of those 'children of the poor,' as, amidst the many hundreds that were in the garden, I only observed one instance of rudeness, in two boys throwing stones at each other. It was instantly checked by the elder people, and the boys slunk away, ashamed of their conduct. The garden was, as is generally known, laid out by the late Mr

Loudon; and the execution of his task does credit even to him. Broad substantial walks lead down the centre, branching off diagonally, and returning up each side in a serpentine form. They are hidden from each other by raised mounds of various forms, sufficiently high to prevent persons seeing over. The named specimens stand singly on the grass, at such a distance from each other as their various habits, as to size and form, will require when fully grown. They are, consequently, conspicuous objects, and draw attention even from the most heedless. In the ground, previously to its being laid out, there were some larger trees: these have been judiciously preserved, and seats placed under them. It is, I think, however, an oversight that these our common trees are not named. That the people pay attention to the names was evident, from the fact that the early flowering shrubs, such as ribes, prunus, &c. were crowded by even well-dressed elderly persons, who were reading the names, and, in some instances, copying them. I would just observe, *en passant*, that the labels contain the botanical name, English name, native country, and year of introduction. The garden is well kept; the walks were smooth and free from weeds: the grass was short, and of a good colour; and the beds were newly raked. Many of the ribes are fine specimens, although the gardens have only been finished three years.

Inauguration of RHS Gardens
June 7 1861

The magnificent Gardens of the Royal Horticultural Society, at South Kensington, were inaugurated by the Prince Consort, on Wednesday. The company assembled was the most numerous and fashionable of the season.

His royal highness took his station at the top of the steps and Dr Lindley, secretary to the society, read an address to the prince, who, in the course of his reply, said: 'We already see, to the south, rising, as it were by magic, the commencement of a noble work, entirely the result of the voluntary efforts of the public; and this garden, itself the offspring of the Great Exhibition of 1851, will hardly be completed ere the exhibition shall have been rivalled, and, I trust, even surpassed, by the beauty and success of that which we hope next year to witness. This garden will then open an additional source of enjoyment to the thousands who may be expected to crowd the new Crystal Palace of Industry; nay, we may hope that it will, at no distant day, form the inner court of a vast quadrangle of public buildings, rendered easily accessible by the broad roads which will surround them; buildings where science and art may find space for development, with that air and light which are elsewhere well nigh banished from this overgrown metropolis.'

Garden Robberies
February 16 1869

Sir, – The letter of the 'Amateur Gardener' in this day's *Guardian* calls attention to what is really a great public grievance. I know of nothing more annoying than to get some morning and find the care of months ending in bitter disappointment by the pilfering of one's choicest flowers and plants. In common with every one in the suburbs who takes a pride in gardening, I have been repeatedly robbed. I do not, however, think all the pilfering attributable to the wantonly mischievous lads and roughs he describes. I have good reason to believe that there are idle vagabonds who live upon that species of plunder many months during the year. These fellows call themselves working gardeners, and you have only to apply to one of them for any description of plant and it will be brought you the next morning. Now, the remedy for this is obvious. Let those who have gardens decline to have any transaction with fellows they know nothing about, and that part of the evil would soon cease. In nine cases out of ten plants can be bought cheaper in Victoria market, and they will have the advantage of having been carefully removed from the soil, instead of hastily torn up. Another class of depredators to be closely looked after by the police in some districts are the 'knockers up.' These fellows, besides doing a great deal of wanton injury, dispose of their plunder to omnibus conductors and men in a similar position. It would require a large volume to contain all that can be urged in favour of flower gardens in the suburbs of large towns, and it is most desirable that the police should be vigilant in their protection, and that the full severity of the law be visited by the magistrates upon garden thieves. The police would also perform a great service if they would, upon finding the gate of a well-kept garden open, close it. By doing so they would not only prevent many pilferings, but would protect the garden from dogs and other animals. Vendors of newspapers, milk, &c. should give instructions to their servants to close all gates after them. Anyone neglecting to conform to this rule I invariably decline to do business with, and the postman gets no Christmas box if he is not careful in that respect. – I am, sir, yours obediently,

> Nemo Me Impune Lacessit
> Park Villas, Queen's Park
> February 15, 1869

The Botanical Gardens, Old Trafford
August 22 1872

The brilliant weather of the last few days, while adding incalculably to the value of the harvest, has done much to renew the floral beauty of our gardens and pleasure grounds, beaten and saturated as they have been for months past by wind and rain. The botanical gardens at Old Trafford of course suffered with most others. During the next six or eight weeks they will present however an aspect of great beauty and attractiveness, in that portion, at all events, which is devoted to large masses of choice varieties, tastefully disposed according to the modern, or bedding out, system.

The bedding out appears to have been managed this year with considerable skill, as would be anticipated from so practiced a hand as Mr Findlay's, and well illustrates the immense advance that has been made of late years in this emphatically artistic department of gardening. When bedding out first came into fashion, some 25 or 30 years ago, and for a long while afterwards – indeed, until quite recently, – the practice was simply to lodge great breadths of colour side by side, varied now and then with ribbons and rainbows red and yellow everywhere predominating, with scarcely an atom of any free or neutral tint, and green proscribed as a heresy. The effect, as would be expected, was most oppressive; but by-and-by it proved to be only another illustration of the well known axiom that a wise thing may be done in a very foolish manner; and 1872 shows a style of bedding out not only not objectionable, but extremely elegant. The old barbaric splendours are retained, but so judiciously toned down with light and neutral tints – blue, lilac, amber, and grey – and green is so well thrown in, that while the glare and glitter that were so painful have disappeared, today we have harmony, softness, and everywhere the agreeable sense of chiaroscuro. This is produced in large measure by the use of plenty of foliage plants – cerastium, perilla, dactylus, fancy-leaved geraniums, &c. – especially of succulents, such as those charming little Mexican echeverias, each a perfect rosette, and more like a piece of sculpture than something alive. Still looked upon by many with disfavour, at the botanical gardens the bedding out system allows of being very fairly estimated, and if contemplated with a bona fide desire and willingness to recognise merit, and the soundness of a principle, the present display ought to win the vote of every one.

The bedding out system has without question greatly stimulated the love of gardening; anything which will so operate cannot be essentially meretricious; it is better to see people fond of a few calceolarias and pelargoniums than fond of nothing at all; it encourages, moreover, a certain habit of tidiness, which before was often sadly deficient, even in gardens of pretension. The mischief is that it encourages, too often, unwise ambition and rivalry, and leads to neglect of what is more thoroughly substantial; not to speak of its furnishing an indolent excuse, every now and then, for discarding the beautiful old simplicities which are the best and unalterable characteristics of every genuine and purely lovable garden.

Meanwhile we can heartily recommend a visit to Old Trafford, where almost as much has been accomplished as may be possible, and with the good taste in default of which neither colour nor quantity count for anything.

Mr Gladstone on Cottage Gardening
August 18 1876

The annual show of the Hawarden Amateur Horticultural Society was held yesterday at Hawarden, and the prizes were distributed in the evening by Mrs Gladstone, the wife of the Right Hon WE Gladstone. In responding to the vote of thanks to Mrs Gladstone, Mr Gladstone said there is not a better nor a more wholesome and salutary village institution in the whole round that can be named than a flower show – that is to say, than a society of which a flower show is the annual celebration. In the first place it is one of those independent institutions which teach the people to exert themselves, and you may depend upon it man is not a passive and mechanical being. You don't train man as a plant, he is a moral agent, and if any good is to be done to him or to any woman and child – and I am delighted to see how many young boys and girls have come forward to obtain honourable marks of recognition on this occasion – if any effectual good is to be done to them it must be done by teaching and encouraging them, and helping them to help themselves. People who pretend to take your own concerns out of your hands, and to do everything for you – I won't say they are quacks, but I do say they are mistaken people. The only sound and healthy description of countenancing and assisting these institutions is that which teaches independence and self-exertion. There is no better kind of exertion than this. It is good for your health, good for your independence – because though a garden is not a very large thing in the life of a cottager, it is a very considerable element of independence – as well as comfort, pleasure and satisfaction. When well managed and of proper size, it makes a sensible addition to his means of living; and, for my own part, I sometimes hope that many of you may live to see the day when there will be no such thing in this country as a cottage without a garden. I rejoice to think that gardens are increasing. We have said before, and I may say now on my son's part as well as my own, that it is our desire to see them increase here. It is not always a very easy thing to make new divisions of land, because, unfortunately, when a bit of land is given to one it is very often taken from another. Land is not a thing which can be manufactured. If we could manufacture it we would make larger gardens, and have gardens for everybody; but as opportunity offers I am glad to think there are many gardens already, and there is every disposition to make them universal.

Retirement of Sir Joseph Hooker
November 27 1885

After Monday next English official science will be poorer by two of its most worthy representatives. While Professor Huxley, as is already known, retires from the presidency of the Royal Society, Sir Joseph Hooker resigns the post which for 20 years he has filled so ably as director of the Royal Gardens, Kew. His botanical work during his well-known wanderings in the Himalayas is of scarcely less scientific importance than that of the Antarctic regions, while it is difficult to conceive that his *Himalayan Journals* can ever be out of date either for instruction or entertainment. Nor must the journey which he made in Morocco with Mr John Hall be forgotten, and its substantial narrative, not to mention his run across America with that most genial of scientists, Asa Gray. Wherever his travels have led him, Sir Joseph Hooker has been able to discover some new aspects of nature's most delicate handicraft, and been able to tell his story with surroundings of real human interest. No one probably did Darwin more service when working out his *Origin of Species*; as an eager fellow-worker and loyal assistant few probably knew the services Sir Joseph had rendered to one of the greatest of revolutionists, as well as the foremost of evolutionists. But it is as the Director of Kew Gardens that Sir Joseph must be specially remembered at present. There he has held sway for 30 years, 10 as his father's assistant and 20 as chief. It is mainly due to them that this old royal domain has become probably the largest and finest garden in the world. Every nursemaid and mechanic, the crowd of Sunday visitors and bank holidaymakers who flock to Kew to drink in sweetness and delight ought to be grateful to Sir Joseph Hooker for the earthly paradise which has been provided for them under his ever watchful and intelligent directorship. No one could have discharged the duties of a trying post with more efficiency, or done more to raise and maintain these gardens as a great national institution – the centre of botany for the British Empire. Few, indeed, know the services rendered to our great empire by Kew Gardens. Not a colony but has reaped advantage from the knowledge and experiments and advice of Sir Joseph Hooker and his able staff. The coffee plantations in Jamaica and the chinchona gardens in India, the forests of Canada and the cotton and wine plantations of Australia – all have found help of the highest value from Kew. The daily correspondence, indeed, between this great botanical centre and our colonies all over the world, not to mention foreign countries, is greater than that of many a government department. The director of such an institution can have but little of that quiet and unworried leisure which is absolutely necessary for the best work in science. And it is this consideration, and not any feeling of failing faculties, that, we believe, has determined Sir Joseph Hooker to resign his trying post at the end of the present month.

Ladies' Fruit and Salad Gardens
February 20 1891

The first of Miss Harriman's ladies' fruit and salad gardens, near Derby, with its excellent dwelling-house, large orchard-house, and plantation of over 3,000 choice fruit trees, is now very near completion, and the first six ladies will very shortly go into residence.

Starting as it does in a thickly populated neighbourhood, there seems every probability of the greater part, if not the whole, of the produce of the garden being taken by people near, who will open deposit accounts with the lady gardeners. On and after April 1 the gardens will be open to visitors every Thursday afternoon on payment of one shilling. It may be well to mention that one example has already been set of a lady lending a large part of the necessary £100 to a less fortunate person who could not command that sum. During April, May, and June, the busiest months of the year, most of the day will be taken up with gardening work. Holidays will have to be taken by the ladies in turn during the winter, when those left at the gardens can with ease do the work of sending off the stored crops as ordered, attend to the plants under glass, and feed the poultry. This new industry promises one pleasant and profitable way out of the present congested state of the 'lady labour market.'

The English Art of Gardening
May 13 1892

We wonder whether the English art of gardening will really revive. The first thing to realise is that flower growing is not gardening and that florists are not gardeners. Yet how much English gardening consists simply in the planting and replanting of countless generations of geraniums, calceolarias, and lobelias, not as touches of brushwork in the finished picture of a garden, but as ends in themselves. Owners of gardens should mind neither their nurseryman's advice nor their neighbour's example. They should, first, consider the country they live in. To every country there is an appropriate type of garden. The Italian garden, an affair of almost strained stateliness, with broad terraces and with statues backed by ilex and box, is not for us. Fauns and Dryads in damp marble look miserable themselves and depress others; the whole design demands a clear sky and a distance of purple mountains. Nor is the French garden, also stately, with intersecting avenues, fit for any place but the flat sylvan spaces of central France. The old English garden, the only really English garden, was expressive in its way of all the character of the English landscape. Thus it began from good trim turf and kempt trees and orderly hedges. There never was much wildness about this country. Small and populous, it has always had need of hedges, pollard willows, and lopped elms. Its pastures, especially its commons, which were always before the eyes of the old masters in garden art, were close cropped and used to the utmost. Hence the qualities of the English garden. Not a copy of English landscape but a close relation and adjunct to it, the garden was small, fenced about like Solomon's, primly square like Bacon's, space everywhere economised, and labour nowhere. 'On level ground or on an even slope the simplicity and completeness of the square have great charms. Its beauties may be emphasised by its treatment in numberless ways and with quite small dimensions. A square, say of twenty-five yards, with crossing paths, seven each way, all of little red paving bricks arranged in patterns, with flower-beds between, the middle crossing emphasised by a fountain or sundial or brimming well, the red-brick wall on one side made with a seat along it where one can sit in the sun, and on the others three clipped yew hedges, with alcoved recesses for shade – such a garden is a true withdrawing room, and with its flowers for all seasons and its simple devices may show an art of gardening more to be desired than the most elaborate and costly arrangements for exotics and bedding plants.' We should not be for the sundial in making such a garden now. Those who used to put an accent on the beauty of their gardens with a handsome sundial did it because they wanted to know the time. We cannot go back on the progress of clock-making, and we shall never get at beauty by hunting for quaintnesses and archaic prettinesses. Gardening is the making and keeping of a garden to fit the country it stands in and the house that stands in it, and not merely the breeding of flowers as stock on a farm, or the making of experiments to find how long a flower will escape death in England which might have lived happily in Japan or the Alps.

Horticulture for Women
July 15 1897

The education congress on subjects of imperial interest was resumed yesterday in the Empress Theatre at the Victoria era exhibition. Lady Georgina Vernon read a paper upon the training of women in dairy work and the outdoor industries. Next in importance to dairy work as a fascinating and paying industry she placed gardening, which could easily be carried on by women in their own gardens. It was terrible in these days to see the number of splendid gardens which were allowed to go to waste. But if gardening was to pay it must not be attended to one day and neglected the next. A garden to be profitable demanded a knowledge of horticulture and constant care and attention, and she advised a course of study at the horticultural college, Swanley, Kent, if this occupation were to be taken up seriously. Unless a lady had a large garden at her command she would find flower-growing more profitable than vegetables, which were imported so largely from abroad.

Miss Hutchings, gardener at Kew, had prepared a paper on horticulture for women, which was now read. She contended that if a woman had a natural liking for her work and the necessary physical fitness she should not be disqualified because of her sex. The advantages of a knowledge of science could not be overlooked. The gardener and the scientist should work together. Even market gardening and fruit growing were being taken up by women, and where they could employ labourers for the very heavy work they succeeded in managing. This year the number of women employed at Kew was three. Too much could not be said of the training which these gardens afforded.

Mrs. Joyce bore testimony to the great value of the Colonial Training Home at Leighton, in Shropshire, from which young ladies has been sent to remote and distant parts. Miss Frear, secretary of the Swanley horticultural college, said that the public had most cordially received professional women gardeners, and if they had now 20 more well-trained students they had places for them to fill. (Cheers.)

The Chelsea Physic Garden
August 17 1898

The news that the Chelsea Physic Garden has been saved from the encroachments of brick and mortar by the London parochial charities will be welcome to residents in Chelsea. It has been suggested that it might be preserved as an open space, but the need for any action in this direction has now passed. The garden was presented by Sir Hans Sloane to the Society of Apothecaries on condition that 50 new varieties of plants should be grown in it and annually furnished to the Royal Society till the number amounted to 2,000. These gardens and the Botanic Gardens at Oxford are the oldest in England, the land at Chelsea being acquired by the Apothecaries as far back as 1674. Evelyn visited the Chelsea garden in 1685, and mentioned as varieties he saw there a tulip tree and a tea shrub. Here, too, it is said, was one of the first attempts to supply plants with artificial heat, the greenhouse having been heated by means of embers placed in a hole in the floor. It was here, too, that Philip Miller, the prince of gardeners, so styled by Linnaeus, spent nearly 50 years. He managed the gardens from 1722 till 1771, during which period the gardens attained a great reputation in Europe. Miller was the author of the much-admired *Gardener's Chronicle*. It is a pity that the gardens are not more accessible to the public, for it is a good step from Chelsea to Battersea Park. Under this new regime, perhaps, the public will be granted greater opportunities of enjoying these quaint old gardens and blessing the good Sir Hans Sloane, thanks to whom this breathing space still remains untouched.

One And All Gardening
January 1 1899

Mr EO Greening, as editor of that cheap and attractive annual *One and All Gardening*, has collected from some well-known persons their views on what may be styled the ethical as well as the aesthetic value of the cultivation of fruit and flowers. As there is at least a small altar to Flora in every human heart, one could easily make a goodly volume out of what notable men and women have said in praise of gardens. Mr Greening's aim has been less ambitious, but still he has drawn weighty testimony from very diverse quarters. Mrs. Fawcett thinks there is a free-masonry about garden-craft. The veteran Academician Mr Sidney Cooper, now in his 97th year, rejoices in a rose tree that still climbs outside his Kentish home and was planted by him in 1848. Mr George Alexander thinks that 'to the hard-worked actor an hour in a pretty, restful garden is an invaluable tonic.' Mrs ML Woods has a pretty allegory about the 10th Muse – that of Gardening, – nameless, but honoured everywhere. Dean Bradley, Sir John Lubbock, and Canon Hole are known to be garden-lovers, but it was not known to everybody before that Miss Braddon, the Rev Charles Voysey, Sir Arthur Arnold, Lionel Brough, Mr Rider Haggard, and Mr GJ Holyoake were also amongst the enthusiasts. Mr Charles Booth, the analyst of poverty, tells us, with true insight, that 'the great charm of gardening lies in the response that the growing things make to affection. Like the bright faces of children, herbs and flowers reflect the love that has been spent upon them.' Canon Barnett, who contrived to have a leafy corner even in Whitechapel, says: 'He who makes a flower grow gets some good for himself, and he also gives good to every passer-by who sees its beauty. The gardener is blessed and blesses. Why is not everyone for some portion of his time a gardener?' The question is one on which town-dwellers may ponder with advantage.

Wood and Gardening: Gertrude Jekyll
April 4 1899

Wood and Garden. Notes and Thoughts, Practical and Critical, of a Working Amateur. By Gertrude Jekyll. With illustrations from photographs by the author. London: Longmans and Co 10s 6d.

Lovers of the garden – and happily the number of them is rapidly increasing – will find this book entirely delightful, while those who are not yet enthusiasts may soon find themselves converted by running over its pages, or even by glancing at the photographs with which the volume is liberally decorated. The author describes herself as a 'working amateur.' Only a person to whom that title is rightly applied could have produced the book. It combines the knowledge and experience of the professional gardener with the freshness and receptivity of the cultivated amateur. The author modestly disclaims the possession of either literary skill or botanical knowledge. Certainly the reader must not expect to find distinction of style or felicity of expression. It is not as literature that the book will be valued. In this it differs from some well-known books on similar subjects; but, although the composition is quite unpretentious and sometimes even heavy, the writer's simple and straightforward manner, combined with her evident sincerity and enthusiasm, atone for much. With regard to her knowledge and experience, however, she does herself injustice. They are both more than sufficient for her purpose, and are clearly the result of long and laborious care. The locality of the writer's pleasance is not revealed, but its character is fully set forth. It extends to fifteen acres, and includes copse, heath, and woodland, as well as many kinds of garden. In her description the writer wisely gives a chapter to each month of the year. This facilitates reference and increases the usefulness of the book. Other chapters follow on miscellaneous aspects of garden work and study. The most attractive are those on 'The Colours of Flowers' and 'The Scents of the Garden'. These two subjects have rarely been so adequately treated in so short a space. The writer's preferences are given to the more delicate odours, such as those of apple blossom, wild rose, and the smaller pansies. She has a good word too for the delicious bog-myrtle, and the tiny woodruff of the hedgerow, whose leaves are almost sweeter dried than when fresh. We are glad to see, also, that she would include in gardens, for the sake of its wonderful fragrance, the often despised night-scented stock (Matthiola bicornis). The chapter on 'Large and Small Gardens' is full of wise and practical suggestions. The garden proper should not be so large as to become fatiguing, but should run into woodland of the orchard type; and, best of all, the orchard itself should not be put out of the way beyond the kitchen garden and stables, but should have direct connection with the lawn or the hardy-flower garden, while the grassy space under the trees should be planted with daffodils, cowslips, hyacinths, primroses, and snowdrops. In speaking of small gardens the writer acknowledges that she has learnt much from observing those in front of roadside cottages. Her example may be well followed. The chapter concludes with the account of a garden only three feet by ten inches, which she made in a box for a poor factory lad in one of our northern manufacturing towns, and the story is not without its pathos. The two things to be chiefly learnt from this book are, first, that the charm of a garden does not depend upon its size; and, secondly, that the finest gardens are those which reflect individual taste and are the result of the owner's personal care.

Out with the Old:
1900–1919

Gertrude Jekyll's *Colour in the Flower Garden*, 1908 * RHS's
Great Spring Show moves to the Royal Hospital Chelsea, 1913
* Women's Land Army formed, 1917 * National Union of
Allotment Holders, 1918

Evolution of the Amateur Gardener
April 3 1903

By a Sympathiser

When daffodils begin to peer
With heigh! the doxy o'er the dale,
Why, then comes in the sweet o' the year;
For the red blood reigns in the winter's pale.

Proud-fac'd April dress'd in all his trim
Hath put a spirit of youth in everything.
That heavy Saturn laugh'd and leap'd with him.

Now that the gold of the daffodils has gleamed in the winds of March and tossed a fugitive beauty from the brown earth, and the birds call from every sap-filled branch, and

> *the chaffinch sings on the orchard bough*
> *In England – now!*

our thoughts turn again to the outdoor life. In the last years we have seen a healthy revival of interest in the garden, though no doubt the keen instinct of the publisher has done something to spread the fame of it abroad. Special spring shows of garden-pictures are becoming increasingly common. In the windows of some of the Manchester booksellers and stationers there is nowadays quite a display of water-colours of old gardens and pleasaunces, 'haunts of ancient peace' that have an irresistible appeal. Already it is plain that the suburban amateur is briskly at work. He is one of a large class of persons eager, competitive, restless till the season of shows sets in. Monster blooms, gigantic marrows, strange devices in large pots 'arranged for effect' occupy their thoughts and form the staple of their speech. Let them be avoided in a railway carriage. They may easily be detected. Their sighs are manifest and indubitable. A carnation, or sweet-pea, or tea-rose in the buttonhole, often a basket or bunch of fine blooms taken to town, a certain fondness for a mode of dress that smacks of country life, a glimpse of a copy of *The Amateur Gardener* or *Field and Garden* or a seedsman's catalogue in the pocket, above all a roving eye that seeks a victim. These things mark the man who has 'taken' gardening. A glance at the button-hole, the remark 'Fine blooms those, sir,' is enough to open the gates of discourse, and thenceforward on that journey let no man think he will get the cream of the morning's paper. Governments may change, ministries may wax and wane, writers may come and generals go, but the amateur gardener flows on forever.

It is of interest to watch the evolution of him. He comes, raw and unspoilt, say from Broughton, Whalley Range, or Longsight, and goes as pioneer to the new Edens, unplotted and roadless, adjacent to

Wilmslow, Cheadle, or Disley. In these early days one sees him surveying the strange mounds of clay and sand which are the embryo of his garden at the 'desirable villa residence.' His look is one of mild wonder, not untouched with despair. But he is shortly seen with a copy of Jones's *Complete Gardener*, a packet of grass seeds, and a lawn mower. Then on an eventful day a set of assorted tools is handed out of the train to him by a smiling guard, who has seen many such arrivals, and henceforth this man, reversing the old description, goeth home to his work and to his labour in the evening. It is the last stage, and soon none is louder than this erstwhile modest and unassuming person in vaunting of his William Allen Richardsons, or 'belle alliances,' or Lottie Eckfords. He can tell you all about creepers. He prefers the Latin names of the shrubs, and his ampelopsis and Dianthus Barbatus are better than any his neighbours could show.

The spell of the garden is subtle and strong. Perhaps it is so strong because our minds turn against the manner of our today's life in towns, because we are not all entirely satisfied that man was created to sit upon a stool, or that in the course of the years to fill many reams of paper with writing and with figures, or to dispose of many hundredweights of cloth, or ship to the uttermost parts of the earth many bales of goods – goods which perhaps weigh much and wear badly – is the realisation of the whole of the divine plan for the 20th-century Englishman, however great a part of it it may be. So that the love of gardens is a protest – a protest against admitting that the crowded city can be the best dwelling-place for us, and that humanity can reach its ideal when it is penned by masses in mean streets. It is a realisation that the town square with its small and smoke-begrimed trees is not refreshing enough for a tired mind, and that it is not when placed in tubs, however ingeniously painted, that shrubs minister their highest pleasure to the man that looks at them. So those who have the power to choose their home have come to make an effort to free themselves and to live properly. The pity of it is that the sane and quickening influence of nature is reserved for those only, that as yet it cannot be part of the national system of education.

Thus it is that the garden becomes increasingly precious and sought after. For the garden brings us back to the living things of the air and earth, and here 'seeds of white thoughts, the lilies of the mind,' are sown. It is, too, a good refuge when you are worried, a place to turn and do some weeding by yourself. And yet all the while it is within hailing distance of your friends, and you have in it the warm, comfortable sense of being near your home, and this makes the especial charm of the garden. For we have become town dwellers, and we are bewildered and out of the way in the great silences and expanses of the country. We are over-awed and uneasy if we make too long a stay in the regions of vastness and with the majestic sights and forms of the earth. And so we grow to attach a peculiar value to the domestic garden. There, after the day's work is ended, we may give ourselves over to the sensations of twilight and silence, and have time for thought and dreaming, if we have not long since grown out of the habit. But always at hand are the companionships without which the garden would only be half what it is.

A good recreation for the amateur gardener at this season, between the seasons, when spring has begun to tempt us and yet the occasional rudenesses of winter keep us still within bounds, is to look again through one's books to discover the garden writings of our poets and essayists. Few of us possess those books of to-day, artistic in form and tempting in type and picture, which set out in charming language all that we cannot possibly do, and which give directions for making and managing suburban plots and 'small gardens' of, say, five acres in extent. It is a counsel of perfection to most of us to be told to reserve two acres for woodland or a picturesque wilderness, or leave an acre for ponds. But one may do well with the poets and essayists, finding their garden thoughts and getting a double garden joy in the search – the pleasure of their open-air thoughts before the warm summer evenings come, and a store of happy phrases and good thoughts to enrich our own garden musings when we sit in the little place afterwards.

Not wholly in the busy world, nor quite
Beyond it, lies the garden that I love.

Park Gardening
August 31 1905

The prime uses of town parks are first to retain open spaces as 'lungs' in our over-crowded cities, and secondly to provide pleasant places for the rest and recreation of the people; but there is a third use which they should subserve, and in which they largely fail – this is in giving lessons in town gardening. The most effective parts of many of the Manchester parks show expensive and mechanical gardening; the turf is cut up by small beds and turf edgings are used everywhere, and all these edges require a vast deal of purely mechanical labour in clipping; the best beds are laid out with thousands of bedding-plants, reared in frames and pits, and dumped into the ground in geometrical patterns which allows of no natural grace and freedom of growth, and are scarcely more flowerlike than those wonderful confections of beads and porcelain with which the thrifty French decorate their dead. There is no true gardening here; any man with measuring lines and a free hand in the matter of expense can fill in a given pattern with a sufficiency of plants in pots. The plants and labour are costly, and the show can, at is best, only last from June to September. What can be said, then, of the more truly garden effects in our public parks? How of the lawns, the trees, the shrubs, the herbaceous borders and rockeries?

Of the lawns it may be said that they are for the most part admirably kept. Lawns are better understood in England than anything else. In one of our most dressy parks there is a long wavy line of shrubbery which exhibits almost every fault of unintelligent gardening; in it laurels, rhododendrons, and privet are packed so close that all form is lost, and the only relief to these sooty evergreens (for privet is often almost evergreen) is made by elder, a coarse shrub which is only seen to advantage growing unchecked by water-side. In front of this dingy mass, in a long narrow ribbon of ground, robbed of nourishment by the roots of the shrubs, is a melancholy row of herbaceous plants, untended, ill-chosen. What wonder if people go away with the impression that a herbaceous border must be a dull, shabby thing, at any rate in Manchester, and that it is not worth attempting? Yet even in Manchester charming effects can be obtained with herbaceous borders and well-chosen shrubs. Such borders do not, it is true, put your eyes out, like the beds on each side of the broad walk at Alexandra Park, but there are humaner methods of astonishing than this. At Peel Park there is a quiet little lawn with a wych elm in the middle and a really handsome mass of golden rod in the curved border round; many of the effects in Whitworth Park are even better, and here we may see a certain amount of real gardening.

If the amount of attention given to carpet beds were given to herbaceous borders they might, with intelligent management, be run at a small fraction of the cost, and they would be source of constant pleasure from their variety at different seasons. But the plants must be given a fair chance. Any dark corner is not good enough for them. They must be planted in good soil, in an aspect which suits them; they must not be dotted in a mechanical fashion at regular intervals, but grouped carefully, with full knowledge of their height, colour, and season of flowering. The best effect is attained by planting generous groups which can be seen at a distance. At Peel Park plants of graceful white veronica are quite lost by being interspersed with coarse and ineffective vegetation, whereas if they had been massed with a background of larkspurs or a foreground of vivid nasturtiums or cornflowers they would have shown their faint silvery plumes to full advantage. Even in a small garden a certain boldness of effect can be attained by careful planning of masses, and in large gardens and parks this is comparatively easy. The plants must be well staked and mulched; they must have dead blooms cut off, and they must be cut down when they have done flowering for the season. Interspersed with the perennial herbaceous plants should be such bulbs and tubers as may be left in the ground. Instead of the strip of turf so commonly used as edging we might occasionally have dwarf flowering plants which are bright in their season and give next to no trouble. The smaller bulbs look very well cropping up through such a green carpet.

A great deal of the success of a herbaceous border depends upon the gardener's careful attention to succession. It should be so planted that when one group is going off another is coming on, and the whole border should never be overblown at once. Here there is ampler scope for a really intelligent and decorative use of half-hardy plants. Does it strike you that a certain corner is rather dull? Have certain anticipated effects not quite come off? A stretch of blue Lobelia erinus may then be softly effective, and will astonish those who have only seen it vulgarised in ribbons and dots. Even the calceolaria can be worked into a scheme of yellows and greens or be sparingly used as a highlight among deep purples or browns. Again, though small beds in grass have a mean effect, nothing can be more beautiful than a few groups of more precious things planted out for the summer in holes made in the turf and filled with rich soil. The exquisite blue agapanthus comes to one's mind for such use, and lovely effects can be got by groups of Lilium auratum, the cobalt-blue plumbago, lilac and white goat's rue, nicotianas (both white and red), white tree lupins, and the more choice peonies.

If in our parks the herbaceous borders are bad, the rock-beds are even worse. Manchester gardeners need lessons in the best ways of treating sloping ground almost more than in anything else, for a great number of their houses are raised more or less above the garden; yet Peel Park, which does so much to encourage gardening, throws away its splendid opportunity for a fine rock garden and its steep sloped is heaped with sickly white stone, while the few weedy plants struggle to exist in no soil to speak of. The chief mistakes here are that there is about four times too much stone and that of the wrong sort, and as much too little soil, and the few plants that are languishing are not well chosen. A rockery should not be all rocks. There should be enough to keep the soil in position and no more, and they should be well sunk in the earth, which should be made very good with peat and leaf-mould and grit of all sorts. Especially the rocks should be porous and of a good colour, so as to look as natural as possible; nothing is better than sandstone.

Many beautiful plants would grow and increase in such a soil and situation.

In the planting of shrubberies there is a great sameness, and there are too few flowering trees. Parks and gardens are used so much less in winter that one might even sacrifice the winter aspect a little if this were necessary; but it is not, for many deciduous trees and shrubs, if allowed to attain their proper size and specific form, are as beautiful in winter as in summer. Of course if the gardener cuts them all over to the same pudding-basin shape they are not beautiful. The fact is that to prune well one must prune thoughtfully and the average garden hand does not like thinking: he would rather take the shears and cut everything he sees sprouting. The monotony is greatly increased by the prevailing habit of planting too closely, so that the trees and shrubs form a compact and shapeless mass; there is the less excuse for this in public parks since the need for a 'screen' is not felt there as it often is in private gardens. In a park naturally and thoughtfully planted we should have new flowers every week in infinite variety: all we can do at present is to see the same pelargoniums staring us in the face from June to September, and the only change we have is when the frost catches them and we return to bare ground again.

HMS

Village School Gardens
September 12 1905

The school garden at Cheadle Hulme is already seven years old. Some of the boys who first worked in it are now in good situations as gardeners, owing much of their speedy advancement to the useful knowledge acquired during out-of-school hours on their little plots in the school garden. At Alsager there has been a school garden for three years. At Siddington there is a school garden directly under the control of the county council, and at several other Cheshire villages

– Wrenbury, Sandbach Heath, Odd Rode, Styal, and Oughtrington amongst others – beginnings have been made. The county council has helped by providing tools and seeds, and the schoolmasters, in most cases, have gladly given up some of their leisure for the benefit of the lads. Already it has been shown that the school garden may be made an education adjunct of great practical value, and the technical education committee of the Cheshire council is now considering the advisability of creating school gardens in every village in the county. The idea is to include gardening in the school curriculum for senior boys, so that when a village boy has passed his standards he may be able to do something more in a garden than root up weeds and pick caterpillars off gooseberry bushes. In a couple of seasons in the school garden he will learn not only the manual processes of tillage, but he will come to understand some of those secrets of the soil which the old-fashioned gardener ferreted out only by long years of observant toil.

Some of the advantages of giving village lads a better understanding of garden work are obvious. The chief one is that a knowledge of the natures of plants and soil and fertilisers enables the cultivator to secure a bigger harvest. In one Cheshire village where a school garden has been in existence for a year or two, the seniors now consult the juniors about the management of their allotments, converted in a body to the new-fangled ways of the school garden by the discovery that their sons had learned how to produce three bushels of potatoes where only two had been forthcoming before. There is no miracle, of course, in such an achievement. All that is necessary is an appreciation of the capabilities and necessities of the soil, care in the application of manures, judgment in ordering the rotation of crops. The school gardens already existing in Cheshire are not worked uniformly. Some of them are cultivated as one big garden, in every part of which every boy at some time or other does his share of work. Others are cut up into plots, and each lad grows his two rows of potatoes, and his beans and peas and cabbages, and perhaps a few onions and some carrots and parsnips. The plot system produces a fine spirit of rivalry, but for practical purposes it is considered that the model large garden is the best training ground, because in it one variety of vegetable or fruit may be grown in several different ways, and the boys may then find out by direct observation which is the most satisfactory treatment. So far the cultivation of vegetables has been the prime feature of Cheshire school gardens, but it is recognised that the treatment and pruning of fruit trees is quite as important as the growing of cabbage plants, and gradually the gardens are being stocked with bushes. But until some definite scheme is shaped by the county council the development must be necessarily slow.

The county council's chief concern in the matter is how to develop a scheme which will not involve too heavy an expenditure. One suggestion is to appoint a number of travelling teachers whose work would be to go from school to school and instruct the boys for a certain number of hours every week. Another is to leave the instruction in the hands of the schoolmasters. Not all the schoolmasters are at present qualified for the duty, but a course of Saturday lectures at the Holmes Chapel college could be arranged to meet this difficulty. Of the two proposals the second seems to be the most promising. A sufficiently large staff of peripatetic teachers would be costly to maintain, and perhaps very uncertain in its working. How, for example, could the travelling teacher demonstrate the proper way to sow onion seed if at the time appointed for the lesson there was a heavy thunder shower? It is possible to imagine a succession of weekly weather mischances which would make impossible for a whole season a demonstration of certain necessary operations. But the schoolmaster, being, like his boys, always on the spot, could choose the weather when it served, and so arrange his other lessons that the running of the school machinery not be thrown out of gear. Travelling inspectors might exercise a general supervision of the gardens and act as expert advisers to schoolmasters in difficulty. By some such arrangement a general system of school gardens might be started all through the county without setting up any elaborate and expensive machinery, and much of the unavoidable outlay – rent of land, extra payment of teachers, expenses of supervision, and so on – would be met by the grants that would be earned from the Education Department.

Handwriting: Jane Loudon
December 8 1906

Is there anyone left, in a Lancashire garden or elsewhere, who recalls the honoured name of Jane Loudon, authoress of *The Lady's Companion to her Flower Garden?* Mrs Loudon was an accomplished lady, who wrote not only on floriculture but on arboriculture and landscape gardening, and illustrated what she wrote. In one of her works she desired to insert a sketch of the Waterloo beeches at Strathsfieldsaye – a picturesque clump planted to commemorate our deliverance from the Corsican tyrant. Accordingly she wrote to the Duke of Wellington requesting leave to sketch the beeches, and signed herself, in her usual form, J Loudon. The duke – who, in spite of extreme age and with perceptions not quite so clear as they had once been, insisted on doing all his own correspondence – replied as follows:

'F. M. the Duke of Wellington presents his compliments to the Bishop of London. The Bishop is quite at liberty to make a sketch of the breeches which the Duke wore at Waterloo, if they can be found. But the Duke is not aware that they differed in any way from the breeches which he generally wears.'

Colour in the Flower Garden
April 20 1908

In *Colour in the Flower Garden (Country Life,* 12s net) Miss Gertrude Jekyll returns to her view of the gardener's art as being primarily that of making beautiful pictures by studied grouping. We can hardly imagine a more stimulating guide than Miss Jekyll for this kind of art. Her skilful placing of shining light blossoms near the entrance to a cool dark glade is one of the effects repeated several times, and always charmingly, in the beautiful photographs which illustrate the book. Cistus laurifolius, with a fern walk beyond; Madonna lilies, by some steps leading into a woodland; St. Dabeoc's Heath, making a patch of white fairy bells ringed with deep green leaves, are all happy thoughts. She has a number of plans of various parts of her gardens, with photographs showing views from certain marked points, so that it is a fascinating pastime to reconstruct the place in the mind's eye. Her grey garden, with its relief of pink hollyhocks and white China asters, is delightful; and the blue garden, where she admits high lights of white lupins and foxgloves and palest yellow snapdragons, would be delicately beautiful too. One feels a little more doubtful about the green garden, which if it were in the full sun would surely be rather tame.

The Woman Gardener
July 29 1908

There are now many instances of women who are living on the land by the practice of *petite culture*. Some are specialists, confining themselves to violets or lilies of the valley; others grow fruit or poultry, while others take up gardening or dairying in a more extensive way. I have paid one or two visits to a woman farmer, no longer young, who is a splendid manufacturer of cheese, which she sells at excellent prices every season. There are, however, few industries so fascinating as the flower garden, which offers many advantages to women who are too delicate to deal with bigger things. In all our large towns and cities there are many persons with little gardens at the front or back of their houses; these people are often supplied by growers in the country or the suburbs who make a point of producing garden plants for sale. There are many which are easily grown, such as wallflowers, violets, chrysanthemums, arum lilies, geraniums, hyacinths, and tulips, and other still less costly, such as stocks and asters, lobelias, pansies, and nasturtiums, which come within the range of the purse of the working man.

I have paid a visit to a woman living a mile or two from an important town, who dwells in a pretty villa which is almost embedded in flowers. The soil is not by any means good, though well manured with artificials, and yet it is crowded with flowering plants, most of which are sown in rows – annuals and biennials – and despatched by post as orders are received. On my arrival I found the lady in her office, with a pupil sitting opposite, dealing with a large number of orders which had been received that morning. The office was a railway carriage. It was divided into two, one half being used for afternoon tea, which is given to visitors, for there are many who call to see the gardens and to spend money on the flowers. There is a small glass propagating house and some frames, in which large numbers of early plants are grown. The best seeds are used, and these only, and they are obtained at trade price. All are sown with care in soil which has been prepared in pots and boxes. At a given time they are removed from the boxes and pricked out in the open beds, and left to grow for sale to customers.

As I was not expected, I can faithfully aver that the business must be a good one, and that other women might make it an example, for in front of the owner was a little pile of postal orders which had been received that very morning. I noticed that the office wall was half covered with packets of labels on which were printed the names of the plants grown in that flower garden, together with instructions for their management. Each lot of plants despatched by post was packed in material for their careful preservation. I learned, what is but common sense, that the earliest buyers obtained the finest plants, these being drawn from the rows to give the smaller ones a better chance to grow. The lady told me that she advertised week by week in selected papers which reached the homes of thousands who prefer to buy plants rather than grow them for themselves – or fail to grow them. Among the largest crops were stocks and asters, phlox and calceolarias, fuchsias and godetias, polyanthuses and roses, carnations and penstemons.

One of the chief objects in a case like this is to provide for all seasons and not for summer only. In the flower markets of the large cities some varieties of plants are sold in boxes holding from four to twelve dozen each, but purchased by the dozen at an average nursery they cost much more; indeed there is no comparison.

James Long

Back-Yard Gardens
Manchester's Flourishing Society
August 31 1910

The Leo Grindon Flower Lovers' Association, established in 1905 by Mrs Leo Grindon to perpetuate the memory of her husband, the well-known Manchester botanist, has done much good work. Mrs Grindon and the Lord Mayor of Manchester presented the prizes awarded to successful competitors in back-yard gardening. The proceedings took placed in Mrs Grindon's own back garden in Cecil street, Greenheys. Formerly an ordinary town back-yard, Mrs Grindon has converted it into a pleasant garden, in which some of Shakespeare's plays have been given with great success. A special feature of the work which the association undertakes is that of encouraging the growth of flowers and creepers in the bare back yards of working men's dwellings, and prizes were given yesterday to numbers of tramway men and dwellers on the Blackley estate, which belongs to Manchester Corporation. Photographs which were shown illustrated some very admirable results which have been achieved, and the widespread interest taken in the movement was indicated by the fact that some 30 prizes were awarded.

The lord mayor, who read a letter from Sir Thomas Shann regretting his inability to be present, said that all assembled, and many people outside, owed a debt of gratitude to Mrs Grindon for the great interest she took in what was really a splendid work. He called it a splendid work because, living as we did in a material age when most of us had to work hard to keep body and soul together, it brought a great deal of pleasure into our lives if we had lovely flowers to look at. He remembered that when recently, with his wife and daughters, he visited Japan they were struck with the gardens in that country and the love of flowers shown by the Japanese. He thought it showed that their civilisation was very advanced. Even living as we did in the lovely climate of Manchester – (laughter) – they had seen what could be done with a little trouble and exertion. He hoped the movement would extend.

Parks and Town Planning
A Criticism of English Methods
February 27 1912

The series of lectures on town-planning which has been arranged by the Manchester education committee was continued last night by a lecture on 'Parks and open spaces in relation to towns,' by Mr T H Mawson, special lecturer on landscape design in the University of Liverpool. Mr Paul Ogden presided.

Mr Mawson, in opening his lecture, remarked that last year he gained some notoriety by saying that the English public parks and gardens, so far as they depended on art and not upon nature, were the worst in Europe. He was sorry he was not able to withdraw the statement. The English parks were absolutely the worst in Europe, in spite of the fact that the art of landscape architecture was further advanced in this country than in any other. We were a race of gardeners and garden designers. The best that had been done in the art had been done in Great Britain, but seldom for the public, nearly always for the private individual. London and the six largest cities in England had spent during the last 20 years millions of money on the formation of public parks and gardens, but not one penny of the money had been spent under expert advice. On the continent and in America a very different state of affairs existed. The reason for the difference was a sociological one. In Germany, in France, in Italy, in America as a man attained wealth and education he drew near the heart of the city, and his endeavour to make his surroundings beautiful benefited the city. In industrial England directly a man amassed wealth he used it for the purpose of getting out of the place where his money had been made. So it came about that nearly all the best landscape gardening in England was on private estates. Even our town garden was treated as if it were a private garden. It was invariably enclosed with an expensive fence with a thick ring of high shrubs and trees on the inside. More attention, he thought, should be paid in planning a town garden to the pleasure and refreshment which passers-by might derive from it.

Instead of having an unclimbable fence, would it not be better to have grass running down to the public roadway, with just a protection of posts and a swing rail? All that was required was some stretches of plain grass and a few straight walks. But that was not the way to spend money. We usually covered the space with shrubs and trees. The great bane was that we did not understand the beauty of plain surfaces, and that we had very little appreciation of our English trees, the most beautiful in the world. We were for ever running to foreign countries to find the latest leopard or monkey-puzzler, or some other thing, which, instead of giving a homelike, restful character, destroyed everything that was good and right in a public park.

Mr Mawson spoke of the need for planning the open spaces of a city with a view to future requirements. He described the two systems of laying out open space commonly used – the encircling system and the radiating system. In the first a belt of land surrounding the city was reserved for parks. This method was to be preferred only in the case of the old towns, where an alternative was difficult. In the second, wedge-shaped pieces of land were reserved, stretching from the very heart of the town into the open country. It was, he thought, easier to adopt this system in England than it was on the continent, where many of the towns were built within walls or fortifications. In most English towns the main roads radiated into the country, with straggling suburbs following their lines, between these main pieces of land, more or less wedge-shaped, which could be bought either at agricultural value or, at most, at the value of accommodation land. He wished that English municipal authorities would do as some continental towns did – make up their minds to a definite policy of development, costing as a whole, perhaps, millions of pounds, and do a little towards it year by year. Mr Mawson advocated the making of boulevards to serve as links between the parks.

Gardening and Golf
May 18 1912

There are many resemblances between gardening and golf. Both give you good exercise, and in both you knock a good deal of turf about one way or another. But it is gardening that gives you the best exercise. It is the first exercise man ever took to, and it is still the best. There is nothing like it for training. If you want to enjoy your supper and a good night's rest put in a couple of hours in the garden when you get home from business. But gardening has another superiority over golf. Every stroke in the game of gardening brings a concrete return in due season. Every hour's work in the garden means that your home will be more beautiful by and by. The colour and fragrance of flowers will surround you, and your house will have that finish and charm which only nature can give. A cottage embowered with flowers is more beautiful than a palace. Have you ever noticed as you walk along a country lane or a suburban road how you pick out for admiration and approval the houses that have good gardens? They look comfortable, prosperous, well-to-do. You feel that this is a happy, well-ordered, pleasant home. The other houses with poor, scrubby gardens look mean and shabby. So look after your garden. It will be good exercise and a joy for ever. And there is no easier way of keeping up appearances.

The Flowers of All Nations
May 21 1912

'Only one branch of gardening is not represented in the show – landscape gardening,' said a man who looked like an expert at the private view of the Royal International horticultural exhibition today at Chelsea Hospital. He was, however, quite wrong. Landscape gardening of a quaint and characteristic sort is there, for one side of the show is in old Ranelagh Gardens, with its curly walks and wooded knolls and 'glades discovered,' as old drawing masters used to say. All that was really wanted was a gazebo looking out on a ha-ha. When admiring any of the eight rock gardens with the Japanese dwarf forests or the man-o'-war, deer, peacock, or cocks and hens in cut box-bushes, or the variegated evergreens, one was constantly coming on a beautiful single red hawthorn in flower or a fine piece of lilac only to find that it was *hors concours*, being part of the old garden. The wonderful avenue of ancient lime trees – one of the major beauties of London at the moment – was also *hors concours*. One felt very proud that the crowds of foreign exhibitors and visitors should see this beautiful piece of old sylvan London, with Wren's ashen grey and red old hospital broadening over it all, and the aged pensioners in their scarlet coats moving slowly about it like perambulating geraniums. The committee could not have chosen a better place to assemble the loveliness of the growing earth than the old Chelsea gardens in May.

It is the largest show of flowers ever held in the world. England had much leeway to make up here. It is nearly 50 years since the last international show, held at Hyde Park on the site of the great 1862 exhibition. Since then there have been international displays in France, Holland, and Italy, the wonderful Ghent show of 1908, the Berlin show of the following year, and the great tulip show at Haarlem last year being the most memorable. The present assembly covers 24 acres, and has one tent with an area of three and three quarter acres. A particular feature is the spaciousness of arrangement and the long vistas ending in great central features, such as the enormous bank of cinerarias built up against the old Peninsula obelisk, which is one of the sights of the hospital gardens. This will face the King as he enters the exhibition from Embankment. In the great tent there is a comely fountain and a huge group of garden statuary with nymphs and fruit and a terminal of Pan. Roses have been arranged in bowers and in long trellised walks. Fuchsias are trained on frames standing straight out at an angle overhead forming a long avenue and making one adapt the poet's line to:

And the fuchsias hold up their arms
When spring rides through the woods.

Enormous glowing packs of azaleas and rhododendrons gather at the sides, and the fatigued eye travels gratefully from them to cool, moist recesses of green ferns of all kinds and varieties, amongst which tall Fiji ferns, rising closely to a height of five feet, provide an attractive foil to an 150-year-old Thuya obtusa in the Japanese dwarf garden. There is about an acre of roses here, including, one suspects, most of the varieties which one speaker at the National Rose Society Cconference today declared ought to be consigned to a lethal chamber. In nothing more than in roses is the difference between the exhibition of fifty years ago and the present one made clear. In those days it was the cabbage rose and the old tea rose that excited the gardeners of the nation. Now it is the dwarf, the climbing, and weeping, and other varieties. Cape primroses, gladioli, iris, sweet peas (now more fashionable and elegant than even the carnation), begonias, and dahlias in bloom in hundreds, each section raising enthusiasms and problems that are too deep for anything but professional words. The outsider in his wanderings through this gorgeous scented maze is constantly in a world of new colours and shapes, and if some of these turned out to owe their eccentricity to the fact that they were queerly but expertly wrapped, each bloom in little hood and swathings, the wonder was by no means diminished. In the vast orchid pavilion one was lost in thickets of strangeness. In the result one could only say, as Mrs Carlyle's servant said on her return from her first visit to the National Gallery: 'Oh mum, how expensive!' The end of this white palace is like a mass of fireworks with golden sprays with a weird muted glow soaring out of Catherine wheels and squibs and zigzags of these fragile exotics of all the colours of the rainbow – no! of the aurora borealis.

Elsewhere one thought of butterflies, or eerie, cloudy jellyfish with a clot or two of blood amongst them, of that new kind of transparent Japanese tea saucers – of anything, in short, but friendly happy flowers. One turned from these begums and ranees and sultanas into a tent which had in its centre a bank of joyful old-fashioned flowers set round with an old-fashioned border. There were nasturtium, phlox, foxgloves, delphinium, Canterbury bells, poppies, old pinks, crimson sweet Williams, petunia, and mignotte. 'Here is old England again,' I said to a busy blue smock figure with a watering can. 'Pardon, M'sieu' – he began, puzzled. It was, as it happened, the French section. The only other exhibit yet in place there was cabbage lettuces. Belgium, Holland, America, Japan, Canada, as well as France, have all separate exhibits.

The development of the rose and the coming of the orchid (there were hardly any orchids in the 1866 show) are two of the most obvious features in the present exhibition. Another is the rock garden, which did not then exist as we understand it. There are seven or eight rock gardens in the Ranelagh grounds, showing how the world is now ransacked for these little plants, which keep their fastnesses from one year's end to the other, an ever-changing pageant of delicate tints. Edelweiss, of course, is there in four or five forms, and gentian like blue velvet (some of it comes from Ireland), and many plants from the Rocky mountains, and a queer little green-and-white strange plant from Mount Popocatapetl, and so on. Then there are water gardens and fruits and shrubs of all kinds and garden ornaments and crowds of other things that will really take you the eight days of the show in which to see them.

JB

Mrs Pankhurst and the Kew Outrage
February 11 1913

At the meeting of the Women's Social and Political Union at the London Pavilion yesterday afternoon, Mrs Pankhurst, referring to the destruction of orchids at Kew, said it was very sad that women should have to destroy beautiful flowers in order to call attention to their movement. Referring to the telegraph wire-cutting, Mrs Pankhurst said it seemed to her that what the women in Glasgow did on Saturday was quite as effective as what the combatants did when they shelled Adrianople, and the women did it without injuring a single human being. They did not want the gentlemen who belonged to clubs in Pall Mall and Piccadilly to be pleased that their windows were broken. They wanted them to be angry. If the government responded to the demand, and arrested her and sent her to prison – as she recognised it was quite right they should in the circumstances – they would still be wasting their energies. Sooner of later the government would have to recognise that the whole trouble arose from the fact that the government, claiming to be a representative government, would not make itself responsible to the women of the country. (Cheers.)

Fashionable Craze for Gardens
June 16 1914

Gardens and dancing and flying continue to be the passions of the fashionable rich, and many people dance during the week in London and garden at the week-ends in the country. The latest development in rich folk's gardening is the children's gardens, and the most expensive landscape gardeners are sent for to design and lay out a garden for Miss Molly or little Lord John, for gardening is now the craze also among children of the great house. I believe that a girl's garden has just been laid out at Windsor for Princess Mary. A well-known English countess left the other day for the continent to lay out the Italian and other gardens of a French millionaire – for a very substantial fee. Lady Wolseley's training college for lady gardeners is now producing many girls who are doing excellent work throughout the country. Even in London people are beginning to cultivate their gardens, and are discovering that flowers will grow now since the abatement of the smoke nuisance. The renewed passion for gardens, I am told, is actually shortening the London season, and it seems as if before long it will be Ascot rather than Goodwood that will mark the season's end.

In the Botanical Garden
June 14 1915

The war has taken away some of our open-air entertainments, but we still have the bands in the parks, and if we need to salve our conscience for keeping them we can reflect how great a boon they are to wounded soldiers. There is even a new band performance on the list. This summer, for the first time, a shilling admits you on Saturday afternoons and Thursday nights to the carefully guarded seclusion of the botanical gardens to hear the band of the Coldstream Guards. People in the mass have not yet discovered this pleasant idling place. Yesterday there was the intimate feeling of a big family party in the circles and chairs under the trees round the bandsmen, who looked in their scarlet coats like a bed of geraniums on the unworn grass. They play in a quiet glade among the bushes and weeping ash trees, close to the fellows' tea enclosure, where wounded soldiers in blue hospital jackets sit happily listening at tables. Filling in the background is the old-fashioned bulbous glasshouse, flanked by examples of the decaying art of topiary gardening. There is plenty of khaki on the chairs, and if people should be tempted to forget the war there is a staid little group of soldiers' wives – and widows – sitting in the shade to remind them of it. The listeners have mostly come in from houses in the stately Georgian terraces round about. Picnicking family parties are common in the cool places, and tennis goes on within sound of the foliage-softened music. In one corner an opening in some rhododendron bushes has been turned into the stage of an open-air theatre, where children are practising dances for some performance. A small girl in a saffron frock and fairy wings trips solemnly to the Waldteufel waltz the Guards band is playing, quite unabashed by the battery of pleased eyes watching her from the chairs.

Garden Expenditure in War-Time
August 26 1915

To the Editor of the Manchester Guardian

Sir, – There has recently appeared in the public press correspondence urging the entire cessation of garden expenditure, and, though the letters have more pointedly aimed at public parks and gardens, such expressions are apt to be dangerous, inasmuch as the gardening public at large may be likely to interpret and apply them to themselves individually. Indeed, that this is happening is evident from correspondence recently received on the subject from prominent and well-known firms, who tell us that their trade is very seriously depressed, and point out that an entire cessation of trade means not only temporary financial loss but the irretrievable sacrifice of many years of labour spent in producing new and improving older fruits and vegetables for our use and flowers, trees and shrubs for our solace and enjoyment. They rightly feel that, as they have catered for our happiness in times past, it is hardly right that they should now be brought to a position in which they can no longer even retain their employees' services. Most of their younger men have enlisted, and they ask, not for the usual trade, but for just sufficient support to keep them going and to meet current expenses which cannot be suspended.

The president and council of the Royal Horticultural Society feel that in drawing the attention of lovers of gardens to this trade aspect of the question they are but again advising that medium policy which, in the long run, is always the wisest, and fellows and gardeners generally are urged not to forget this when framing their economies. – Yours, &c.

W. Wilks, Secretary
Royal Horticultural Society, Vincent Square,
Westminster, London SW, August 24.

A Country Diary: Kew
May 11 1916

Kew Gardens, May 10.

Nowhere, surely do the bluebells grow more luxuriantly or look more ravishingly beautiful than they do under the beeches in the ground of the Queen's cottage at Kew. Here the varying thicknesses of sheltering boughs make varying shades of colour in the sea of flowers – now deep blue, now pale, now lilac of the most warm and tender hue. It is the most fugitive colour to catch and describe, but it hangs in the memory to solace and encourage. It is like a butterfly's wing. When you get the first glimpse of it through the trees on a sunny day, it seems incredible. Looked at close, each fluted bell seems one colour; pale or bright, it is blue. But the bracts are red and the effect in mass is shot, and now one and now the other of the two colours prevails.

London Squares for the Wounded
May 24 1916

With a little goodwill and management there ought to be no difficult in making many of the London squares available as rest places for convalescent soldiers. The suggestion was made a few days ago, and it has been actively taken up. Some of the squares that are near hospitals are already used in this way. What is wanted now is an appeal to the sympathy of the residents who keep the gardens in so many squares as a domestic preserve. Most of the West End squares are controlled by committees of residents, and I hear that some of these committees are now willing to allow the neighbouring hospitals to have keys. If the squares were thrown open to the soldiers no doubt the residents would be making them happy. They might give tea parties in rotation, for instance.

There has long been a feeling that too little use is made of these quiet gardens. It is the rarest thing in the world, for instance, to see anyone in a Bloomsbury Square garden except a stray nursemaid. It is certain that the wounded soliders would use the squares more gently than the squads of recruits that took possession of them in the early months of the war, and trampled the grass bald and used the trees as amateur hat-pegs. The squares are now in their perfection, the old lawns have renewed their youth, and the gardens are bright with hawthorn and chestnut. There are far too few sitting-down places in London. When one sees the wounded soldiers sitting on the steps of Westminster Hospital, for instance, or making their way painfully about the street – and they will do anything to get away from the hospital for an hour – one feels that throwing open the squares is one of those things that has not happened only because it is too obvious.

Miscellany
May 12 1917

A little knot of business men in a Manchester café were talking about the conversion of their flower beds into vegetable patches. One unblushingly admitted that, in spite of the example of Miss Gertrude Jekyll, he had determined to stand by his herbaceous border, and could give sound business as well as aesthetic reasons for doing so. 'I cannot afford to throw away pounds' worth of good stuff which I know how to grow in order to attempt to grow what I know nothing about: nor do I see the utility of breaking my back again when you chaps are growing far more than you'll know what to do with. So what I propose is that I'll keep some of you supplied with flowers if you'll keep me supplied with vegetables.' A bargain was struck at once. 'What I was afraid of,' one of his friends remarked, 'was that while we would have been giving vegetables away all summer through, my wife would have been spending fabulous sums on flowers.'

Digging for Victory: 1920–1939

National Garden Scheme, 1927 * Institute of Landscape Architects inaugurated, 1930 * Sissinghurst opened to the public, 1938 * Dig for Victory campaign, 1939

The Curse of Adam
August 25 1922

'No, I never visit herbaceous borders.' The peace of heaven lay upon the Cheshire lawns, but the wrath of man boomed forth in the colonel's voice. 'This modern craze for gardening is a certain symptom of the decay of England.'

'God Almighty,' quoted our hostess reprovingly, 'first planted a garden.'

'He did, madam, and found immediate cause to regret it.' The colonel addressed himself fiercely to the attack. 'The effect on our first father was precisely that which brings ruin to the nations who follow in his steps. He grew absorbed in his work, intoxicated by his successes, blinded by his petty interests to morality, chivalry, and truthfulness. He was, in short, a typical gardener, and dismissed, rightly, at a moment's notice. And ever since his day you find that an excessive interest in gardening betokens a people on the verge of moral and social bankruptcy.

'O yes, dear lady, Babylon had hanging gardens, I know. I know also that as soon as they hung satisfactorily the Medes overran the empire and wrested it from their creators. The Greeks were no gardeners. Why, their idea of a suitable punishment for badly behaved young men and women was to transform them into shrubs; they used the daphne and narcissus and laurels as warnings, not as domestic pets. I've forgotten my classics, but I expect you'd find it was just when they were beginning to be sentimental about flowers and talk about violet-crowned Hymettus that they began to quarrel and decay. Anyhow the Romans of the early Republic had a good sound antipathy to gardens. Don't you remember how properly disgusted they were when they found their ex-general among his cabbages? It wasn't his love of biennials that took Julius Caesar over the Alps. No, it was the worst of the Caesars, Caligula and Tiberius and Nero, who planned gardens on the Palatine. The corruption spread, of course, though I'm glad to say you find Pliny in exile because he would talk about his fruit trees. But by the third or fourth century every governor of a province was busy with the gardens of his villa, and the way was prepared for the invasions of the barbarians. Anyone, even a barbarian, could do for a man with a garden.

'Now isn't it a wonderful thought that from that day till the 12th century or so you'll hardly hear a word of a garden, except possibly in some monastery's chronicle here and there? Too many wonderful things were happening; the nations were emerging from chaos, the church and the law from chaos, gothic architecture out of debased romanesque, the Crusades out of feudal wars: in days like those, men weren't going to waste their time making holes in a bit of ground for a seed, and watching a pink or blue thing come up out of it. No, it's not till the 13th and 14th centuries that you begin to find the poets prattling about gardens again. And alongside of their raptures about roses and eglantine, daffodils and gilly-flowers, you find an England of enclosures and class hatreds, of futile civil wars and contemptible foreign policy. Why, the very word roses stands for one of the most despicable little wars in history!'

'Aren't you forgetting the Italian Renaissance?' asked one of the patient audience.

'Not at all. The Italian cities were all very great in art and literature, but politically they were doomed quickly enough. They had a bad influence on us for a bit under Henry VIII, but then you find in England a spirit strong enough to resist. It's an interesting phenomenon about the puritan, the man who really made England, that he didn't care about his garden except as a place to grow things to eat in. In the great period of England, Queen Ellizabeth's reign, the adventurers were out on land and sea, and gardens grew fruit or were filled with shrubs, sensible things men didn't fiddle over. England became great, and it's only with the foreign, specially the Italian, influence of Charles I's day that men began to trim their yews and get bulbs from Holland and the rot sets in again. Oliver Cromwell saved us for a little; did you ever hear any speech of his about gardens? With the Restoration every man's thoughts turned to planning and planting, as you see from Evelyn and Pepys, and we lost our wars by land and sea.'

'Principally to the Dutch, who were famous gardeners,' suggested someone.

'Oh, they had their gardens, I'll admit, but their bulbs were money-making concerns. A utilitarian garden doesn't demoralise as an ornamental garden does. Besides they'd have been better without them. They wouldn't have declined as they did in the 17th century if it weren't for that national blight. As for gardens in England – well, William III was looking at his garden at Hampton when his horse threw him and he died. What worse can you say of a garden that that?'

'Still, we recovered a bit. When Walpole sent everyone mad on turnips in George II's reign, and people left off worrying about flowers and put up arches and grottoes, men's minds grew nobler. A turnip or a potato under a grotto doesn't demoralise you; the grotto's done for life and a potato's career is simple and void of charm. Then you find us cut on the high seas and in India and America every morning bringing despatches of victory. And meanwhile the French monarchy was crumbling under the last few Louis, who did nothing but plan palaces and avenues. They fell at last before the storms of Rousseau and the romantics, and they were very windy, you know, calling Europe to a return to nature. All Europe might have been ruined if the gardening microbe had been let loose then, but mercifully the romantic school raved principally about heather and wild fir trees and waters, so we remained healthy and won Waterloo.'

'Well, the Victorians loved their gardens,' said our hostess defiantly.

'Not as you do,' returned the colonel. 'They let loose their gardeners among the lobelias and dahlias, but you don't find the great scientists and statesmen and authors and politicians running about themselves with bits of bass in their mouths and cuttings of catmint hanging out of their pockets. No, the gardeners bedded out calceolarias and the butlers arranged the fuchsias in epergnes, and left our great men time to get through the mutiny, and the Crimea, and the Factory Acts. No, it was about fifty years ago, partly through the pre-Raphaelites, partly, no doubt, through the infernal skill of Germany, that the gardening microbe was let loose among us.'

'Since when,' I ventured, 'we've won the great war.'

'We were so weak, sir, that we could not avert it,' returned the colonel stoutly. 'We only extricated ourselves by the aid of those non-gardening people the Americans and those utilitarian gardeners the French.'

'But what are the secret vices of gardening?' asked someone wearily.

'They're self-evident, dear lady. A gardener becomes over-attached to one spot of earth, fearful of absence, fearful of risks. He sees the work of his hands prosper, and he becomes wrapt in a cloak of secret self-satisfaction, of private interests, and all the ritual of a secret code. He digs his soul into his plot, and he becomes the prey of all the greater races, the wanderers, the adventurers, the explorers. When a man settles down in a garden he settles downward in evolution. I should like to see all the gardens swept from the face of England, except' – he paused to bow courteously to his hostess – 'this one, dear lady, and …'

'Thank you,' murmured the lady maliciously; 'and ...'

'And my own,' admitted the colonel. 'It's my principal hobby, you know!'

WFP

Gardens Underground
July 18 1924

It is always pleasant to hear every year that the inspectors, linesmen, and other people on the underground are not too tired by their rather depressing life to think of cultivating their gardens. The directors made their journey of inspection to-day to select the prize-winners along the line.

If the prizes go for conquest over natural difficulties the best should go to the east end. There are some marigolds on the upside of Whitechapel station which stand out like a good deed in a naughty world, and there is a neatly arranged garden at the Minories which is about the only garden of any kind in those regions. South Kensington has always had a high reputation in the underground gardening world, and there is a linesman there who can do wonders with antirrhinums and dahlias that fight valiantly against the eternal gloom and smoke. One feels sure that this worker has found a perennial pleasure which compensates for all the depression of mechanical life.

Farther out west the best station gardens are very rich and bright. There is one at Walham Green which could hardly be beaten in a Surrey village. The station gardens have to struggle into existence on any little patch of the embankment which the traffic leaves free. The underground company gives a small grant for stocking the gardens, and sometimes supplies the earth. One wonders whether something might not be done to relive the glazed aridity of the tubes by encouraging little greenhouses on the platforms.

The Fourpenny Packet
April 17 1928

Some years ago I was privileged to listen to a dramatic story from an old countrywoman. She told how her gay garden had attracted the notice of some passing equerry when royalty had been visiting her village, how he had stopped to offer her congratulations, how she had replied, 'All done with fourpenny packets,' and how the equerry ran after the Queen (no less) telling her that she must come and see what could be done with a fourpenny packet. For myself I have no such lofty ambition; I do not much desire to attract the admiration of equerries, but I established the old lady in my mind as the chieftainess of our clan in that she had testified to the fourpenny packet even in the presence of her majesty. It is true that we have no definite organisation; there is no Ancient and Loyal Fraternity of Fourpenny Packeters; we have no password, no rules, no conditions of membership, but I like to think that we have definite characteristics and that the amateur who raises flowers from a fourpenny (it may be a sixpenny) packet of seeds has a definite place among gardeners,

We are not people who have succeeded in life as the world counts success; we do not possess 'places'; the true fourpenny packeter does not even hire a gardener on one day in the week. Such as it is, his garden is his own and it has a way of weaning him from other recreations. You will not find the fourpenny packeter playing golf very often at this time of year; at Easter he was not lured by any of the advertisements of the holiday resorts; his instalment-partly-paid two-seater did not add to the congestion on the roads out of London. In a rather ragged old jacket and a pair of grey flannel trousers arrived at the stage of life in which a few more stains or the tear made by an envious rose thorn are neither here nor there, he might have been seen hoeing, raking, preparing seed-beds, kneeling beside his borders surrounded by gay-hued fourpenny packets, fashioning labels, visualising July and August, By the last day of his holiday his back was aching considerably and the preparation of the ground for the patches of seed was a thought less perfect than on the first day, but he was content. Seed time had been honoured once more, the first stage in the yearly miracle accomplished; the 'sowing in the spring where intended to flower' was done.

The fourpenny packeter has the best of it. The farmer drilling spring corn or roots or broadcasting seeds in the older fashion would be surprised if nothing appeared and is angry and dispirited if fertility is low. The opulent owner of acres of garden may remark to one or other of his helots that he would like a patch of clarkia here or nigella there and troubles himself no more with the matter; like John Forster at the luncheon table, he will say 'Let there be flowers' and (unlike John Forster) he will get what he demands. This is a dull way of gardening in which the only emotion stirred easily is one of annoyance; it reminds me of a purse-proud magnifico who once conducted me through his greenhouses, hearing that I had some small love of flowers. Wherever I remarked on the fineness of any bloom he would sneer and say that he was afraid he must get rid of his gardener; he had measured the petals and they were definitely smaller than some he had seen at the shows. But the fourpenny packeter never loses the thrill of seeing the first seedlings pushing through the ground; it is at such moments that (however solitary of habit) he will call someone to share his delight; it is one of the characteristics of the fourpenny packeter that he is not selfish; he would rather say 'our borders' than 'my borders.'

I believe it to be the fact that fourpenny packeters are very strong among small practitioners of the arts. The struggling writer, artist, musician will have a garden, as likely as not, even though it be no more spacious that the window ledges which Thomas Gray celebrated. The adventures, the hopes, the fears, the modest successes of the fourpenny packet garden are essentially those of the struggling practitioner of the arts. I cannot associate the successful man with a fourpenny packet garden. Just as he sends his work to an agent whose business it is to sell as profitably as possible so I imagine him handing over the real business of gardening to a hired man, taking all the praise when interviewers surprise him (by careful arrangement) in his 'old world garden,' but really interested only in results, whether in flowers or cheques. The fourpenny packeter, whether in letters or in gardens, has much more of happiness if also much more of failure. He envies neither the rarer flowers nor the great fame of the other; he has done what he set out to do, at least in part; next year he will have finer flowers (but still from a fourpenny packet): next year he will write better stuff (but still not clamant for interviews and pufferies). There are one or two people whom he will conduct, not ashamed in pride, round his garden when the time of flowering comes; there are one or two people whose praise of anything he writes he will value, but he will make no vain boastings. Whoever chooses to admire shall be told – 'All done with fourpenny packets!'

H. T. Kemball Cook

The Hyde Park Wizard
May 5 1928

In the little house in the middle of Hyde Park lives Mr Hay, most Scottish of gardeners, the wizard who is waving a wand and unrolling carpets of the most brilliant flowers before our eyes in the royal parks. Through the severe spell of early spring Mr Hay has cherished the 170,000 British tulip bulbs (the largest show of its kind ever seen in London) which are bursting into flower. Already in the sheltered flower walk of Kensington Gardens blossom early spring tulips, discreet in their shrub-surrounded bays, but they give little idea of the massed glories about to break forth at Victoria Gate, where 50,000 Darwin tulips are unfolding, or of the colour that will soon blaze out in the single-shade bed near Hyde Park Corner, where already a faint haze of pink, yellow or red wavers above the green.

Mr Hay is not the only man from north of the Tweed who lays out our London flowerbeds for us. If a name means anything, the superintendent of Regent's Park, Mr Campbell, is another who has come to teach us the greater gardening.

The life of a horticulturalist is no easy amble from bed to bed, trowel in hand and dreams of glory in his head; nor is it one of dignified repose in an office. Nor only is he concerned with the most intimate details in the lives of his trees, his flowers, and his grass; he is also in constant touch with all the main growers and with the horticultural market. He does not disdain detail, and may even be seen occasionally pursuing with net and spray those pests who ravage his trees.

But to us who feast our eyes upon the delights spread lavishly before us the park superintendents must always remain the supreme practical gardeners – the men who cause that honest commercial bulb on which the amateur gardener lavishes time and care in vain to blossom into a thing of beauty, a joy that will be with us for weeks if heaven and the winds are kind.

Spring-Cleaning the Estate: The Post-War House
April 26 1929

The annual business of spring cleaning is an arduous business in whatever house, small or large, old or new, it is performed. Of the nature of its arduousness no information is needed, for every reader of these columns, whether man or woman, has had, no doubt, an ample experience. There is, however, a type of house, almost wholly the product of the new post-war age, in which, in spite of its newness, the annual spring clean is found to be the most arduous of all. This is the kind of house which one finds standing on all the new housing estates, and the spring cleaning of it is particularly wearying and lengthy because the greater part of the work is done outside and not inside the house.

On our estate, a small one as these things go, the very air is quick with the cleansing properties of spring. It is not choked with the dust and racket of the beating of a hundred carpets, nor are the pavements and front gardens littered with the paraphernalia of the army of decorators who are at present in full occupation. These things would be the chief signs that spring had come in many a district, but not here. We judge the coming of spring by observing signs less subtle and more tangible. When housewives begin to set forth with buckets full of a substance looking like red paste, and begin to treat the low brick walls of their gardens and the walls of the houses as far up as they can reach with their brushes to a liberal touch of rouge, then we know that spring is here. When the husbands come home from the office carrying a series of young forests under their arms, and when lorries begin to arrive at about dinner time on Saturdays loaded with long wooden laths, then we know that gardens are to be restocked and refenced, and these things are the very harbingers of spring.

Fashions in Trees

The annual rite of spring cleaning finds us all a little conservative, and we all tend to play the game of follow my leader. Who sets our fashions I do not know, but once they are set in the spring we follow them with an eager obedience that is almost slavish. Last spring someone bought a laburnum tree and proudly planted it in the front garden. A fortnight later well over half the houses in the road also sported baby laburnum trees. This year, however, laburnum seems to be unfashionable. The rhododendron has supplanted it and is all the rage. Every day at present one see market gardeners dragging rhododendron bushes over their shoulders, trailing their leaves in the dust of the roads, evidence that more and yet more families have decided to mark the opening of gardening season by planting rhododendrons in their front gardens.

Another thing which is keeping most of the householders on this estate busy just now is contracting for loads of soil. The loads are brought in little Ford vans and then deposited unceremoniously on the footpath. Then the children bring their spades, and the very tiny ones use their grubby hands, and valiantly labour to hurl the soil over the garden wall. Then they weary of it, and begin to use the heaps of soil as sand-pits, until they are torn away by their parents, and the rest of the work is left until father comes back from town. But these children are having a splendid time just now, for on one road alone on this estate there are, as I write, no less than ten heaps of soil gracing the footpath.

But our conservatism in spring fashions has, alas! its limits. In our own houses, we thought that we would pose for once as the leaders of a fashion. Instead of buying rhododendrons we bought five poplar trees – little ones, of course – and planted them in a splendid row. Then we happily retired from our labour and awaited the results. But to our chagrin no one whatever has followed our carefully set fashion. Rhododendrons are everywhere, but there is not a poplar tree to be seen on the whole estate, except in our garden. It proves that no rule is without its exceptions, and I suppose that we must take it as the just reward of overweening ambition. But it is very distressing.

RBL

A Woman in Manchester: The Long Evenings
June 8 1929

These long June evenings fill the suburban roads with pleasant sounds. There comes a time when the last of the people who are going out in the car have gone and the stay-at-homes – both man and bird and beast, as the Ancient Mariner ungrammatically expresses it – settle down to their tranquil occupations. In gardens there is the genial sound of someone clipping a hedge, and perhaps the scuff and whir of the lawn mower or the lapping trickle of the hose. Where there is a hose there is usually also a barking dog and the excited shriek of a child, trying, with intense preoccupation and busyness, to distract the attention of authority from the approach of bedtime. Between that and the gardening age are the white-clad people on their way to the tennis club. Canvas chairs are out on the lawn, and somebody has a portable wireless set that spreads a thin and persistent patina of music over the medley of sounds. Enthusiasts drift into neighbours' gardens to compare the growth of delphiniums and stocks. Blackbirds sing and big velvety bees hover over the lupins.

Shaping Nature
February 12 1930

The Institute of Landscape Architects, which was formally inaugurated yesterday by its first presidential address, should make a useful contribution to a handsomer England. Mr Thomas H Mawson reminded his hearers of the great days of their art – days linked inseparably with the laying out of princely estates by landowners of taste. The work of probably the most notable of all practitioners, Sir Joseph Paxton, is well known to the north and midlands, for the grounds of Chatsworth, with their arboretum, vast glasshouses, fountains, and model village of Edensor, stand as a lovelier memorial to him than that Crystal Palace by which he is better known. True, the architects of landscape were apt in the heyday of 18th century formalism to gild the lily without scruple, and with results sometimes more wonderful than lovely. Those who know their Alton Towers, for instance, with its astonishing wealth of regimented evergreens and its inscription to the Earl of Shrewsbury who inspired the design, 'He Made the Desert Smile,' may remember the dry comment of William Morris that the desert was commendably polite in refraining from laughing outright. But it is as little likely that the landscape architect of today would commit such follies of formality as that a great land-owner could be found with the funds to command them. What is unquestionable is that democracy, in a day when parks, public and national, take an ever more important place in popular estimation, will be but poorly served if it cannot command the skill in handling landscape that was once the privilege only of the landed; and the new institute is welcome as a help to supplying that skill.

The Garden Widow: Her Doleful Plaint
May 8 1930

Not everyone believes that home grown vegetables reduce the housekeeping bills, or that gardening is always a soothing occupation leading to peace. Sometimes, whatever its lovers may say, it brings about friction in the home. Evelyn, for instance, whose husband gardens, has a way of pointing this out, and declaring that there is a lot to be said in justification of her predecessor's little adventure with the serpent. She was a grass widow, and bored. Almost certainly she wanted Adam to go for a walk or share in such gaiety as Eden afforded, and he told her he had to pull up peasticks or burn rubbish or engage in other recreations appropriate to the apple-gathering season. He probably fussed, too, if Eve touched flowers or fruit until he thought fit, so that there was a particular attraction in taking an apple. No, says Evelyn, gardening out is only to be undertaken on a commercial scale, with factory inspectors and trade unions behind it, as even a day's outing is impossible if the watering cannot be neglected for a single evening. Talk of being tied up by a nurseless baby! A garden is worse than twins. Moreover the whole family is upset by the rage exhibited when a horse has stuck its head over a wall and eaten a chunk out of a favourite bush, or two cats have settled a dispute in the middle of a flower bed.

Then there are the vegetables themselves. The golf widow murmurs, but she is not expected to cook and eat the balls, as well as listen to descriptions of the game. They are put on one side, or lost. In vain FitzAdam protests that Evelyn may benefit from the vitamins and salts and such-like substances; she simply replies, with deadly truth, that they are both tired of everything he grows before it is ready for the table. Lettuces and cauliflowers are on sale in shops from February onwards, and she is sure they would have scurvy if they waited for FitzAdams productions. Wholesalers bring jam-making fruits to the door – a much pleasanter way of getting them than spending hours in the broiling sun stooping over currant and gooseberry bushes. For each householder to grow his own greenery appears as much a back number as if he had to shear the wool from a sheep before he could have a suit of clothes.

And as for the financial aspect, loads of manure are expensive, and often seeds and plants are bought in duplicate, creeping or crawling or flying creatures having devoured one sowing or crop.

Gardener-employer acquaintances say that every cabbage they cut costs a shilling. FitzAdam hints that this reasoning is illogical, as he pays no wages, and besides, all writers on domestic economy say the use of home-grown vegetables reduces the housekeeping bills. Evelyn's invariable retort is a quotation of the market price of each one in the garden and the suggestion that the total be compared with the last account from the seedsman. So that they are merely making on the swings what they lose on the roundabouts.

MLS

Garden Luxury: New Use for Battleship Timber
July 11 1930

There is no horticultural section to the Royal Show in the sense that there are sections clearly defined for the various departments of agriculture and the modern appliances so essential to it. There is the flower show in the two large marquees, of which a review has already been given in these columns, and in the immediate neighbourhood are a number of stands devoted to garden sundries ranging from the modest penny packet of seeds to the resplendent conservatory and equally imposing greenhouses and garden houses.

But these by no means exhaust the interest of the show as far as the gardener is concerned. Around the entrance and tucked away in the most unlikely byways are a hundred and one things that will enchain his attention if his steps happen to move in those places. And perhaps it is as well that this is so, for otherwise he might miss some of the very things for which, though not primarily intended for his particular benefit, he may have been searching and puzzling his brains over for a long time.

To name a few there are wire fence devices which might be made of great use in the training of climbing and rambling plants; extending ladders which are needed by all who have high wall plants and fruit and other trees to spray and prune; galvanised metal receptacles which would be ideal for the storing of artificial and other fertilisers, soot, and wood ashes; stout three-legged milking stools invaluable to the gardener whose back and knees are not as supple as they once were; cheap automatic latches, as useful on the garden as on the field gate; expensive Australian 'monkey-jacks' which haul up tree stumps and roots with a diameter of eight or nine feet with less strain than it takes some of us to upturn a well-established lupin or hollyhock; small harrows, as useful on the lawn as anywhere else; and so on, almost without end.

On the stands – and there are many of them – wholly devoted to the needs and fancies of the gardener one cannot say that there is much in the shape of outstanding novelty, but there is a great deal to make one wish that one's banking account was a much more substantial affair than it is. Apart from the more 'common or garden' tools, which are strangely invisible – possibly because the makers think that by this time everybody has what he wants for the summer – all the old accessories in the nature of ornaments – birth baths and feeding tables, sun-dials, seats, fences, gates, frames, greenhouses, radiators, lawn-mowers (motor as well as hand), rose arches, and pergolas – to name only a few – are to be seen in bewildering variety, and in some instances attractive departures in the materials brought into use are to be seen.

The revolving garden house which, the heavens willing, enables one to be in sunshine or shade the day long, seems to be becoming more popular; concrete and glass and steel are limiting the claims of wood on the frame and greenhouse; and ordinary glass is giving some way to insulating glass. There are substantial greenhouses, too, so constructed that the purchaser is assured that by no stretch of imagination or even law can they ever be regarded as landlords' fixtures.

The multitude of teak chairs, tables, seats, and similar articles all made from battleships – there can be no doubt about it for the names of the vessels are given! – is such that one begins to wonder what will take their places when the League of Nations gets its way and all our warships are put to such good use. On one stand some of the possibilities of reinforced concrete in the making of pillared pergolas, bricks, and paved paths in a variety of colours are admirably demonstrated.

Gardens, Young and Old
August 2 1930

On the subject of gardens most gardeners would hold that I have very little right to speak. I do not like digging, am a poor hand with a scythe, weed but fitfully, mistrust all rakes, and am, in fact, much better at enjoying gardens than at making them or at keeping them in order when made. I do not evade my share of the work in the garden by pleading conscientious objections (as does one friend of mine, who says that he likes nature and that the more you garden the farther from nature you get), but I escape just the same, because my efforts, though well meant, are feared by the true gardener almost as much as a plague of slugs, mice, locusts, and chaffinches combined. I am not allowed to do any gardening beyond plucking off pansy blossoms that have passed their prime. This, authority and experience teach me, is the way to keep the pansies flowering freely all through the summer with blossoms of the largest size. So, when I think of it, I go and do it, and, when visiting the gardens of my friends or when my friends are visiting me, I earn easily quite a lot of respect, by stooping (when somebody is looking) and carefully picking off a few blossoms, with the remark that they have probably been overlooked. But, just because from my youth up my activities in gardening have been generally feared and therefore forbidden, just because gardening has been, as you like it, beyond or beneath me, I have been free to think about gardens. It is quite true that I have nothing to say on phosphates, leaf mould, pruning (which I think rather cruel), and such things, but, to make up for this, I have something to say on the relations between gardens and man.

Gardeners proper may disagree with my observations. But (on paper I am not afraid to say it) gardeners proper seem to me to be creatures like moles or worms, so busy moling or worming that they are incapable of seeing much beyond the dirt they play with. To them a garden is simply a garden. It is to them what a battlefield is to a general or a chessboard to a composer of problems. It is the arena in which they can enjoy and display their activities. From year's end to year's end they are at it, digging, hoeing, sowing, pricking out, bedding out, pruning, grafting, mowing, and looking over nurserymen's catalogues and the lyrical invitations of the Dutch bulb-growers. These activities recur continually, and the busy gardener leaves it to me consider, from outside, his relation to his flowers. He is himself almost too busy to perceive what he is doing, or how he and his garden change. Intent on growing his flowers, he may not suspect that his choice of them varies with his years, so that his garden may reflect his own life-story.

The born gardener begins in childhood, at an age when the past seems negligible, the future fantastic, and the present extraordinarily lasting. His flowers then, his favourite flowers, are virginian stock, asters, nasturtiums (especially Tom Thumbs), marigolds, sweet peas, and all the other cheerful, showy annuals that can be grown from penny packets (or have penny packets gone up in price like all else?). Then, perhaps, when the time comes, he will add a few seedlings from the shop, violas, monkey-flowers, or snapdragons. An aunt may give him a geranium or two, a calceolaria, or one of those exotic begonias. These things will keep his private bed alight until the winter, when he forgets it and them until spring sunshine send him to the penny packets once again.

This liking for annuals (for the other plants mentioned are hardly likely to survive his treatment of them, nor does he expect them to last) reflects very well his unconsciousness of his own mortality. For him a few months extend almost for ever. It is also noticeable that in childhood he chooses the gayest of annuals. I regard as only of the first signs of growing up a readiness to sow some mignonette, a flower of sterling qualities but lacking in the direct garish appeal of some of the other penny-packeters. I do not pretend to lay down rigid rules on such matters. Any child may fall in love with any flower. But, in general, the proper places for annuals is in the child's garden, and the child's instinct takes him to the annuals first of all.

As he grows up he begins to acquire a taste for flowers of a more wifely and less flirtatious character. These annuals that smile through a few weeks of summer and then are gone for ever, like pretty girls who wave from passing trains before disappearing into eternity, begin to lose interest for him in comparison with flowers that will stick it out through the winter and welcome the gardener with the returning spring. The youthful but no more childish gardener is not quite in so much of a hurry to get an immediate return, but comes to think highly of flowers that are at their best, not a month or two after sowing, but in their second year, like sweet Williams, canterbury bells, and wallflowers. Perennials, like phlox and michaelmas daisies, grow in favour as the gardener grows older. It is remarkable that though even very young people like roses to look at, to smell, or to give to each other, they leave the growing of roses to their more patient elders.

Bulbs, grown by everybody, seem at first sight to evade this kind of classification by the age of their admirers. But it is not so. For bulbs can be either annual or perennial, according to the treatment they receive. For example, children love growing a bulb in a glass, in winter, keeping it in the boot cupboard till the lower glass is filled with roots, and then promoting it to a sunny window to watch the green spike rise and burst with its astonishing miracle. Soon after that, when the flower fades, the bulb begins to smell most horribly and is banished from the nursery. Somehow or other it never appears again, and next year new bulbs are brought in to put in the old glasses. Those bulbs whose fate it is to delight a winter nursery are quite clearly annuals. For older people bulbs are not annuals but perennials. They too grow a few bulbs indoors, for creative purposes, but they have an increasing sympathy with the outdoor bulbs, which die away so completely and then, year after year, confound the pessimists by reappearing, as the older people do, in their accustomed places.

The general principle that these observations seem to establish is that as man, growing older, becomes more and more conscious of his mortality, instead of seeking by a choice of short-lived plants to flatter his own longevity, he prefers those which may more easily outlast him. This principle is by no means upset by those who do not desert the annuals as they grow older. They may grow a few for various reasons, for the sake of their children, or as a sentimental tribute to their own childhood, but the annuals are no longer enough for them, and their deeper affections are for the less fugitive inhabitants of their gardens. This truth is most clearly illustrated in the planting of flowering shrubs, and especially of trees. Old men plant trees, not young, though it is obvious that the young man who plants a tree has a better chance than an old man of living to enjoy the shade of it. When a young man plants a tree it is, as a rule, to humour a much elder man than himself. The youthful heir to the great estate does not naturally rush forth on his 21st birthday to celebrate his coming of age by planting a tree. But his ageing father, having taken late in life to planting trees, makes his son do what he now wishes he had himself done thirty years before, and so plants a tree by proxy, and, by proxy, will enjoy it 30 years after. The passage in which Scott's enthusiasm for tree-planting shows at its height was written by him within a few years of his death. I did once hear of a small boy planting trees on his own account, and was much interested, until it appeared that mercenary motives were involved, and that he was setting up as a nursery gardener and selling his trees at exorbitant prices to an aunt. I never feel greater confidence that I am what insurance companies call 'a good life' than when I notice that, though I think a row of greengages ought to do well at the bottom of the orchard, year by year I forget the planting of them until it is too late. If I had planted them when first I thought of it I might by now be counting the ripening fruit upon their branches and hating jays and blackbirds. When, at last, I do plant them, or rather insist on their being planted, for I shall not be trusted with the spade, I shall take as a decided indication that I am getting old.

Arthur Ransome

The Jail Garden
August 19 1930

Gardens tended by women detained in Holloway Prison is a dream of Miss MD Stubbs, of the National Gardens Guild, that has come true. Inside that grim place for wrong-doers are three big gardens where summer flowers are in bloom, bringing their fragrance to beautify the drab prison life.

Only a short time ago one of those gardens was a dumping ground for coke; another was a rubbish heap; and the third consisted of a long strip of rough grass having a sycamore tree, a wasps nest, iron railings, and a drain pipe. How the transformation was wrought was told to a reporter yesterday by Miss Stubbs, who explained that the Prison Gardening Association works in conjunction with the National Gardens Guild.

'I have been attending Holloway prison for the past two years,' Miss Stubbs said. 'The prisoners come voluntarily to my lectures and classes, and do all the gardening themselves. We have three classes, each lasting two hours, every weeks, and my pupils are from 25 to 70 years old. Some are only strong enough to pick seed-pods; some wield a pick-axe to break up the hard ground. They are very friendly and keen about gardening. They have told me that they look out anxiously each morning to see what the weather is like. If there is rain, they know there will be no gardening in the evening. Usually then, I give them lectures. In one of the plots they grow lettuce, which, I believe, they are allowed to have for tea.

'I shall never forget the first lecture I gave when 23 prisoners filed in with an officer behind them. She left them with me, and locked us all up for an hour. Women nowadays are well treated in prison. The cells are now called rooms, the wardresses are known as officers, and there is a bell in every room which the prisoner can ring in case of need. Every room has electric light, and the prisoners are allowed to use it till nine at night. The women's health is well looked after, and they are allotted work in accordance with their strength.

'One woman wanted me to give her hints about stocking a garden because, she said, her husband had bought a house which had a plot at the back, and when she came out she wanted to be able to lay it out. Another woman who had been gathering seed-pods told me that never again would she buy a pot of stock in flower for eightpence thinking it would provide her seed for her little garden. She knew now what a penny packet of seed would do.

'They are friendly, decent people, these unfortunate women. One of them particularly wanted flowers planted in a plot because, she said, the hospital cells overlooked the plot, and it would be something to cheer up the women patients. To be able to get out in the open-air among the growing life of plants and flowers gives these women a fresh mental outlook. It teaches them that there is something more in life than the sordid little things that have occupied their thoughts. Many of them feel their imprisonment very keenly, but work in a garden makes them forget and shows them there is still beauty of life, that life is still worth while.'

A Gardener's Grumble: Exchange No Robbery
October 23 1930

This is the time of year when I long to possess a thrusting, unsnubbable nature. Like all gardeners, I have spent the sunny hours of the autumn days digging and dividing, replanting and discarding, planning once more that garden beautiful which ever eludes my grasp. And – this is where the thrusting nature would come in – I have cast my eye covetously upon various plants in my neighbours' gardens.

Mrs Smithers opposite specialises in a particularly beautiful mauve and gold pansy; my beds are a summer riot of a rather rare crimson viola. Through the medium of her rather unattractive children I have arrived on speaking terms with her, but she little knows, as we converse on this and that, that I am longing to shout, in schoolboy fashion, 'Will you swop some pansy cuttings?' Of course, I can't say it; it isn't done in our road.

I still shrink shyly past the gate of Holm Nooke, the scene of last autumn's humiliation. For, emboldened by desire, I dared to stop one day and address the fierce-looking lady who was spraying roses in the borders.

'Excuse me,' I began, 'Could you tell me the name of that lovely pink with the crimson spots? I do so admire it.'

'Dianthus rosea splendens,' she boomed. I was favoured with one short scornful glance, and then the fierce lady continued her elimination of lesser pests. And yet, if only she had met me in the proper gardening spirit, we might have been a tremendous joy to each other. If she had given me some of those delightful pinks, I would even have responded with some slips of a brand new variety that no one else in our road has even dreamt about.

Why cannot we, in the interests of our cherished bits of gardens, throw our deadly husk of grown-up reserve and false delicacy? If only we could attain some measure of frankness I can picture our road on an autumn Saturday afternoon as happy as an exchange and mart as any boys' playground, with its stamp and cigarette card 'swaps,' its harmless barter.

But I don't feel very sanguine somehow. We are hedged closely in and away from each other by more than our carefully clipped privet. And I am afraid that my best hope lies in my own courageous trowel on some dark October night ...

HMM

Catalogues: The Flower Seed Order
January 24 1934

Once upon a time the gardening year crept upon us quietly, almost secretly. It just came. You went to bed one dark moist night, slept the clock round, strolled out into the soft earthy garden and – what did you see? Nothing much until you went to look, poking your fingers among the mould and the cosy covering of warm brown beech leaves. Then you came upon the first glossy, gold aconite, wide open, flaunting itself in a new green frill.

Next day a bright blue hepatica popped up. Soon you were drinking your midday coffee out of doors on the sunny side of the house, free of furs and goloshes, and watching the snowdrops unfold. Over the garden wall kindred spirits exchanged roots and ideas. The little acres were re-planned – 'roots where tops is and tops where roots is,' according to rural custom. Rubbish was tipped into trenches and little heed paid to those who croaked about the weather – 'we shall pay for this later on.' Spring was here, without any blowing of trumpets to announce the event.

Gardening in those days was a leisurely affair, free and easy. Contentedly, the same old-fashioned flowers, mignonette and marigolds, seeded themselves all over the place. Little pansies were everywhere, and no one minded that they were so small because they were so sweet. Heartsease they were called then, not show blossoms with fancy names. You were careful not to tread upon the Madonna lily patch, and you hunted out bits of old flannel on which to sow mustard seed and cress. And that was about all the preparation that was made for spring.

Fireside gardening

What a change has taken place! Christmas cards and seed catalogues come by the same post. More often than not they bear the same floral device. Snow, robins, and swinging bells in lighted towers are out of fashion. Rose arches, rock-garden designs are in, for greeting purposes, as if to tempt you to order, every spring, a newer and more extravagant list of seeds and specimens.

And what a joy those catalogues are. Truly a gay guide to fireside gardening. As you get busy with paper and pencil the evening is gone, but the time is not wasted. Later on, when the hot sun forces up unnumbered seedlings, you will know how and where to plant them before they fade.

It is great fun making imaginary picture gardens. I knew a girl who made a blue garden. It was paved with old flagstones and enclosed by a rough limestone wall. The catalogue offers unlimited blue shades from A to Z for this pretty fancy. It also gives free inspiration all the way through. You may plan the whole year ahead. Also there are novelties to be watched for and noted down. Who failed to grow the new double-scented nasturtium last summer? Not long ago it was too costly for ordinary impecunious garden-lover. Into my scrapbook go all the notices of recent flower shows for reference, annuals, biennials, perennials – all call for different cultivation, some for the greenhouse, others for outdoor sowing.

I encourage the notion each spring of growing some flower new and strange, and last year grew, for the first time, that queer flower salpiglossis. How it lasted! In the autumn a few slips off the old plants were stuck in a frame. They are alive. This year I have marked Zinnias and that South African perennial Arctotis Scapjgera. Only lack of space prevents a tick marked against every variety of seed offered. One must draw the line somewhere when dealing with such an entrancing problem as the flower seed order.

TT

Keeper of the Cacti
January 31 1934

Tomorrow Mr Cobbold, who has been curator of the cactus house in Alexandra Park since it was built, retires from the corporation service. He has an even longer connection with the cactus collection, for he was employed by the late Mr Charles Darrah, who started it. When Mr Darrah gave the collection to the corporation in 1906 Mr Cobbold went with it. Since then the collection has grown, not so much by purchase as by exchange with other collections. Just recently, for instance, there has been an exchange of specimens with a United States collector. The Alexandra Park collection is one of the finest in the world: it is certainly the equal and in some respects the superior of the collection at Kew. Mr Cobbod will be succeeded by Mr H Hall, who is now assisting him and who had had experience both at Kew and abroad.

The different types of cactus require constant care – one variety has to be cross-pollinated by hand: the curator has to take the place of the insects which should carry out this function. Mr Hall will have to take over all these duties from Mr Cobbold, but he is likely to escape one troublesome duty which bothered his predecessor. Mr Cobbold in the days of the militant suffragettes had to guard the cactus house from violence, and one occasion an attempt was actually made to blow it up. A good deal of damage was done to the house, but fortunately the plants escaped lightly.

Roses Round the Door: Advice from Experts
January 16 1935

Mr Eddie Cantor recently informed me through my three-valve wireless set that you cannot grow roses round the door unless you plant them there. Dean Hole began his famous book on roses by saying that the man who would grow roses successfully must have roses in his heart. Having brought some new rose trees (or is it bushes?) and asked my expert friends how to stick them in the dirt, I find that neither Mr Cantor nor Dean Hole has said all there is to say about growing roses.

In the first place I was brought up on the idea that lots of clay was good for roses, and as my new garden is full of the stickiest clay imaginable I began to fancy my chances for the local championships. When I met Hodgson (who writes about roses) I led up cunningly to my new batch. 'What sort of soil have you got?' he asked. 'Clay,' I said triumphantly. 'That's a pity,' he said, 'a great pity.'

Thus I gathered that the clay idea was just a legend. There was a chance for me if I broke up the clay thoroughly, digging at least three spits (or it might have been spats) deep, and incorporating into the shattered clay all the 'top sod' I could get hold of. With roses in your heart and top sod in your clay, you could grow almost any rose known to horticultural science.

I had not the heart to tell him that it was as much as we could do to keep the top sod on our little patch of lawn, never mind sparing a bit for the roses. Although several visits have been made during the dark weather to a neighbouring meadow, there are still a few bald patches. If we try seed, our sparrows call in their neighbours during the busy season. They simply love the scares, and perch on them when their little stomachs are full – which is seldom.

So I guided the talk on to varieties. 'What have you got?' he asked. It took me a while to find the paper. 'Mabel Morse,' I said. 'Mabel Morse' he admitted to be a beautiful flower but a poor grower. And anyhow it was no good for my district. 'Not even with top sod?' I implored. He was adamant. Not even with top sod would it do in our district. I began to see what Dean Hole meant.

What Hodgson does not know is that my neighbour, who never puts top sod into his clay (and knows little more about roses than that the roots are the bottom of the tree or bush), grows 'Mabel Morse' splendidly. His brother brought him the trees and gave him two injunctions: plenty of manure and cut them well back in the spring. Without even sticking to that he fills his bowls and hands us an odd bloom or two over the rails. When I have planted mine I shall read what the gardening books say.

TT

Gardens on Display: The Efforts of the Great
June 13 1935

The opening of private gardens to the public on payment of a small fee devoted to the cause of charity is probably one of the most popular movements of the day. Innumerable people take advantage of it and, with so many facilities for transport, the numbers are increasing and everyone with a pocket-handkerchief of a garden wants to see what people are doing on a grander scale. One point which emerges is the large number of fine gardens in this country with, usually, a house to match. Another is the dislike of the really formal garden, except as a setting to a house or where everything is so big that some sort of order must ensue. Even so, gardening in England is singularly informal as compared with that in France, and a much larger proportion of the space seems to be given over to flowers and flowering shrubs which are the chief characteristic at this time of year.

Owners of gardens themselves must regret the necessity for fixing dates a long time beforehand. Many of the rhododendron and azalea gardens recently have been much spoilt by the weather, whereas a few days earlier they would often have been at their best. Rock gardens are a perpetual interest, whether the particular form of Himalaya suits the garden or not, and everyone who possesses even as much as a few clinkers does not spare criticism or admiration of his most magnificent neighbour. Garden-lovers on the whole seem on the elderly side. The assemblies at the various gardens are much the same as those who go early to the horticultural shows. Gardeners are seen there and children are taken. Gardening is less amusing and perhaps too stationary for the 20s. In some of the bigger places, teas may be obtained for a sum which means additional profit to whatever fund is being supported. Probably more might be done in this respect, especially where a certain amount of organisation is bound to take place. At one garden there were at least 200 cars, all neatly parked in the meadow, directed by an ex-sergeant major. Helpers are also needed in the display of the ground. The one-time show place has developed into a multitude of show places, great and small, all of which seem to attract the whole of the countryside.

Gentle Pleasures
August 8 1935

The Latin folk say we make a pain of our pleasures. Perhaps that is why the French are so fond of walled gardens. A walled garden suggests seclusion; you may potter there without even the excuse of a spade stuck in the earth near by, and the outer world is shut off from you, so that your eyes are not tempted to wander and your mind to roam from the flowers, the mossy walls, and the pleasant paths.

The hillside garden has its charm, especially if the sea is visible in the distance through trees, but here you are on view; some neighbour may hail you from the road, and a garden should be a place of peace. Your feet should know every inch of a path by 'feel'; there should be a seat in a corner that catches the sun all day, so that you seat yourself on mellow warmth. You find yourself gazing at the hollyhocks swaying gently in the faintest breeze, or at the pansies, with their soft velvet faces along the border, and the world that has seemed inimical becomes suddenly a friendly place.

To lie on the ground, flat, your back stretched on the grass and the coolness of green blades on your face, seems to give strength; it is as if the earth pulsed strength into you. 'Let me get my bare pads on the soil and I will face the world.' There is something in that. As we draw farther from nature it is well that we should have her, even if tamed a little, on our doorstep in the shape of a fine old tree, a grass plot, a pool, and the brightness of flowers. In a garden, if you walk it towards evening, as the birds pass from evensong to silence, all things seem to conspire to gather round you in gentleness. The first night-beetle hums by on heavy wings, the soft-bodied moths drift over the flowers, perhaps a late bee goes by, and an owl sails to the tree with ghostly wings.

PHJ

The Walled Garden
August 7 1936

To the great and good are given walled gardens set in the middle of more garden, and innumerable gardeners. But some of the Georgians, who had the knack of building a large house on a limited space, made the walled garden one of the features of the house. They did not hesitate to set the house almost on the street, with all the pleasantness of looking out and seeing what was going on. Or they had a small garden in front and enormous gates, which equally could be looked through, and a magnolia, which somehow clothed the house beautifully. The walled garden would have one big tree in a corner of it: it did not shade the house too much, but suggests rooks and greensward. The garden provided a great deal of wall-fruit and then gave itself over to flowers that could be picked without breaking the heart of the owner. A walled garden in Sussex today is full of gooseberries trained against the wall, pears with a bias cut against the wall, apples, and so forth, all of good stock. The rest of it is lawn, with flower-beds at the moment crammed with tall sweet Williams, spiraeas, campanulas, anchusa, columbines, snapdragons. From the front door with its portico there is a view through the house into the walled garden, through a wide doorway into a farther garden, and up a grass path to the end.

H

Kitchen Gardens
November 7 1936

It is sad to reflect that our kitchen gardens are becoming smaller and of less importance as the years pass. Gardens were at first planned and tended almost solely for the cultivation of herbs and vegetables, flower gardens being almost unknown. Gradually the kitchen garden, owing to its economic importance, developed into a garden of pleasure as well as one of usefulness, and it was often planned on an extensive scale. With the coming of flowering shrubs and the many varieties of flowers, the kitchen garden once more reverted to a place for purely utilitarian ends, and flower gardens as such came into evidence. Now, with quick transport, comparatively cheap vegetable, and tinned foods, the kitchen garden is quickly slipping out of existence in private gardens, and we are thereby losing much interest in gardening and, indeed, in good eating also.

Let us see how we can combine, in the comparatively small garden, the pleasure of growing good fruit and vegetables in beautiful surroundings. In most gardens of a small size those vegetables which are grown usually become tucked away as far from sight as possible, and are screened off in disgrace from the rest of the garden by a laurel hedge, or even more unsightly diamond-shaped trellis.

Draw a rough plan of your garden and see whether it is not possible to redesign the ground as a whole and thereby make your garden seem more extensive and important. Your main paths will be the first consideration and these should be sufficiently wide to allow two persons to walk comfortably abreast. If it is possible to have smaller paths for the wheelbarrow to one side of the garden then this main walk can be of turf. These paths should divide the garden into convenient-sized plots.

A garden in Surrey
Since this is to be a flower, fruit, and vegetable garden combined, the main pathway must be made attractive. In a famous 16th century garden at Albury just such a broad grass walk runs under slender iron hoops, spaced about 10 feet apart, up which are trained cordon apples and pears. These are planted in pairs, opposite each other, to give a uniform appearance. Beneath this and on either side of the grass are borders, four feet wide, in which are planted bold groups of low-growing gay flowers such as violas, petunias, and pinks, and they are arranged for the convenience of culture in blocks of one variety. This arrangement looks excellent and makes the tending of the flowers a straightforward business.

At the point where this path meets the other main path, which cuts across at right-angles, the occasion is made for a circular dipping tank. This has a simple, flat stone rim, 18 inches above the turf, upon which are stood oblong terra-cotta pots full of those flowers which need the protection of a cold frame during the winter; these include fuschias, heliotrope, maiden's wreath, hydrangeas, and cannas. The smaller dividing paths could well be edged with low box or, if slugs are feared, by narrow borders of low-growing flowers such as dianthus, auricular, or iris, and these could in turn be backed by espalier or cordon fruit, trained on well-designed square trellis. Red and white currants and gooseberries lend themselves to being trained as single, double, or triple cordons, and are a happy decoration to the minor paths; and the wineberry and improved blackberry are also attractive.

The vegetables are planted in conformity with this design. This is not the place to discuss which varieties should be chose. Bear in mind, however, the decorative beauty of rarely grown delicacies as the elegant sweet corn, the lovely coloured seakale, and the handsome foliage of the globe artichoke. The beauty of a well-designed kitchen garden that combines both grace and utility is a subject which needs a book to itself.

A

Flowers in the Grass
April 29 1937

I once read an article on gardens in China in which it was said that the Chinese do not care for formal beds but prefer to grow flowers informally among grass. The hint was, somehow, fascinating and led to much speculation on what sort of flowers and what sort of grass and how. Then speculation led to experiment.

Daffodils and snowdrops in rough grass and crocuses on the lawn are one of the commonest as well as one of the most beautiful sights of spring. Primroses and polyanthus are less often seen but have proved equally attractive, especially along the edges of a grass path bordered by rockery. Cutting the grass round about the plants is rather a nuisance, but the owner of a small and precious plot does not mind resorting to shears and even to scissors.

There is another small flower that will grow on the lawn without any help at all and that is the daisy. There is a certain advertisement for weedkiller in which a perky little daisy is shown gazing up innocently from its dainty rosette of leaves at a hand from which are falling some grains of a poisonous substance. The murder of plantain or thistle I can endure, even that of the dandelion, which is a handsome flower but given away by its course leaves. But that evil treatment of the daisy makes my blood boil. I have never found anyone in the country to support my plea for the daisy; but in the city of Hanover, distinguished for its beautiful public gardens, it is permitted to grow, not entirely unchecked, but with a freedom in some contrast to that of the humans who look on it.

Cow Parsley
Another experiment took place in a garden where there was a largish area of grassland left wild for children to play in. The owner, however, was anxious to bring the meadow into some sort of relation with the rest of the garden; so we took up, here and there, irregular patches of turf and filled the spaces with a good light soil in which we sowed seeds of various annual poppies. Then, in order to smooth the transition from the garden proper to the poppyfield, we collected from among the grass all the plants of parsley we could find and set them at the back of the herbaceous border. 'Dim was the cow parsley in the meadows,' wrote Virginia Woolf in that most poignant of war-books, *Jacob's Room*, poignant because there is no war in it, only a story of peaceful development that is abruptly terminated. Well, all the fragrance and luxuriance of high summer is in that phrase, and so it was, also, in the foaming white flowers that made the background to our border and the introduction to our meadow.

At present it is the classical spirit that is uppermost in gardening, though I suppose at any moment we may be toppling over into surrealism. Indeed, something of the sort was indicated the other week by the BBC's well-known garden expert when he described a friend's rock garden. This was said to include marble mantelpieces and some chimney-pots. And last summer, in Germany, I myself saw giant sunflowers growing in a window box. They sprouted at the first floor and flowered at the second. But, generally speaking, we are being told to consider form and design and to regard gardening as almost a branch of architecture. Romantic and literary gardening is, I am afraid, out of fashion, and flowers in grass is an essentially romantic notion. And to me literary. William Morris's story, '*The*

Hollow Land, written while he was still an undergraduate, but remaining, I think, his greatest achievement in literature, ends with the words: 'And before us lay a great space of flowers.' My picture of that panorama of the Hollow Land was not just one of fields of flowers, but of a mingling of flowers with many coloured grasses, a sort of supernatural meadow. This fancy inspired my experiment with poppies, snapdragons and other ordinary flowers, together with decorative grasses, annuals and such perennials as the common green and white ribbon grass and pink Glyceria spectabilis and pampas. I also used plants with grass-like leaves such as iris and montbretia. Some barley, too, was sown to make a patch of autumn gold in the background.

Personally, I was pleased with my meadow, though no doubt to others it may have appeared rather formless. But that is the position with all gardens. What the onlooker may see as an undistinguished agglomeration of plants is often to its creator his entrance to the hinterland of dreams. Dreams are of many kinds, memories of childhood often. These dreamers are the people who plant wallflowers and mignonette and other scented plants, because scents somehow evoke memories more effectively than either sights or sounds. Then there are would-be travellers who try to obtain subtropical effects with the aid of concealed flower-pots and yuccas tied up for the winter in sacking or, more practically, confine themselves to gardening under glass. We have to think of Cinderella's coach when we look on old Henry's giant pumpkin at the show, and to remember that even the squarest and most conventional front garden may be somebody's supernatural meadow.

MED

Banker-gardeners
July 12 1938

For whatever reason, gardening is a favourite pastime among people who work in banks. Perhaps it is that the spying of incipient weeds is like spotting the doubtful client, or that an orderly array of beds and borders has kinship with the exactitude of figures. With the exception of Barclays bank, all the 'big five' now have their thriving horticultural societies. Lloyds bank – which is the latest to take to gardening – only formed a horticultural society last year, and already, by the time of that society's second show, which is taking place now at the head office in Lombard Street, its membership is 1,250. It has been the worst possible year for gardeners, yet apparently the judges declared the roses on exhibit admirable by any standards or for any year, and they praised the delphiniums and sweet peas.

On an average, a bank garden measures about 40 feet by 30 feet, and most of the owners are their own spare-time gardeners. In the Lloyds Bank show messengers as well as branch managers are represented, and so keen are some people – in both the upper and lower grades of bank employment – that they have changed their homes simply to have better gardens. Some of them go in for kitchen-garden produce as well as flowers. These, curiously enough, are not the lower-grade men, who might do it for profit, but the higher staff, who, it is said, do it for fun.

Tap Water for Gardens
June 24 1939

When a number of persons were summoned at Stoke-on-Trent yesterday for illegally using tap water for their gardens, the Potteries stipendiary magistrate (Mr W McGregor Clarkson) said, 'It seems such a pity that gardens have to go, because they mean such a lot in the lives of so many people.' Mr C E Herbert, prosecuting on behalf of the Staffordshire Potteries Water Board, said it had not been possible to buy water for gardening purposes since April 1, 1938, owing to the shortage of water, and the board regretted the necessity of taking the prosecutions.

The stipendiary magistrate dismissed several of the cases for lack of evidence and imposed fines in others varying from 5s. to 15s.

Lawns and Order:
1940–1959

Soil Association founded, 1946 * *Gardeners' Question Time*, 1947 *
Festival of Britain, 1951 * CE Lucas Phillips' *The Small Garden*,
1952 * Percy Thrower's *Gardening Club*, 1956

Home-Grown: Help for Allotment Holders
January 29 1940

The excellent work which is being done by the Friends' Allotment
Committee and the Central Allotments Committee to help the
unemployed, partially employed, and seriously impoverished people
to obtain and cultivate their allotments and gardens is indicated in
their annual report for last year and in an accompanying appeal for
continued public support.

There are now 2,622 societies, representing 102,892 persons,
receiving help from the committees. Last year they received 77,204
collections of seeds, 2,481 tons of seed potatoes, 669 tons of fertiliser,
14,228 tools and 5,596 gardening and cookery booklets. The men
themselves contributed £22,255 toward the cost, and to that public

contributions added £9,122, and the government a similar sum – a total cost of £40,033. The produce which resulted was valued at about £600,000. For the coming season the expenditure is estimated to amount to £45,600. Towards this the men are expected to contribute £24,600, the government will grant up to £10,500, and the committees hope to receive £10,500 from the public.

Digging Overdone
April 20 1940

The admirable practice of digging for victory can be carried too far. If the patriotic householder decides that a few rows of beans shall mark the place where his miniature lawn used to be that is his own concern, and his landlord's. But when it comes to the Ministry of Agriculture taking over for potato growing under its war time powers a recreation ground that is in constant use by the youth of the district, public policy is involved. In the case which Sir Lawrence Chubb referred to yesterday the playing field was one of those acquired under the George V Memorial scheme. It cost £6,000 to drain, level, and lay out, and when finished was able to offer to schools in the area six cricket pitches, six football fields, and 24 tennis courts. It is not only that the expense of restoring it to its original purpose will be out of all proportion to its agricultural yield. The ground was performing as a playing-field a function quite comparable in importance to the producing of food. Fresh air and exercise are as needful to the city child as fresh vegetables, and it is to be hoped the precedent thus set will not be followed elsewhere. There is abundance of idle land that could be turned to food production grounds. Successive commissions of experts, for instance, have established the fact that anything up to 3 million acres of the Scottish deer forests could, if properly handled, be brought back to their former agricultural uses. Steps are now being taken to advise local agricultural committees of the best means of utilising them. With more foresight the agricultural area could have been greatly increased by this spring. But whenever it is undertaken work on this scale should make needless any interference with little bits of land that are already put to their best use in providing health for the younger generation in the towns.

Half an Acre: Making a Vegetable Garden
June 12 1940

The war, or rather the consequential exhortation to dig for victory, has solved the problem of the half-acre paddock at the back of the cottage. In its day it would seem to have been many things to its several owners. Straying tufts of forget-me-not still hinted at the outline of a border; odd blooms popped up unexpectedly and incongruously in the rank grass. But in the final year of uneasy peace, when the cottage was mainly a week-end camp, we were content to present and preserve an air of respectability at the front and let nature frolic as she would in the paddock. The Scotties at least delighted in it, for a rabbit was often to be startled and give noisy but always unsuccessful chase by Jock and Jenny. And we did gather a rich and entirely untended crop of raspberries. Our lettuce perished before the rabbits, but two marrow plants brought forth their fruit in almost embarrassing abundance and harvest festival dimensions.

With the evacuation of the family to the cottage the unshorn face of the paddock soon became an eyesore. When the government called for the growing of more food it became also a thing of shame. The first job obviously was to break up the turf, and 20 minutes' work with a spade was sufficient to show that before any appreciable amount of a surface of the nature of coconut matting had been lifted by the combined energies of two women, two children, and a week-ending male, all sowings for a 1940 crop would have been in vain.

It was the daily help who suggested the solution of the problem. Her husband, she said, could produce a plough if we could produce a horse. In fact, he produced both, and before their arrival I undertook to get rid of the jungle-like grass crop of 1939 which the great frosts had left flaxen as a patriarch's bear. That was really my only positive contribution to the primary act of digging for victory, and, if not heroic, it was at all events spectacular. It was the simple accident of dropping a match which suggested that fire might accomplish twice as quickly the work of a scythe. Twice as quickly was the grossest of underestimates. For a few moments I walked behind a thoroughly well-behaved fire, checking its course here, encouraging it there. Then suddenly the wind freshened – and there was the fire leaping ahead at an alarming pace, racing towards one neighbour's woodpile and hen run, breaking through the hedge in a crackling encircling movement over the garden of the empty house on the left, with a range of greenhouses in its track. Disaster seemed inevitable, but beaters arrived, and the casualty list did not extend beyond the raspberry canes and the hedge.

The horse came the following day, and I felt sure I had seen him before. He was, indeed, the horse chartered by the rural district council to cart the dustbin contents to the spot where they are hidden from view. He is a very large horse and apparently a strict trade unionist. Or else when he looked round and discovered the strange piece of ironmongery attached to him his sense of dignity was outraged. At first he stuck his toes in and refused to budge an inch. Then, 'encouraged' by much tugging from behind, he made his firs furrow like a Roman chariot charging into action. With continued 'encouragement' and much shouting the job was done.

That was several weeks ago. Now the potatoes are coming along in 18 rows, the beetroot is showing strongly, and although the carrots are a mystery and the first two rows of scarlet runners, sown against the weight of local advice, were nipped by a May-morning frost the townsman never heard of, their successors are already running an exciting race with the peas. We are eating our own radishes and spring onions and shortly the infuriating experience of paying fourpence for a lettuce will be no more. The celery and the marrows are in. It has all been good fun and good exercise, and we are getting proud of it. In fact, we now refer to the cottage as the farm.

One for Luck: Strangers in the Garden
July 4 1940

Very often when we are buying seedlings the market gardener will throw in an odd plant, as he says, for luck. Occasionally, too, the gardener will find that he gets new plants without being sure how they have arrived. Nature works her will in many ways. Sometimes the birds will carry seeds and drop them; perhaps in return for food and drink provided, but more often, I fancy, because they are carrying more than they can hold.

This spring we got a nice display from a small plant of daphne mezerion. We do not remember planting this, and it is almost certainly a gift from our feathered pensioners. Next year it will be a good sized bush, ready to transplant to some more suitable place in the garden. In our small front garden there is a young laburnum which must be the offspring of the bigger trees in our neighbours' gardens. It just butted in and will have to be moved, as it is treading on the toes of a young lilac bush. Nearby there is a plant of the white campanular, also a gift from the gods.

Not all visitors are welcome. These last few years the rose-bay willow-herb has flourished in extraordinary fashion on commons, in hedges, and even between the crevices of neglected pavements. This pretty weed sends seeds most plentifully and can be seen in season floating in the air like a miniature snow storm. It sneaks through garden rails, over walls, and between crevices, and if not carefully controlled will fill any garden in a month or two. Fortunately, it is easy to pull up and should be dealt with ruthlessly.

Some of the cultivated varieties of garden daisies have a knack of returning to their ancestry if left in position for more than one season and filling the lawn with pretty but unwanted flowers. There is a story of an old lady who chided her gardener because her lawn had not as many daisies on it as had her neighbour's, but I am afraid it is a fifth column yarn, though I hate to cut off the head of a single daisy with my small lawn-mower. Agreed, sentiment should not enter into gardening.

Lots of young hawthorns invite themselves into my garden because of my kind face, but the head of the household tosses them over the wall without ceremony. After all, the proper place for nature to do its worst or best is in the bush or the wilds. Our tiny garden must be sparing with its hospitality, as space is strictly rationed. Still, I like to leave a visitor alone until it discloses its identity. Generally it turns out to be a weed, but I am hoping some day to find that a rare plant has, out of millions, chosen me to be its host. Now I must weed out the dandelions reluctantly. What a lovely flower they are if properly grown!

TT

A 'Dig for Victory' Exhibition
September 8 1941

A good deal of useful information is to be gained at the Dig for Victory exhibition which will remain open at Harrods for another week. One of the stands is an information centre, where talks full of good advice will be given and films shown of war-time gardens. Girls wishing to get practical training as gardeners will hear at the stand of the Women's Farm and Garden Association about its apprenticeship scheme, the many openings for trainees, the present demand for women gardeners and prospects of permanent employment after the war. The National Allotments Society has made an impressive display of vegetables grown in London suburbs, magnificent runner beans, marrows, pumpkins, and smaller stuff piled in a great mound.

The Autumn Garden
October 4 1941

The autumn garden is always both a rich and ragged place, and never more so than in this year whose drenching August rains made for a richness of a miscellaneous growth instead of for quick ripeness of the grain and fruit. With labour everywhere scare and domestic hands too busy to add nettle grasping to their other labours, the gardens have run amok. The eternal tendency of flowerbeds to display a shaggy foison in October and the unshakeable resolution of the weeds (what an ethical example!) have been confirmed by climate and by circumstance. The autumn's special symbol, the chrysanthemum, the golden flower, burns beside the sere and stooping veterans of the vegetable jungle, the pea-sticks and the bean rows of our war-time larder gardening.

For connoisseurs of melancholy there is no place so happy as the autumn garden. The brave pretences of the robin's pipe – for this bird seems ever to be rediscovering April when September comes – have a gaiety which is merely poignant amid the gathering mists and cruelly abbreviated afternoons. Vainly he sings against the pibroch of the rising winds and falling leaves, whose fluttering descant 'from all the woods that autumn Bereaves in all the world' creates the symbol of transience. It is a dance of dissolution. Yet there is a rare particular beauty about all this presage of a general decay.

It is a beauty that comes with quiet modesty to our woods and gardens. The American fall – 'fall' is good old English for autumn and we would do well to take it back as part of lend and lease – is a conflagration. The woods take fire at the first touch of frost and blaze like a city bombed. An American Shakespeare would have written of the sere, the scarlet leaf: our vegetation goes more gently through a yellowing and mellowing process. Our autumn has more of gold and less of red, though the vermilion has its carnival on the berried hedge and will at last infect the leaf. It is a beauty changeful, undisciplined, and profound that comes to us now, and something of the same kind seems often to happen in the lives of artists. Their ageing minds become autumn gardens, untidy with a growth of phrase and fancy both exquisite and random.

Perhaps Thomas Hardy was never greatly vernal; even when he danced at Cremorne in 'Jullien's grand quadrilles' you feel that he was more sensitive to November's sombre hints than to the fair assurances of May. But in the autumn of his life you get the finest fullness of his spirit. The Dynasts is scarcely a tidy piece of work, but what an autumn garden of the pensive spirit at large among its immensities! Shakespeare's last plays contain some perfect examples of this entangled October beauty. *Cymbeline* is a jungle of trailing briars and of blossoms without peer.

The English are supposed to be a beevish [sic] and insensitive people, and sometimes they seem to earn the title. Yet the English have always shown a certain shy genius for sadness. Their simplest folk songs have a tender yearning and seem, like the ghosts in Virgil, to stretch out their hands in love of the distant, the unattainable shore. Whoever wrote

But all the music he could play
Was over the hills and far away

created something of pathos and of beauty which has echoed forever in our poetry. 'Over the hills and far away' might, of course, be a cheerful summons to meet a new dawn. But essentially it seems to signify a departure into the mists of the unknown. It has the savour of an autumn dusk.

Even when the spirit of the age seems most vigorous and blithe, when the poets are in tune with the nightingale instead of moping with the owl, as happened in the 1590s when the old Queen watched her young men flash in wit and song as well as in affairs of State and war, the cult of melancholy makes its strong appeal. Partly then it was a pose – and how dull life would be if nobody ever practised 'spruce affectation' or allowed his mental foppery to cut a caper! To cultivate self-pity can be maddening if done heavily and by a fool, but done by an artist it is often the stuff of the loveliest writing.

From *Hamlet* to AE Housman we have had a great deal of English railing and glooming and unpacking with tremendous words the heart with rue that's laden. Shakespeare's Hamlet, it must be remembered, was, in feeling as in phrase, a fashionable young Tudor nobleman. His melancholy was as much to the manor born as were his scholarship and swordsmanship to the fashion trained. Grievance indeed he had, but without it he would surely have found cause for cursing.

Melancholy, the breath and being of the autumn garden, is as much the spice of life as is any form of jocundity. Popular taste everlastingly dotes on tunes and ditties of parting and of death. Melancholy at its worst creates the closely united mawkishness of the Victorian ballad and the Victorian funeral. 'Why,' asked Dickens's Mr Mould, 'do people spend more money on a death than on a birth?' The answer was written in Mr Mould's account books. What he undertook was not merely to bury the dead but to satisfy the living. He gave them sadness with splendour, a forest of plumes. There is a smack of the old and grandiose funeral about an autumn garden, Mr Mould's 'baton tipped with brass,' without which his mutes would have seemed meanly underfurnished. The horticultural plumes abound. The emblems of floral decay are eloquent of a more general dissolution. We, who find pleasure as well as beauty in the autumn garden, are yielding, no doubt, to a whim and cosseting our grief in the tradition mode of the poets with a breaking heart. But there is more to it than a gesture. The autumn sights and the autumn noises, the tangle of wilting greenery, the leaf assuming its gold lace, brief song of robin, and cawings of the rook wood are not merely food for our affectation. They make a superb pattern of unpatterned and untidy things.

Ivor Brown

English Avenues
January 31 1949

The elms of the long walk at Windsor, attacked by disease, were felled two or three years ago. This winter the lime or linden avenue at Trinity College, Cambridge, has been felled. At Christ Church, Oxford, the Broad Walk has been patched up and the mile-long horse-chestnut avenue in Bushey Park has many of its gaps half-filled by young trees. The great elm avenue at Wimpole, in Cambridgeshire (which 40 years ago was nearly perfect for its full three miles) is now sadly the worst for age, and the three-mile Grand Avenue of beeches in Savernake suffers falls whenever there are severe gales.

This last avenue was planted in or about 1722, and here is the key to the decline at the present time of many avenues. England's great avenue-planting age was roughly from 1660 to 1740, and any trees other than oaks and yews planted within this period are likely to be fully mature or over mature today. At least one of Britain's surviving avenues of lindens – that at Buxted – was planted as early as 1630, but there seems little doubt that the widespread taste for avenues came from the continent, where linden avenues became specially fashionable in the time of Louis XIV (1643-1715). Evelyn described the linden tree as 'of all other, the most proper and beautiful for walks,' but later the species was blamed for putting on its leaves too late and shedding them too soon, and many planters preferred elms, hornbeams, beeches, and other trees.

Most of the long avenues of England, such as the avenue of elms in Blenheim Park, were a part of the older tradition of gardening founded on straight lines and geometry and executed on a grand scale. Though gardens were then enclosed, long vistas were much admired and the human eye was invited by avenues to gaze far beyond the garden, through park and forest into the distance. Sometimes the trees were clipped to a great height on the inner side. The word 'avenue' itself, though not unknown, seems to have been less employed than it is now. Celia Fiennes, for example, when describing what she saw on her famous tours between 1685 and 1705, usually refers to rows of trees where we should say avenues.

During the second quarter of the 18th century the newer school of irregular landscape gardening came into favour, with William Kent as a leader. Among the supporters of the new fashion were Pope, the writer, and Hogarth, the painter, and the ultimate chief executive or executioner was Capability Brown. Nature was said to abhor a straight line, and Brown accordingly slaughtered straight avenues by the dozen. However, fair numbers of avenues survived the assault. There are still pre-Brown avenues at Hampton Court, where Brown was in charge for a time. A generation or two after Brown's death, in 1783, there was some reaction. Lombardy poplars appeared and won favour, and Sequoia gigantea (giant redwood) was introduced under the popular name of Wellingtonia. Notable avenues of both these trees, and of some others, were planted in early Victorian times. There were and are some winding avenues. The mile-long avenue of oaks at Bucklebury, in Berkshire, is a remarkable example, but many winding avenues were mere devices to make a drive or approach of a hundred yards seem like two hundred yards.

Today almost any well grown avenue, whether straight or serpentine, is likely to be admired by the general public, yet there are aspects of the popular attitude which might perhaps be examined by a psychiatrist. There seems to be a curious reluctance to accept the fact that trees live only for a term; there is an almost childish inability to grasp the inevitability of death. The possibility that the tree is dangerous or unsightly cannot be entertained. Hence the many unsatisfactory, one might almost say craven, attempts to patch up avenues. Over-aged trees are left till they fall, and then the gaps are planted with young trees. A perceptive writer recently described the old elms of the Broad Walk at Oxford looking 'more pathetic than lively beside the young trees planted to fill the gaps.'

The cliche about 'exploring every avenue' is a minor curiosity. In most avenues there is little scope for exploration – an exercise which might better be directed to thickets, jungles or the confusions of human minds. But the phrase can be justified etymologically, because the idea of an avenue is an approach, and there is much to be said for exploring various approaches to a problem. Further, it is worth remarking that all good avenues should be approaches, leading somewhere. Perhaps a case might be made for smaller avenues of pleached trees as mere garden walks, but a big avenue, detached and by itself, is usually a little absurd. The avenue proclaims, in effect, 'You are coming to something.' An important but commonly overlooked point is that the older avenues of Britain and western Europe were designed, and the trees were so spaced, that they might be enjoyed by people who were standing still or riding or driving at speeds under 12 miles an hour. And that is how they should be enjoyed today, for, as Mrs Brenda Colvin wrote in her book *Land and Landscape* last year: 'An avenue of familiar proportions having evenly spaced trees, is quite wrong for fast-moving traffic. The trees, flickering past the eye like the earliest attempts at motion photography, have a physically tiring effect.'

Anyone who intends to plant an avenue might bear this in mind.

JDU Ward

Summer Bedding: Avoiding Monotony
April 30 1949

In most gardens, small as well as large, summer bedding is practised either as an addition to the herbaceous border and shrubbery or in place of one or the other, and for this as well as for them plans should be made well beforehand, especially where new ground is being used. In earlier days summer bedding was too often confined to one pattern – an edging of golden feverfew or white alyssum, backed by blue lobelia, yellow calceolaria, and red or scarlet pelargonium; all good plants, of course, when used in moderation, but tending to monotony when used in this way generally. Fortunately, under the onslaughts of such innovators as William Robinson, Gertrude Jekyll, and their followers the monotony was broken to such an extent that even in our smaller public parks the old pattern rarely reappears. In his *English Flower Garden* Robinson suggests that the best rule in arranging the beds is to keep the scheme of colour as simple as possible. He accepts a 'brilliant blaze,' but not a 'discordant' one. 'One or two colours,' he writes, 'used temperately and with careful judgment will produce nobler and richer results than many colours purposely contrasted or wantonly jumbled.' As an example of 'simple harmonies' he instances a scheme ranging from palest pink to deep crimson such as may be provided by pelargoniums and verbenas. Similarly, Miss Jekyll tells us that 'one of the most perfectly satisfying examples of colour harmony' she ever saw was in a Midlands garden, which was treated in one harmonious colouring of full yellow, orange, and orange brown, with a free use of such half-hardy annuals as French and African marigolds, zinnias, and nasturtiums.

With the numerous varieties of flowers and foliage plants now at our disposal, there is no excuse for monotony. Besides those already named, ranging, for example, from pink to crimson – to mention a few, – there are antirrhinums, pentstemons, begonias, stocks, fuchsias, the splendens and fulgens varieties of the salvia, dahlias, the Drummond phloxes, petunias, pinks and carnations, gladioli and love-lies-bleeding; in yellow, orange and brown calendulas, gleam nasturtiums, gazanias, tagetes, dahlias, and begonias; and in blues ageratum, cherry-pie, Salvia patens, nigella, violas, asters, nemophilas, nemesias, and varieties of other plants already mentioned.

BL

Congenial to All
July 1 1949

About 37 acres of Battersea Park down by the river are to be turned into a pleasure garden for the Festival of Britain in 1951. Mr Gerald Barry, the director of the festival, gave some facts about the scheme today, but the detailed plan has not yet been worked out. At Battersea, it is stated, there is to be a 'complete open-air area of entertainment' (whatever that is) 'providing for all tastes and pockets.' Space will be 'devoted to the traditional and conventional activities associated with the fairground and amusement park, and in this respect the festival office already enjoys the full co-operation of the National Amusements Council. 'Care will be taken to avoid excessive noise and to give the gardens an atmosphere congenial to all.' It reads as though somebody in Mr Barry's office has been studying not merely the ideas but also the prose style of the late Prince Consort.

The plan itself, however, is promising. There will be open-air cafes and restaurants, music-hall entertainments, concerts, spectacles. The area will be laid out as 'an outstanding example of landscape gardening' and at night there will be illuminations. The gardens may be approached by boat. It is going to cost in all nearly three-quarters of a million, and the government and the LCC will put up the money. There might be a loss of £100,000. One wonders, however, whether the fairground section of the garden will not ruin the rest. The site is a small one, and if the fair is to have 'traditional and conventional activities,' as promised, it is going to make the traditional and conventional din. A more modest scheme omitting the fairground would surely have been more in keeping with the site, the neighbourhood, and the occasion.

Height Limit for Flowers? Keeping the Gardens 'Tidy'
February 10 1950

Bridlington Town Council, which recently decided that front gardens on the new Bessingby estate, where 700 houses are to be built, must have lawns with flowers but no fences or gates, may impose more restrictions on the gardens. Its property committee recommends that tenants should not be allowed to place any erection in the front garden such as bird baths, sundials, rockeries or similar structures standing above ground, or to grow tall shrubs or flowers there above a certain height which has not yet been specified. It will probably be made known when the matter comes before the council on February 22.

A member of the council said the idea of the gardens was to have as much open space as possible in front of the houses. The council wanted the gardens to look nice, neat and tidy, without being too rigid. If tenants were allowed to grow what they liked they might let their imagination run riot.

Mr Morrison 'Cross': Festival Gardens' Loss May Rise to £1,500,000
March 20 1951

Mr Morrison gave what will presumably be his last reply to a question about the Festival of Britain in the House of Commons today, and it was most distressing to him and to the house: certainly he could not have left this reply to his successor. He had to announce that the estimate of the cost of the Battersea pleasure gardens, which he reported at about £1,625,000 on March 6, was now put by the board of Festival Gardens Ltd, at about £2,500,000. So sharp an increase in so short a time had made him 'cross,' and he was having the position investigated. The estimated loss on the undertaking for six months' working had risen from £572,000 to £1,500,000. The Treasury is to advance the extra capital needed to complete the gardens, but the spending of this money will have to be covered by a bill.

Ministers must wish heartily that they had spared themselves this blow. The Battersea gardens project has attracted more criticism than any other part of the Festival. Extra expense is bad enough, but extra expense which must be incurred before there is time to secure parliamentary authority for it is worse.

Pleasure Gardens at Bath: Echo of Jane Austen
August 27 1952

Miss Austen no longer lives in Bath. If she did, would she refer to the whole business in tones more generally associated with Lady Catherine de Bourgh? So say the traditionalists, who now stay indoors at night. The city is debased by the goings-on in the Sydney Gardens, by the illuminations, the occasional fireworks, the dancing, floodlighting, and children's corner. What makes it even worse is the proximity of the revels to Bathwick Hill, whose residents have interchanged from time to time with those of the Royal Crescent. In future, the traditionalists assert knowingly, the traffic will be one-way.

The idea of a Sydney Gardens pleasure park is so old that, when it was revived at the beginning of this year, resentment immediately manifested itself among those whose spiritual home is the late Victorian age. In the late 18th century it was fashionable to attend the gardens, if only in search of light refreshment. 'There is a public breakfast every morning in the Sydney Gardens,' wrote Jane Austen to her sister, 'so that we shall not starve.' But that was an age when Bath was fashionable and a trifle sinful rather than a spa and quite respectable; today it is neither, and the rate has increased to 22s 3d in the pound. If the city council do not lie awake at night pondering over ways of making money, it is simply because the climate encourages them to sleep the clock round.

Bath has only recently emerged from the restraints of middle-class tutelage, and the social setup reflects confusion. A few thousand feel faint at the barest mention of the future, 10 times their number are offended by any reference to the past; the remainder, who rule the city, are indifferent – and always vote Conservative. Since Britain's finest Georgian monument has little to offer the more wealthy visitor by way of amenities (the large hotels are still occupied by civil servants, nurses, and a vast vacuum purchased by British Railways), the pleasure park was inevitable whatever the inhabitants might say. If the silks and satins of aristocratic Bath have been put away for all time, then it is fitting that Gainsborough's darling should be provided with workaday jeans. Bath is still a standing invitation to the comic dramatist who might furnish a sequel to *The Rivals*, and the classic comedy of the past six months opened appropriately on the heights with a socialist councillor protesting that the pleasure park would attract the 'wrong type of people,' trippers from as far afield as South Wales and Swindon. A public inquiry was held at which a man from Whitehall politely awaited complaints; needless to say, those living close at hand did not condescend to put in an appearance, possibly because they feared contamination by the wrong people.

The second act of the comedy (which the legal adviser of certain publicans says may be transferred to the high court) introduced a fresh batch of characters who threw up their hands in unison at the prospect of a licence being granted by the magistrates. The free churches, the temperance ladies, the publicans, and the police all resisted strongly, though for different reasons, but to no avail. The deputy town clerk of Leamington, a resort which opened its pleasure gardens last summer for two months and showed a profit, assured the magistrates that all is quiet and serene in Mr Eden's constituency. The temperance ladies might have reminded him that even Miss Prim's innocent beverage exploded at Leamington.

The Sydney Gardens are situated at the far end of Pulteney Street, and form an elegant back garden, complete with loggia and mock Roman temple, to a discreet 18th century house. At 8.30 each evening the lights are switched on and the public admitted at a shilling a head. Flowerbeds are picked out, petal by petal, by concealed ambers, and the trees by embracing floods which make them seem as theatrical as the properties of a Beerbohm Tree production. And while the younger visitors blend steps primarily American and only remotely Viennese to the music of a Gypsy band, their elders fluctuate between the refreshment tent (sadly unlike those of the Canterbury Festival) and a state of pleasant bewilderment.

They find it hard to credit that Bath, staid and stuffy by tradition, should permit natural dignity and good manners to go cheerily hand in hand with the base, common and popular. The most affecting scene of the week is reserved for Saturday evenings when the male pensioners, sedate in their best caps, line the inner walls of the Roman temple whose seats demand a Spartan fortitude. Leaning speculatively on their sticks, the pensioners have shown themselves appreciative of the temple's lighting, white on the outer stonework and crimson within, and probably feel that the stage manager has enabled them to experience the lustre of sin without bothering too much with its basic requirements.

High above the canal, which bisects the Sydney Gardens and which has been much criticised by the Conservatives on account of its fountain and glittering, artificial water lilies and swans, juts the loggia of Sydney House. Perhaps it was a mistake to invite teenage art school students to decorate it in what might tactfully be described as an anti-baroque manner, but at least it encourages one to turn away to the northern slopes of the city, to Camden Crescent, where Jane Austen lived and wrote. Parts of Bath have scarcely changed since Jane took her cousins to the Sydney Gardens, where 'regular horse exercise' costs half a crown a month, and swings, the use of a bowling green and a swimming pool only seven and sixpence for the season.

'Even the concert will have more than its usual charm for me,' continued Jane, 'as the gardens are large enough for me to get pretty well beyond the reach of its sound.' So it is to-day. The pleasure park is pleasing to the eye and not unduly disturbing to the ear, and if the children lack the Emett railways which adorns Battersea Park they are rewarded with very Emett-like expressions of surprise on the faces of the drivers as they travel past on the old Great Western line. Socially, the pleasure park is a success, financially it depends upon the abatement of the rains which have afflicted it often since its opening.

If the park sustains a loss, then its opponents will dance a gleeful minuet and the city fathers retire in disorder. This would not be beneficial to the city, which is badly in need of an organiser. Its annual arts festival will never emulate Aldeburgh or Glyndebourne so long as the philistines have to be placated and Geraldo offered to offset the presence of Beecham. But the pleasure park is different, and may help, however indirectly, to remind people that Bath is more than the commercial town it has almost become and could well be the showplace of England. All in all, it is pretty certain that nowhere else do citizens march forward to lower rates by switching on fairy lights and indulging in gaiety, beer, and an atmosphere approved of by Jane Austen.

Kenneth Gregory

Flags and Flowers: Mr Cuthbert's Weekly Gardening Talk
February 21 1953

While we are all busy in this eventful coronation year preparing the flags and bunting for the joyful occasion, we must not overlook the wonderful opportunity this event offers to make our gardens as gay as possible. Surely there can be no better way in which to display our loyalty and our faith in the future. Nature has endowed us with a multitude of brightly hued flowers within the reach of everyone and there could be no more charming method of symbolising our feelings than to make our gardens a galaxy of colour. Many of my readers have had the same thought in mind, for they have been writing me for advice on planting their Coronation gardens, and I do not think I can do better for the benefit of all keen gardeners than to make some suggestions which may be helpful.

For window-boxes and hanging baskets there will be the obvious choice of geraniums, white marguerites, and lobelia, and for the traditional show of red, white, and blue it would be difficult to beat. For those whose temperament or artistic leanings look for something more subtle, then for this same purpose, the salmon-pink geranium with the fragrant heliotrope, cherry pie, and again the white marguerites, make a charming combination. If you have a special bed which is a focal point in your garden, it would be well worth while trying your hand at carpet bedding for there is nothing that looks more effective and showy. Such a bed can be circular, square, or rectangular.

It does not matter which, for you can plan the motif of your carpet bedding and adapt it to the space you have available. You may arrange your plants in a geometrical design on it, or, if you are more ambitious, why not try to delineate the royal cipher or the crown? The plants I suggest you try for this experiment are phlox drummondii, which will provide the bright red, sweet alyssum for the white and purple, lobelia for the blue, tagetes for the gold, and cineraria diamond for the silver.

My Guide to Gardening: 'The Real Labouring Stuff that Blisters are Born Of'
May 13 1955

I have never had the slightest desire to write a gardening book. But if I did it would be on gardening – not gardens, mind you, but the real labouring stuff that blisters are born of. I know exactly the form it would take: I know equally well that no publisher would ever accept it. Of course, Ronald Searle would have to illustrate it – and that's as likely as my writing it. But what fun it would be seeing someone else in the attitudes I am obliged to adopt. And on the dust-jacket, as a symbol and a warning, would be a long-legged, tousled Amazon surrounded by every known tool from flail to hatchet against a background of jungle growth and tangle. And, above in letters of red the title God Wottery. It would not be a technical treatise nor a psalm about nature. No, mine would be a manual on gardening as the single woman sees it through bi-focals in middle age, with no time to work in it, no leisure to enjoy it, and no money to spend on it. But it would be devastatingly practical in its do's and don'ts, giving chapter and verse on how to make the darn thing yield – or bust!

There would be hints on flirting with the seasons as they flash by with nothing done: on summer days spent in macintosh and hood with slugpot and sugar tongs; on GROWTH spelt in inch-high letters as indication of its zeal; on planting peas and watching marigolds come up; on a catch crop of dandelions on paths and grass; on bonfires –

oh, a lot about bonfires and the neighbour's washing, cheating with paraffin, and soggy mounds four feet high. There would be paragraphs on pests, starting with the talkative neighbour who thinks you are there on all fours for his benefit, to Things-that-move-quickly-in-the-soil (subdivided into those that crack or splash when destroyed). Naturally there would be a catalogue of essential needs such as gum-boots and a deck-chair, barrier cream, tweezers and iodine, a vacuum flask, and a few master-tools which can readily be adapted to all purposes by the addition of adhesive tape and a 'bit o' band.'

This unique book would also deal with how to make dinners and catch elusive tradesmen when 40 paces from the house; and what to say when the phone rings and you leap those 40 paces down a terraced garden to ground level, fumble for the backdoor key, remove boots, and pad hot-foot to a far room to lift receiver and hear, 'That Sandy Lane garridge? I want a taxi at once!' There would be a further section on taking pains listing the manifold pains inflicted as one works (in alphabetical order) to include backache, bruises, bumps, cuts, and grazes, and working through to wrenches, withers and whacked. All this for the edification of those who think they are gardening when they go delicately round in the wake of a violent male nipping off pansy heads and tying up lupins. The hacking and hewing of the single gardener, the heaving and dragging, tugging and tussling that goes on is nobody's business – but it makes biceps like puff sleeves. Add to that prickles and thorns … I think, perhaps, it might be advisable to give life-size diagrams of the more usual – roses, rasps, goosegogs, neighbour's holly, rusty nails, bits of glass and crockery, &c. This chapter would be called Those Blood-stained Secateurs.

This, of course, would lead to a section on starting a museum. The things that turn up in the best-regulated and dogless gardens! Ours was virgin soil, but I'd give a lot to know who buried stems of clay pipes, bent ironwork, limpets, and a crop of blue and white china. As an addendum, here I would mention dustbins. Garden rubbish, you must know, is frowned upon by all binmen, so a deal of artfulness is called for. Horrid things like sprout stalks, which will neither rot nor burn, are obvious fodder. The thing to do is to fold them in (to use a culinary term) between layers of ashes and tins, topping off with some old corsets and a hat or two – not forgetting a handsome Christmas box in season.

But stones! What to do with stones deserves a book in itself. I might possibly work in a competition at this point offering a prize for the best suggestion. We have eight long paths, four rockeries, and an empty field – at least, it was empty till it was sold as a building plot. The man who bought it and I don't talk. You soon learn you have no more control over what grows in the garden than you have over the fauna that infest it – cats and dogs are legion and each has its own particular right of way and hunting lodge. You may decide to grow antirrhinums – but up come some marigolds from last year; you take infinite pains with your lettuce bed and all you get is chickweed and slugs; you put in night-scented stock seeds near the house and the first thunder shower shoots them down the grate. I give up! Nowadays, if a thing takes a fancy to a place it can have it and I pretend the effort is mine.

Take rasps – take as many as you like; I can't get rid of them. 'They'll never grow here,' everyone told me. 'They're greedy eaters. Dig 'em up and put 'em in the sun.' I did, with blood, sweat, and swears, every sucker. Into that border went hardy perennials and they rooted as well. But that July we had as fine a set of raspberry canes among them as we'd ever had. And enough fruit to jam.

The more I think about it, the more I realise the promise of this unwritten book. And not only the promise, but the size of it. It would take a lifetime to produce – and two-thirds of that are gone already.

Kathleen Binns

The Gregarious Gardener
January 25 1958

'If I were Sir William Joyson-Hicks, which, thank God, I am not, I should lie awake at night thinking how dangerous to the real prosperity of the country was the diminution in the number of allotment holders, because I am sure that allotment-holding provides an antidote to bolshevism.'

That was Sir Francis Dyke Acland presiding at the annual conference of the Allotments Organisation Society and Smallholders Ltd, in London in 1927, and he was complaining of the government's indifference to the fall in the number of allotments after the first world war. By 1930 250,000 had dropped away from the 1920 figure of 1,330,000 and by the time the second world war began the figure was down to 900,000. In 1943 the Ministry of Agriculture carried out a survey among those digging for victory on 1,700,000 allotments, which showed, it said, that 96 per cent wanted to go on cultivating allotments after the war. Now the number of allotments is down to about 900,000 again, and the faithfuls in the movement complain of the government's indifference. But an antidote to what these days? Television, or fretting about the future, or still bolshevism, perhaps?

Even so, 900,000 allotment holders are a lot of people and they are well organised in a down-to-earth, unsentimental kind of way. The statute book from 1887 to 1950 is littered with acts to define their rights. These vary from the fundamental – for instance, that allotments must be provided by local authorities on the application of six registered parliamentary electors or ratepayers – to the less obvious – that rooms in public elementary schools may be used free of charge with the consent of any two managers for the purpose of public discussion on any question relating to allotments under the acts. (Sounds as though Lloyd George might have got that one in.) Among those defending and seeking to extend these rights are the National Allotments and Garden Society in England and Wales, and the Scottish Allotments and Garden Society.

The NAGS includes some 4,000 local associations with around 300,000 members, and 120 affiliated local authorities. It 'aims at getting allotments, and gardening generally, recognised as an essential element in civic life – not as a temporary expedient to meet emergencies such as war and unemployment.' This is a fine aim, but the history of two post-wars and the depressed 30s is against it. The society has won for allotment holders the agricultural subsidy on lime and fertilisers and grants for taking water to allotments. It receives a (falling) government subsidy and has representatives on the Ministry of Agriculture's allotments advisory committee. It is a member of the International Office of Allotment and Garden Leagues. In 1951 it took over from the Society of Friends the scheme for providing seeds and fertilisers at low prices for the aged, the unemployed, the blind, the disabled, and the widowed. It has recently begun selling seeds at a cheap rate to members of affiliated societies, runs a cheap insurance service for huts, and a cheap duplicating scheme. There is an annual conference, numerous booklets, and a monthly journal. Associations affiliated to the society take out a 2s 6d share and pay a yearly affiliation fee of 6d a member.

And village produce associations was added to the title and work of NAGS a few years ago. But there is also a National Federation of Village Produce Associations, which receives no official help. The associations were a food-growing, live-stock rearing, wartime movement. Since ministry support was withdrawn in 1951 those associations which entered the fold of the national federation have increasingly developed as a family counterpart of the women's institutes – one subscription covers the whole household and the activities for men, women, and children. They include lectures, shows, films, garden judging, digging matches, digging of old people's gardens, and home-grown suppers. The federation, to which the associations are affiliated at a yearly cost of only a penny a member, provides a bulk-buying service for the associations, issues a news letter, and holds an annual conference which sets off with a supper of traditional dishes supplied by the counties. There are about 13,000 members in this movement.

Just as the war shortage of food led the government to encourage vegetable growing, so the post-war shortage of dollars led it to countenance tobacco growing. The National Amateur Tobacco Growers' Association was founded in 1948 to take advantage of the government's concession that an amateur could grow tobacco for himself without a licence. There was a later concession that a grower could each year have 25lb of dry leaf cured at a bulk-drying centre duty free. (This would work out at about 30 cigarettes a day.) The association provides seeds at 1s a packet or plants at reduced prices, gives advice on growing them, and offers curing facilities. (Costing about 3d an ounce this gives a final cost for an ounce of tobacco of 5d.) There is an entrance fee of 1s 6d and a yearly subscription of 5s. Fixing life membership at £3 3s suggests that members are not expected to smoke themselves to death with undue haste.

Requests for the addresses of secretaries of the societies mentioned in these three articles will be answered as soon as possible and the (s.a.e.) offer still stands.

GFS

Fundamentals
November 15 1958

'The garden's full of furniture and the house is full of plants!' sing Flanders and Swan, and the audience howls with glee. 'Ever-so-very-contemporary' is the fad, thus neatly pilloried, that came to Kensington by way of Scandinavia. But as old as the garden of Eden is the first principle of the lost art of gardening – the interpenetration of house and garden, and the unity of both with their setting – that came to christendom by way of the Alhambra. The lost art, mark you, not of horticulture but of gardening; of making outdoor places to live in as much as to look at: not just places to grow plants in, but places in the making of which plant growth has a part to play.

The quality of the garden as a whole, as distinct from its contents, depends on its creator's grasp of the unchanging principles of landscape architecture, which themselves derive from the universal laws of nature. It is natural, therefore, that *Garden Design* (Country Life, 52s 6d) should be written by Sylvia Crowe, president of the Institute of Landscape Architects; that it should start with the Assyrians, the Han dynasty, the Villa Lante, Versailles, and Stowe; and that it should prove far more stimulating and helpful to the tillers of suburban plots than any previous work in its field, though the bulk of its examples are taken from country estates.

What the author finds missing from the modern garden is the serenity, the 'look of easy inevitability', that comes from an understanding of the fundamental principles of unity, decisiveness of intention, and relation to the human scale. And of these the greatest is unity – the acceptance of the discipline imposed by the character and limiting factors of the site, if it has any, or the carrying through of a unifying idea, expressed, in the inward-looking small garden, in a focal point. Our fault is that we have not yet learned to use creatively the wealth of new plant material at our disposal. 'It is impossible to have too great a variety of plants to choose from,' says Miss Crowe, ' –provided a choice is made.' All this is just, and her practical advice fires the imagination. But if her affection for hosta (funkia used to be its more appropriately repulsive name) is the sign of a 'true gardener', I confess myself a mere plantsman.

Planning and Planting the Landscape: The Patient Work of Sylvia Crowe
September 14 1959

The English genius for landscape which flowered so brilliantly in the 18th century has skipped so many subsequent generations that one feared the strain was lost for good. In recent years, and particularly in the years between the two wars, it seemed that no visual crime was too gross for us to commit as miles of countryside were raped for ribbon development, hundreds of trees pulled down to make way for drab housing estates. But there are signs that the tide of taste is again coming in, and one of them is the growing school of landscape architects. Most of these (their institute, founded in 1926, has nearly 200 members) are employed on designing private gardens, but one or two have obtained posts with the more enlightened municipal authorities, and a few have been consulted on really large scale public projects.

Among the distinguished members is Miss Sylvia Crowe, who is landscape consultant to both Basildon and Harlow new towns and to the Imperial College development in South Kensington. She is a past president of the Institute of Landscape Architects which she helped to found. Her list of assignments since she founded a private practice at the end of the war is impressive, since it includes restoration work in Lincolnshire after the 1953 floods, work for colleges in Oxford, the laying-out of public gardens at Mablethorpe and Sutton, and the churchyard of St Mary's at Banbury. She has also worked on housing the United States Air Force in Britain and the nuclear power stations at Trawsfynydd.

At a first meeting she gives an impression of being immensely patient, which is just as well since some of her landscape schemes take 50 years to mature. She is quiet and self-contained, and even when contemplating some monumental piece of public stupidity remains fair and detached. Nevertheless her criticisms are devastating. 'Most municipal authorities when they speak of landscaping mean cutting out little flower-beds and putting in geraniums and roses,' she said sadly. 'That has nothing to do with landscape. A good landscape should flow smoothly round one, and you can't get that effect by cutting things up.' Urban landscape, she goes on to point out, has two functions. Partly it is there to provide a visual relaxation, something peaceful to look at to counteract the frantic elements of town life. Partly it should be making the best possible use of available land to give people opportunities for physical relaxation and enjoyment. She quotes one of Harlow's many good examples.

'I remember in one place we had a disused gravel-pit. One could have just filled it in, of course, but it occurred to us it would be a splendid children's playground – plenty of opportunity to dig. So we left the gravel, but put a path through the middle for people who wanted to take a stroll or take the dog for a walk. Then houses, you see, overlooked the area from just here – small children mustn't be isolated – and the tenant's common-room over there with a nice view.' Her pencil scribbled energetically over a block as she talked: like most architects she ekes out her conversation with little drawings done from a vertiginous, god's eye view. She mentions that another use of planned urban landscape is to discourage street accidents. Lines of prickly shrubs on a tempting kerb persuade people to use a subway or a safer crossing almost without their realising it.

First hand experience in the new towns has shown Miss Crowe that vandalism is not as bad as it has been painted. Many of the residents of the new towns come from parts of east and north-east London with a terrible reputation for destructiveness, but with few exceptions they have shown pleasure and pride in their new surroundings, and have taken to gardening with English passion. She thinks the attitude of the children may have something to do with intensive pep talks in the schools, but attributes most of the success to the spell of good landscape. 'It's important to get the place looking really nice before people arrive,' she says. 'If you stick them down in a house in a sea of mud and rubble you can't blame them if they've no respect for it.' She comments that where young shrubs continually get trodden down it is largely her own fault, either because she has put them in the wrong place or failed to protect them properly during the growing period.

Working from an office in Gloucester Place, it suits her also to live in London, but she has her own terrace garden, leading out to a communal garden where she works when she feels like it. She uses this for experiment, trying to discover which plants will thrive in London, which under trees, and which in what she technically describes as 'dry shade.' Her real love, one feels, is gardens, and until the war, when she went into the forces, she had spent most of her working life designing these. But all her pleasures revolve round the joy of looking at things, and in describing her interests she distinguishes carefully between 'travel' and 'seeing places,' a pastime which she carries out with an intensely analytical eye. Those of our grandchildren who share this tranquil pursuit will be lucky to see the fruit of Sylvia Crowe's labours in its vintage years.

Monica Furlong

Peering Over the Hedge:
1960–1969

Dr DG Hessayon's *The House Plant Expert*, 1960 * Ministry of Agriculture's publication *Chemicals for the Gardener*, 1963 * Soil Association launch campaign for natural gardening, 1968 * Dutch Elm disease kills more than 25 million trees

No Entry
August 27 1960

Walking on deep litter among the sweet peas at the RHS Gardens at Wisley, the expression 'alien corn' comes suddenly to mind. Here were great tall plants with main stems almost as thick as my thumb with splendid blooms on long stalks. They were magnificent, but they were not, to me, sweet peas; and I wanted to get back to my own modest row, produced from two shillingsworth of mixed seed, which was then giving, and continued to give for two months, a profusion of lovely flowers to brighten both the garden and the house.

I have no affection for the inordinately big, whether flower or vegetables. I drive past the Chelsea Flower Show every day when it is on, but never stop and go in. It would probably simply daze me. The little local show, with vegetables and flowers in the main room and honey and cakes in a small side room, I occasionally visit: the kind where everybody knows everybody, where there are homely accents, where the MP and his wife stay long enough to pretend an interest and then clear off to the relief of nearly everybody including themselves. There is a nostalgic but indescribable smell, compounded of the hall itself (it is different in a marquee) and everything in it, including strong tobacco smoke. Yet, in 40 years of adult gardening I have never yet made an entry in a show, and I have wondered about the reasons for this, for during most of that time I have belonged to one horticultural society or another. When as a boy I was learning to play the piano and went to a concert to hear some great virtuoso, I always came away feeling (rightly as it turned out) that I could never be a pianist. In the same way I have never regarded myself as a gardener but rather as a stumbling learner. However that may be, there are two real reasons, one practical and the other perhaps plain silly.

The practical one is that I grow flowers for pleasure and vegetables for eating, and cannot spare time to give special attention to ensuring that suitable specimens are ready for showing at the right time. I simply refuse to disbud flowers to give larger blooms. I refuse to allocate a special plot for show vegetables and nurse them devotedly. I have seen people feverishly dig up root after root of immature potatoes, or nearly decimate a row of carrots, to find half a dozen specimens for a show entry – all for a prize of a few shillings and a little transient glory.

The silly reason for not entering, applies only to flowers: I simply don't like to think of them competing with each other, for they are nearly all incredibly lovely, both as whole blooms and in their individual parts. Perhaps we see the beauty of the individual parts more clearly in childhood. There is more time to look, and perception is clearer, scents are sharper, too: at Wisley I put my nose to many a rose without discerning any scent. Such perception may return in odd moments as it did to me one blustery March day years ago when I picked up a narcissus from the pavement in Bond Street and stood there gazing at it oblivious of the passers-by and their possible thoughts.

And how many friendships are jeopardised at the local show! There are jealousies, mutterings about the judges' incompetence, and whispers that old Joe never grew those carrots himself. Old Joe looks smug and says nothing. There are often one or two relations of Bob Pretty at any of these functions. Which suddenly reminds me that I overlooked our show this year. The schedule arrives so early and I don't keep a diary. It would have been nice just to look in. But I don't suppose I will ever submit an entry, any more than I will ever play Chopin's so-called raindrop prelude to my satisfaction. Omar Khayyam asked to be buried 'by some sweet garden side' and so he was. The garden, not the show, is the thing.

WT

Lightening Labour
April 1 1961

An early Easter and the spell of fine weather that began three weeks ago has accelerated the demand for gardening instruments. One manufacturer of garden rollers reports that over the winter he accumulated larger stocks than ever before in 25 years, and already he is out of stock and five weeks behind with his deliveries. A manufacturer of watering cans said that throughout last season his problem was how to meet the demand, and he resolved during the winter to make sure that when the present season began he would have a large stock. But wholesalers and mail order firms which usually order 1,000 watering cans are now ordering 2,000 at a time, and he also is in grave danger of falling behind on his deliveries.

The search in the garden is for a lighter and more efficient instrument. The light metal wheelbarrow has largely replaced the wooden one in small gardens, and now there are polythene and glass fibre wheelbarrows. The rubber hose is having competition from the PVC hose, 60ft of which can be carried in loops by a woman without undue effort. The roller with spikes in it, which has been used for many years to condition playing fields, is now often replaced by the ' lawn aerator,' a graceful instrument which does not look out of place in a small garden. The plastic watering can competes against the metal one, and those who want a polythene watering can with a telescopic spout are catered for. Sometimes the desire to produce a non-metallic instrument as light as possible arouses the scorn of manufacturers who have been making gardening tools for a quarter or half a century. But the gardener who knows the limits of the new materials will find that they can be put to a good purpose.

Old established firms are by no means the last to take up new ideas. One firm, which now makes a wide range of pruners and shearers, began in the business of sword making in 1772. When swords were withdrawn from the battlefield, the company turned to safety razors, and when the shortage of brass after the second world war prevented the manufacture of safety razors, the company developed its gardening instruments. It has won two Design Centre awards for them, an award for a pruner in 1957, and for a type of hoe in 1959.

Experiments in the use of metals can be as enterprising as those in the field of plastics. A company noted for its spades, forks, rakes, hoes, trowels, and similar tools concentrated in the past on two different qualities of instrument, the cheaper one of standard alloy steel and the other of stainless steel. Last season it introduced a range of instruments described as 'chrome armoured' intended for the gardener who wanted something better than the alloy steel, but something less expensive than the stainless steel. The response to this experiment has encouraged the firm to extend the new range. The comparable prices of a typical tool of the three qualities would be: alloy, 30s; chrome, 57s 6d: stainless, £5 10s.

There is no need nowadays to buy a pruner which weighs down the hand or nips the fingers, and it is not inevitable now that garden shears should loosen the nut that holds them together. But some people believe these are small matters, and that the best thing that ever happened to gardening was mechanisation. Electric hedge trimmers are said to cut a hedge 10 times as fast as the muscle-powered instrument. The increase in their sales is not so remarkable as that for motor lawnmowers. This may be because grass needs more attention than a hedge. A firm which was selling a few hundred electric hedge cutters a year just after the war increased its output to 6,000 a year in 1950, but since then the number has fallen to 5,000 a year.

The chief triumph of mechanisation in the garden belongs to the motor mower. Statistics are sparse in the garden tool industry, but one of the gardening magazines has produced figures which show that, against the rapid rate of increase in the sales of motor mowers, the sales of pushed mowers are increasing by only a small amount. The claim of this magazine is that the manufacturers of pushed machines sold about 427,000 in 1954 and 440,000 last year, whereas the sale of motor mowers increased from 25,000 in 1954 to 120,000 last year. One of the manufacturers of motor mowers challenges the figure of 120,000 for last year on the ground that this represents only double what his own firm produced. He would put the total sales of motor mowers last year at nearer 200,000.

Biology Lessons Come to Life: Parrs Wood Gardening Centre
August 2 1962

'Dig for Victory,' the slogan that turned wastelands into farms and lawns into potato patches, has had fewer more rewarding results than the establishment of Parrs Wood gardening centre, where children from the sootier and more maze-like zones of Manchester find out where a potato really comes from and what a good lawn can really look like. The need for some kind of see-and-touch-and-smell contact with the earth and what grows in it arose when the gardening centre

– seven and a half acres and the former stables of Parrs Wood House, east Didsbury – were in use in the war for teaching teachers to promote Dig for Victory. Mr FG Lucas – now Manchester's organiser for rural studies – was lecturing there and the interest generated, underlined by tales of wide eyed and baffled evacuees in the country, resulted in the formal establishment of the centre in 1948.

Now that it is in full and fruitful summer flight, cloistered with heavy trees, with every square yard in gainful employment, it is difficult to imagine how the concept of the countryside could be better evoked for children from the barren greyness of Ardwick or Miles Platting. Eighteen secondary schools in areas like these provide the centre with 30 classes a week. Each school has its own substantial plot and the teacher of rural studies in the school shows his own class the best way of making their garden grow. The plots are not ambitious frenzies of expertise – beans here, cabbages there and potatoes all over. Simple stuff, but it does the job of putting a third dimension on a biology textbook with complete effectiveness. Mr Fred Brocklesby, the teacher in charge at the centre, is a teacher by profession, but he has a great affection for farming. He sees the centre as a bit of a levelling institution with something of the man-to-man atmosphere of the farmyard rather than the master-to-pupil relationship that the children bring with them from the classroom. When they see you with your boots dirty and shovel in your hand the business of teaching becomes a good deal more matey, he said, only to be slightly contradicted by a group of super enthusiasts down from the smoky city to wash a few pots out who, although on holiday, were all full of Yessir, wellsir, y'see sir ... but at least they were bubbling with the willing exuberance of people who have done something well, not the panicky stalling of inferiors confronted by menacing authority. If the plots teach the children about the texture and feel of good English soil (it is good soil at Parrs Wood), Mr Brocklesby has ideas for bringing a few animals to give the centre a more complete farming atmosphere. Already the chickens have arrived – it is the very arrival of animals into the world which can, Mr Brocklesby feels, give children an insight into basic experiences not to be had from the television or juke-box in Hulme. For the present the mystery of birth is limited to watching a chicken peck its way out of a shell. Soon, on a patch of ground recently prepared for the purpose, a few goats and pigs may make their appearance. These, alive, warm and moving, will, Mr Brocklesby thinks, grip the imaginations of the children even more strongly than the weekly progress they see on the plots.

Apart from Mr Brocklesby, the gardening centre has two horticulturists as instructors and four men to do the day-to-day work in the green houses, where some exotic experimental plants, like bananas, are persuaded to grow. They also produce the flowers for prize days, trees and shrubs for grounds, cope with demands for items like sterilised soil for use in the laboratories of the 400 city schools and, of course, the centre provides advice for all. Evening classes are laid on and are oversubscribed – especially by women, who make up 90 per cent of every class.

With a finger in more than one educational pie the centre is fully worked. Looking far ahead it is possible to imagine that all the older schools that now send children down to Parrs Wood for two or three years will be moved to new building with grounds of their own. This is so far away that no definite plans have been made to deal with it, but it is possible that Parrs Wood gardening centre might become a minor field research centre for fairly advanced biological experiment by grammar school pupils. Mr Lucas might be allowed to prove his contention that a square yard of land can yield £1 per year (or £4,840 per acre per year) but for the time being the centre remains a pleasant classroom in the country for the townees.

Art and Nature
August 4 1962

In this century two different yet complementary styles have emerged in the world of garden design. First, there is a variant of the now well-recognised back-to-nature school of William Robinson and Gertrude Jekyll which was further developed, in the woodland garden manner, by the late Mr T Johnson, of Bulkeley Mill, near Conway, Mr EHM Cox of Perthshire and others. This style, disciplined to suit the small as well as the large garden and to enable the creation of bosky shrub beds where no natural woodland exists, is now ably demonstrated by such sensitive and visionary landscape architects as Mr Walter Irvine, of Wirral, and Mr James Lever, of Sussex.

Developing parallel to this school the present-day romantic style which uses a formal layout of walls and edgings, decorated with statues, topiary, gazebos, ornamental tanks and pools to discipline and contain a seemingly artless exuberance of plant growth. It is a scheme of informal and beautiful plantings held within the confines of a skilful architectural design. Fine examples of the 20th century romantic design are to be seen in some of the gardens open to the public under the National Trust and the various garden charities. Among the most notable of these gardens Sissinghurst Castle in Kent, Hidcote and Kiftsgate, near Chipping Campden, in Gloucestershire, Hill Pasture, near Broxted in Essex and Lyegrove, near Badminton Bodnant, in North Wales, though somewhat different in character, also exemplify the use of natural plantings confined by magnificent architectural features. Few of us can recreate the Bodnant terraces or the old walls and courts of Sissinghurst within our own gardens yet each of these contains ideas which may be adapted even to the most modest suburban or town garden. More important, by visiting such gardens as these one can absorb the climate of thought and design which leads to inspired planting on one's own account.

Pests and Poisons
September 21 1963

Four months ago I received a copy ('presented for review with the compliments of the Director of Publications. Her Majesty's Stationery Office') of a booklet, produced by the Ministry of Agriculture and entitled *Chemicals for the Gardener* (1s 3d). I will not pretend that it has taken me until now to recover from the shock, inured though I was to the coyness with which HMSO and most of the departments it serves shrink from publicising their publications – not one of the Ministry of Agriculture's admirable growers' bulletins on fruit, vegetable, and flower crops (which gardeners would find more useful than any textbook) has ever before or since been presented to me for review. It would, on the other hand, be no pretence to say that I am reluctant to invite readers to make expeditions to the only two establishments in London where most HMSO publications can be bought, since in my experience both are more than likely to be out of stock of anything one wants within days – sometimes within a couple of hours – of its advertised publication time, and less than likely to get it reprinted unless a substantial proportion of their frustrated customers leave written orders. But I must confess that the main reason for my own malfeasance on this occasion has been my unwillingness to enter into the controversy provoked by Rachel Carson's *Silent Spring.*

My unwillingness persists; yet I can hardly touch upon the topic of pest control without committing myself to a few limited generalities. One is that no gardener can logically object to 'upsetting the balance of nature,' since that is just what gardening is; but to do this by creating physical conditions that favour the growth of wanted rather than unwanted organisms is more sensible than to concentrate on killing the pests whose spread one has unwittingly induced. Another is that well-nourished (and especially well-watered) plants can often take pest-damage in their stride and outgrow it; one should therefore be content with a modest degree of control over those insects whose only offence is to share one's taste for garden plants, and seek to exterminate only those (such as aphids) which carry incurable diseases. A third is that the timely use of physical weapons – a jet of water, a finger and thumb – is much simpler and more effective than a belated declaration of chemical warfare: but if one must resort to chemical weapons one should make sure they are potent, persistent, and well aimed.

All this adds up to the simple proposition that you should not use chemicals in the garden without knowing what you are doing; and the more you know the less frequently will you need to use them. Subject to this proviso, however, I can see no sense in abstaining from their use when you do need them, or in selecting any but the most effective for your purpose on such grounds as that the more effective ones are inorganic, or commercially profitable, or that nobody really knows exactly how they work. The same can be said, after all, of most of the drugs we let our doctors use on us. This, of course, is not to deny that the need to resort to chemical controls would arise less often if more money were invested in research into physical and biological methods of control, or that the reason why this does not happen is simply that knowledge commands no market. Those whose concern is only to make the best of what is available should study the ministry's booklet – but not uncritically.

It surprised me, for example, that the ministry should recommend for general use against aphids a number of preparations containing DDT, which also kills pollinating insects, and derris or pyrethrum, whose effect lasts only a day or so, but not a systematic insecticide which is both persistent and selective, killing only the parasites that suck the plant's sap. It is not in fact, necessary to spend any money, or more than a few seconds time, on the control of aphids on plants such as roses and broad beans if you keep a look out for the first colonies. Far more troublesome, I find, are the ants that bore large holes in rose buds. On the other hand, ants in the potato patch seem to do nothing but good: they reduce the soil to the fine tilth that makes for the free swelling of fat and shapely tubers which they do not themselves want to eat. Here I would rather leave them alone than use the preparations approved by the Ministry, all of which are of the type whose toxic elements do not break down either in the soil or in the human body.

Most gardeners take a different view of vertebrate pests, according them a prima facie right to live. I myself regarded moles with affectionate tolerance until a row of hills paraded across my lawn; now I fumigate the run beneath each fresh hill, yet still they come. I am still willing to concede a reasonable ration of fruit and vegetables to the birds, but thankful that the ministry has found (though not yet publicised) a dope that enables unconscious pigeons to be gathered like mushrooms, while less greedy breeds are left to recover. I am all for preserving a full range of species, but I should be well content to see the woodpigeon become as scarce as the bittern. The ministry – intimidated, no doubt, by the public reaction to the effects on wild life of the use of toxic seed dressings – has nothing to say in its booklet about the control of avian or mammalian vermin. Neither, of course, does it venture a word about that most destructive of all garden pests, the domestic dog which can do more damage in five minutes than a million aphids could manage in a year. I hasten to make it plain that I am not advocating the use of poisoned meat. The dog, after all, is not only as innocent as the aphid: it has, unlike the aphid, a human master who could, and surely should be held responsible for its effective control. Few dog owners, after all, would deliberately and in their own persons invade their neighbours' gardens and trample or uproot the plantlets lined out in seed-beds or hardening off in boxes and open frames. Yet that, in effect is precisely what they do whenever they let their dogs loose to exercise themselves unsupervised.

Derek Senior

Gardener's Garments
March 28 1964

'Whenever a new sport becomes popular,' says Alison Adburgham, 'fashion is on the ball,' and illustrates a functional outfit for the bowling alley. Fashion writers often show us what to wear when sailing, golfing, ski-ing, swimming, and playing tennis, not to mention riding and skating. We are even told what to wear on the beach, presumably après swimming. In all this welter of advice not one word is offered to show that designers or fashion writers are aware that a recent survey has shown that gardening is the most popular outdoor hobby of them all. Who advises us on what to wear for that?

I hope that the outfits at flower shows will remain as richly varied as they have always been, but there is a great need these days of do-it-yourself gardening for a neat and serviceable costume that will land up on all the varied jobs that the enthusiastic gardener has to do, particularly if the garden lies, as mine does, on a windy slope to the north. It might even tempt the reluctant gardener into going out on a cold windy day to prune or dig. The old lady who bought a mink coat because she wanted something light and warm for gardening had the right idea, though a Terylene anorak intended really for sailing is a versatile and less expensive substitute. A garden apron is an abomination. It gets caught on twigs, blows about, and is rather too long or too short for kneeling. The ideal skirt has yet to be discovered. Pleated Terylene though easy to wash, blows about, and it, too, catches on twigs. So many jobs in the garden necessitate kneeling, that slacks, even if one is slim enough to wear them, look inelegant, and besides, the knees wear out. The ideal might be a gored, thorn-proof skirt of tweed. This I have never found.

Gloves are often a necessity, though the most vital jobs are usually those which need bare hands, to the detriment of our appearance later. The gardening gloves sold optimistically 'For Ladies' in the seedsmen's shops are always too short in the wrist, which gets unmercifully scratched when pruning. And what about headgear? A brim is often necessary, especially when spraying, so headsquares are out. If I could find one, and had the courage to wear it, an old-fashioned sun bonnet might be the answer. But it would look distinctly odd with the anorak, and even odder with jodhpur boots. We badly need some enterprising dress designer to help us with our problems. Where is the Teddy Tinling for the woman gardener?

Margaret H Swain

Garden
August 1 1964

It may have been the temptation to make a Latin pun on his name which led Parkinson, best of the 16th and 17th century gardening writers, to call his major work *Paradisi in Sole*; but it is a fact that at the time and earlier the words 'paradise' and 'garden' were almost synonymous. But the garden of the English poetic imagination, a paradise of nature tamed to the harmonies of art by rational benevolence, existed only as a dream, expressed here and there in verse, perhaps in paint, but not in the gardener's own materials.

For gardening in England began with a series of aberrations of the kind which any great artist may suffer at the beginning of his working life, and in the course of which he learns the technicalities of his trade while trying to discover what he should be doing. There were Roman, monastic, Flemish, Dutch, and other gardens in England, as there are now English gardens in France or Portugal. The latter, particularly, were, in Tudor and Jacobean examples, sometimes turned into what seem to have been monstrosities by the English desire to get some poetry into them. Perhaps only the knot garden, a product of the middle early period of Italian and Flemish origin, had merit: it was, at least, the only example of the abstract yet to emerge in this art.

Then, at a time when the greatest of the English gardeners, men like Sir Thomas Hanmer, were beginning to feel their way towards an English garden which really would give expression to the paradise dream, came another diversion in the influence of the Frenchman, Le Nôtre. No man ever had a more significant name: for his work was inappropriate to any people but the French, his gardening was a branch of the most grandiose kind of architecture. Italian gardening is architectural, but not in the French sense of creating, with masonry and trees, colossal frames in which men and women could effectively strike those attitudes which compose social pictures.

The garden immanent in the English soul was never conceived as a setting for human attitudinising. Ideally, it would never have more than two people in it. The time for it had not come, and the English imitated, but Englished, the repulsive symmetries of continental models yet could never quite achieve the Ozymandias spirit of Le Nôtre at his most arrogant. It was not their bent to crush nature under tons of masonry or to drill her trees into rectangular patterns. It was rather to show her how, by curbing her temperament and putting her best work into a single composition, she could improve on the products of her untamed genius. The real work of English gardening began, then, in the 18th century with the production of ideal, picturesque landscapes by such amateurs of genius as Hamilton and, towering over the rest, Hoare of Stourhead, a masterpiece which can still be seen as he made it, and by such professional garden artists of talent as Capability Brown and Humphrey Repton.

It is true that the inspiration of this movement was the paintings of certain Italian, but chiefly French-Italianate, *paysageistes* of the Roman campagna and other Italian landscapes; above all, Claude Lorraine and Poussin. William Kent, universal but second-rate artist, had something to do with that. The English artists, instead of painting landscapes, made them with earth, stone, water, and trees. But in so doing they departed from their models and went towards what they could see in their spirit's eye. The Chinese had been doing the same thing for about 2,000 years; but a study of dates in influences shows clearly that the English landscape movement was well under way before its artists had knowledge of what China had done; and William Temple's horticultural chinoiseries were no more Chinese than Chippendale's in cabinet-making.

Stourhead remains the masterpiece of the school; you may see sublime examples elsewhere, at Stowe, at Sheffield Park, here and there all over Britain, but nothing to equal it. Still, it was not the dream realised: it was too native for that, and paradise, after all, was elsewhere, was exotic. The representative Englishman was not Pope, with his urbanities in both verse and the gardening which he practised at the same level of excellence: it was still Shakespeare with his woodnotes wild, yet tempered in romanticism by an ironical self criticism inspired by the best Italianate models. Not until the 19th century was the horticultural Shakespeare born. William Kobmson and born in Ireland, of all places, which owes him, at some removes it is true, the lovely romantic gardens of Mount Usher, Rowallane, Garinish and more, all as 'English' as Dublin's best squares.

What, since Robinson's work, has the English garden emerged as? Here is a recipe: make a landscape in the 18th, but late 18th century style, a 'picture' composed of natural elements only. Let it be in the spirit of the work which was done after Uvedale Price and his disciples had broken the already soft and gentle lines of Repton's best works, excepting about the house where, in a mildly formal garden, tribute can be paid to Latin urbanity, to the superb Italian tradition in garden design. But now into this, using the technical skill taught us by such great 19th century horticultural scientists as Loudon and Paxton, plant not representatives of our native flora only but rather some of that immense wealth of plant material which the industrial and landed rich of the past century paid for, material collected from every corner of the world by the French priest Delavay, the German Siebold, but chiefly by men of British race, botanist-adventurers like Douglas, Fortune, Forrest, Farrer, Wilson, Comber, Kingdon-Ward, who sacrificed comfort and risked their lives during years to send to Britain the loveliest species of the

Himalaya and Andes, of Yunnan and Szechuan, of Rockies and Pamirs. In what spirit will you do this? In the spirit of a man who re-creates, in a garden, the Coral Island of boyhood reading; of a sophisticated townsman who recreates the paradise of the race's simpler youth in which the rules could be ignored and the flora of England and China, India and Peru, could be seen in a single, perfect composition, 'natural' as only art can make it. You will need, to succeed, the soft and equable climate of England.

Where and when is this garden to be seen? The best months are, of course, May and June, when, and especially in the west from Caerhays in Cornwall to Inverewe in Scotland, the floral riches of Sikhim, Nepal, and West China, mingled with those of Europe and North America, give fullest expression to the passion for the natural garden in which, according to Hippolyte Tame, the English are at their greatest in art. Still, the best gardens are good throughout the year. The great ones need no naming here, but two of them should be mentioned as coming nearest to the realisation of the paradise dream: Bodnant, and Tal-y-cafn in North Wales, and Dartington Hall, in Devon. There is an interesting comparison here, for whereas in Bodnant the formal part, the tribute to the classical, and the altogether English romantic garden, are quite separated, at Dartington a remarkable and entirely successful synthesis has been accomplished: it is landscape garden in the 18th-century tradition into which have been planted with rare discretion the less flamboyant of the exotics; pastoral and lyrical have been brought into harmony. This great work of art has been brought to perfection within a quarter of a century, in itself a remarkable achievement. Hidcote Barton Manor, in Gloucestershire, is open all summer, as being now the property of the National Trust. This masterpiece of the last and finest phase in English gardening was the work of Lawrence Johnston, who made another famous garden in the south of France, La Serre de la Madone; it excels in design, in the theme of 'anticipation and surprise,' achieved by the making of many small gardens within the great one; yet also in the art of bringing into the garden the surrounding and distant landscape, in this case the heart of England.

In making use of the national gardens scheme guide book, do not pick out only the big gardens to visit. As an example of what can be done on a medium-sized scale in this art, I would suggest, in the south east, Withersdane Court; it is the property, and a part, of Wye College, near Ashford in Kent, the agricultural and horticultural college of London University. In the south west, my example would be the Garden House, Buckland Monachorum, where in two decades Mr Lionel Fortescue has created an astonishing example of the English romantic or paradise garden on a scale which has not called for great wealth but for a strictness of taste in the choice of forms and colours which are even more rare. Knightshave's Court, the Heathcoat- Amory's garden near Tiverton is another fine example of the paradise school. See, if you possibly can, Sir George Campbell's Crarae, on Loch Fyne, where the rocky and precipitous little valley of a small river has been wonderfully 'gardened.' You may from there go on to Tarbet and get a ship which will land you on Gigha; there, Sir James Horlick has turned a great part of the island into a garden in the spirit which I have tried to define here. Islands, of course, are perfect for the English garden and on Tresco in the Scilly Isles generations of Dorrien-Smiths have, by virtue of a frost-free climate, carried the dream as near to perfection as it can be taken.

The influence of the great private gardens is apparent, and more so every year, in municipal gardening; witness the fine rock gardens with an interesting collection of alpine plants made by the municipality of Harrogate in its city; the way in which a new generation of public gardeners is raising the quality of plant material used in the parks. The same thing is happening in other public institutions: the design and planting, for example, of the grounds of the new University of Exeter will result in a garden of the kind I have been describing; so that, even though there be few such gardens made by private men, the style will not be lost or kept only in the old examples. The English gardener will continue, in Poe's words, to recognise 'in the multiform and multicolour of the flowers and trees ... the most direct and energetic efforts of Nature at physical loveliness', and to perceive that he would be employing the best means in the fulfilment of his destiny as a poet '... in the direction or concentration of this effort – or more properly in its adaptation to the eyes which are to behold it on earth.'

Edward Hyams

Grass-Root Resolutions
January 1 1966

Even if one has no intention of making new year gardening resolutions, there is no harm in working out what they ought to be. If the aim is solely to improve the quality of the garden, my own list would run something like this:

1   Replan and replant large patches of sloping bank in front of the house, since thymes, alyssum and Dryas octopetala have now naturalised themselves so thoroughly that last summer the whole place had begun to look like the wildest of wild gardens;
2   Dig up and reseed lawn, sloping the edge down to meet path which runs round it, leaving no drop in levels between them, and thus growing more grass and less clover, daisy, and milfoil. Or, top up drive to meet edge of lawn; then order and use selective weed-killer regularly;
3   More drainage pipes out of shady dry wall at back of house, or plant some ramondas in them. Or at any rate do something about them, since no moisture has ever been seen to drain out of them yet, and they look like some primitive sewage system;
4   Make determined effort to use available time and energy to better advantage. For instance, decide to spend all spare moments keeping down weeds, and not to wander off to look at things when supposedly forking out ground elder on the orchard banks.

If new year resolutions ought properly to be concerned with the wellbeing of the gardener instead of the look of the garden, the entire list instantly changes and becomes this:

1 Presumably I'm gardening because I enjoy it. I therefore resolve to use my time and energy to the best advantage. Whenever I feel like it, I will stop forking out ground elder and will wander off to look at things;
2 I will not pop out to do a bit of weeding unless I am dressed for the job and I will never, never pop out in my slippers;
3 In cold weather, dressing for the job shall somehow not involve looking like one of those Michelin men;
4 I will use barrier cream regularly under my gardening gloves. And in the summer when I am wearing sandals I will use barrier cream on my feet.

But now the whole thing begins to sound rather like the list of tasks in *Under Milk Wood* that Mr Ogmore and Mr Pritchard are required to repeat in unhappy, dead duet: 'We must take our pyjamas from the drawer marked "Pyjamas".' And becoming a gardening version of Mrs Ogmore-Pritchard is an unattractive prospect. There are just a few resolutions, more practical and more practicable that might actually prove beneficial both to the garden and to the gardener. These for instance:

1 I really will try to order plants in reasonable time. Or failing this, remember to specify, 'No substitutes; please leave on order.' In this way I might end up with fewer plants that I don't want;
2 I will also try not to have ambitious ideas for schemes that are beyond my capacity and beyond the English climate. Or if I have those ideas, I will reject them. Instead of aiming for imagined excellence, I will aim in the garden (and out of it, too) for competent mediocrity. If that sounds impossibly dull, I can only say that one bushy berberis is better than a group of fuchsias killed by the frost.

My resolutions have so far not taken any account of other people. My husband keeps suggesting that we should put a notice on the gate saying 'Do come in if you'd like to'; this is because passers-by stop at sun-rose time to look at the garden from the road. But I should never have the nerve to assume they wanted to come in, and it would be so disappointing for them if they actually did; although I suppose it would encourage any gardener to see all that ground elder. No, we have far too much to do yet before we're ready for that notice. So instead I would just make one altruistic resolution:

I resolve that in 1966 I will not pester my husband to do things in the garden ... well, not more than once a week anyway.

EM May

Snobs and Border Incidents
May 23 1966

Gardening rivals croquet as a forcing ground for the baser emotions. There are those who just like flowers and pretty gardens: and good luck to them. For them, the Chelsea Flower Show (which opens tomorrow) is an innocuous feast of horticultural delicacies. They jostle peaceably around, collect a few catalogues, admire the plants, and retire with their damaged corns suitably impressed by what God, man, and Mammon can do together. But for the rest of us, a day at Chelsea should send us, if we are Catholics, to our confessors. Envy certainly: the desire to humiliate our neighbours, certainly: and snobbery, without a doubt. Not to mention greed at the Waterperry strawberry stand, malice (if we happen to see a plant that could be better grown), and also sloth. For the net effect of Chelsea is to leave me, for one, convinced that there's no point in setting spade to my garden ever again. And look what the place did to the Duke of Edinburgh – watering all those poor photographers?

Envy, of course, one is conscious of and takes steps to combat. The whole marquee is full of couples convincing each other that they wouldn't want to grow begonias as big as soup plates, or roses of that particularly vivid complexion. And the desire to outdo one's neighbours is offset by the equally traditional gardener's habit of pressing cuttings of their favourite plants on their neighbours complete with copious advice and – I trust – a genuine desire to see their gifts thrive. Not that gardeners aren't the most frightful thieves. Respectable middle-aged persons who are scrupulously honest in all other departments of their lives, think nothing of taking cuttings from strangers' shrubs, or stealing seeds from public botanical gardens – though actually digging up other people's plants is frowned on. I have gardening friends whose excitement in life is pinching bits from other gardens, even though they would certainly have been offered cuttings on request. 'Stolen fruit is sweeter' relates not to small boys scrumping but to members of the RHS.

But snobbery is the really ineradicable gardening vice. Most gardeners do their best to disguise this snobbery with mutterings about skill, or aesthetic pleasure. I myself have a line of argument that my aggravating habit of referring to common plants by their latin names is merely for accuracy's sake (though I am aware that referring to the michaelmas daisies as Aster nove belgii doesn't actually hide the fact that they're growing in a soil composed of old bricks and bits of broken toys or that my remembering to pronounce camelia with a flattened second syllable doesn't make the wretched thing flower. There is a counter device here to reverse the gambit and only refer to plants by a folk name. I have heard an expert botanist floor her rivals by talking about old man's bugwort or the Bolivian rose vine. However, real gardening snobbery is composed for the most part of all the old class/money attributes. The snob plants to grow are, by and large, those which thrive in the lime free damp soils of the south west and the north, like the Chinese species rhododendrons or the meconopsis family. You may or may not like the vast rhododendrons of the Grande series with their great leathery leaves and waxy flowers, but there's one thing for sure – you need an estate to plant them in. And indeed, most of the plants admired especially by the gardening fraternity do not flourish in, or near, the towns in which most people live.

Different flowers do have different snob ratings: the different stands at Chelsea, and, even more, the fortnightly RHS shows provide a splendid field for the keen student of the British class structure. The rhododendron and azalea shows dominated by the aristocracy; members of the peerage vie with each other for the prizes and most of the visitors are either remarkably well dressed, or expensively under dressed. It was in this category of shrubs that until fairly recently a Gentlemen v. Players situation existed and plants were catalogued into those raised by nurserymen and those raised by the gents. And Messrs. Hilliers have provided at Chelsea the best snob-experts stand at the show – an exhibit of the leaves of rhododendrons.

Cacti, succulents, and alpines appeal apparently to the retired professional classes, particularly the military. Roses, irises, delphiniums are all the province of the middle classes. Though again within the ranks there are class distinctions. Shrub roses, no doubt because they use more space than hybrid teas, are OK. Species irises, too, have a snob value, particularly the sinister brown and black ones which are so difficult to grow. And at the bottom in spite of – or perhaps because of – their cheerful colours and comparative ease of cultivation are the dahlias. I once admired a magnificent bed of large decorative dahlias in a big Scottish garden. 'The gardener's boy does them,' sniffed the garden owner. 'They're very showy.'

Of course, a little ingenuity and the gift of the gab can confuse any snob intellectual, social, or gardening. The classic remark, 'You should have seen it last week', is merely an elementary example of the technique. I once planted some forgotten tulip bulbs in April and when some miserable, stunted little flowers appeared in August, I explained that they were a rare, autumn-flowering species. They aroused considerable interest: but one doesn't often have to resort to lying. There are also, of course, plants that are actually dead easy to grow and impress all but the experts – like Gentian septemfida and most of the botanical tulips.

Undoutedy the real charm of Chelsea is eavesdropping. I have heard husbands persuading wives that the lawn should be paved and putting forward Machiavellian arguments for idleness. I have listened to housewives planning to spend their family allowances on orchids and heard an inoffensive-looking old gentleman say with venom in his voice that he hated pinks. But my most treasured remark came from a middle-aged lady who said reflectively: 'I do like Lady Mohr – but I think she's got a dirty beard.'

Lady Mohr is an Iris.

Val Arnold Forster

A Country Diary
October 21 1966

Hampshire: My attention has lately been turned to slugs. My garden has a plentiful supply. I have encountered at least nine species, ranging in size from the large, black Arion ater to the small and most destructive Aon hortensis. Slug killers of various kinds make little difference. True, they kill some, but since the population of slugs is enormous, others soon replace those that are killed. The Henry Doubleday Research Association of Braintree, Essex, has estimated that the weight of slugs in a garden of one acre is in the region of 180 to 300 pounds. The weight of food consumed must be considerable. The value of manure from an equivalent weight of live stock would be appreciable, so slugs may have some secondary value to gardeners. They eat not only our cherished seedlings but also a lot of decaying vegetable matter and the faeces of animals. Fertosan is a proved slug and snail killer. It probably kills other things also, but it is very limited in its activity. Other slugs from the vast populations from untreated ground soon invade the treated areas. The best safeguards against too many slugs are, or were, toads, frogs, and slowworms. These have been exterminated in this locality by the vast amounts of chemical sprays and manures.

Hedgehogs still survive. They are very fond of milk, and will regularly come to lap it up at night time. Soon they will be hibernating, and I am about to provide a large box, stuffed with straw, to tempt one to spend the winter in my garden and eat my slugs in the spring.

EL Grant Watson

Cottage Garden Flowers
June 24 1967

It is ironical that at a time when cottage gardens are fast disappearing from the countryside there is a growing demand for the simple flowers that flourished in those overcrowded little plots. And for cottage style gardening, too. We don't mix our flowers so indiscriminately, or plant them among cabbages and gooseberry bushes, but the happy informality of cottage gardening is popular today. There are advantages in close planting beyond the effect of lavish permanence. Close planting conserves moisture and I think many plants are happier when they are grown close to one another. Most of us want gardens that need as little care as possible and plants that can be left to increase slowly without yearly attention. Cottage plants had to look after themselves; otherwise they would not have survived so many years of casual treatment.

Fair maid of France (or Kent) is a typical cottage plant whose small white double flowers gave it the older name of bachelor's buttons. It is an unassuming little plant that has of late years become very popular – and scarce. Its botanical name is Ranunculus aconitifolius fl. pl., and there is a single flowered form which is easy and generous but misses the restrained charm of the double. It is not a plant for the heavily worked garden because after flowering it disappears completely, and can easily be damaged while resting underground. It is slow to increase, but if it is left to itself its dark, well-cut leaves reappear faithfully each spring and the flowers last for many weeks. Another plant now enjoying a comeback is Dicentra spectabilis, sometimes called bleeding heart, lyre plant, or lady in the bath. If ever a plant needed the safe shelter in a shady cottage garden this one does, for its roots are as brittle as glass.

There is nothing fragile about lady's mantle (Alchemilla mollis) now high in the popularity list. It would survive anywhere for its roots are tough and tenacious, and it is a generous seeder. Not long ago it was considered too common for any but the lowliest gardens, but now we meet it everywhere. With its grey-green pleated leaves and endless succession of tiny green flowers it fits in anywhere and is much esteemed by flower arrangers. Astrantias, too, are good mixers and happy in sun or shade. The flowers, composed of a mound of stamens surrounded by bracts in white with pale green and soft pink, give the plant its cottage name of Hattie's pincushion. Some gardeners probably find the colouring a little too delicate for their taste: hence the less complimentary name of melancholy gentleman. The lungworts have always been popular in village gardens, although only the most common form – Pulmonaria officinalis – was generally grown. Now the connoisseurs have discovered there is great beauty in those handsome spotted leaves and discriminate in favour of the best marked foliage. The small blue, pink, or reddish flowers open early, often when snow is still on the ground, and last for many weeks, but it is after the flowering that the leaves assume their best plumage.

I often wonder if the heavily planted cottage gardens had a restraining effect on plants with running roots. Certainly the delightful clustered bellflower, Campanula glomerata, did not seem to be such a nuisance in its humble setting as it is when planted in an open garden. Luckily there are better forms available today which do not run. Many other good garden plants that we enjoy today came to us from cottage gardens. I can remember the time when even the ubiquitous Stachys lanata was to be found only in such places. Nearly 30 years ago the local nursery telephoned to me to ask if I could possibly induce one of the cottagers in our village to let them have a clump of it.

Margery Fish

'Natural' Gardening Urged
September 21 1968

An intensive campaign to dissuade amateur gardeners from using artificial fertilisers and pesticides has been launched by the Soil Association. The association says that with the intensive use of chemicals on agricultural land, private gardens have become a valuable refuge for wild life, especially birds. Gardeners are being urged to experiment by using only natural organic fertilisers, and to learn how pests can be controlled without spraying. The association has become a rallying point for those who are worried about the reliance placed on pesticides and fertilisers. Independent research is being carried out into possible contamination by chemicals. The association intends to emphasise the cheapness of 'natural' gardening. 'Most gardens probably have enough green stuff for compost, together with household waste to provide sufficient organic fertiliser', said the spokesman.

Baden Hickman

Pilferers Force Plant House to Close
April 1 1969

'Gardenlifters,' who are to gardens what shoplifters are to shops, have forced the Northern Horticultural Society to close to visitors one of its alpine plant houses at Harlow Carr, Harrogate. The annual report says that members of the society and the honest majority of visitors must suffer 'for the sins of the small, selfish, and dishonest minority of visitors.' The gardenlifters were in a bus party which, by mistake, got into an alpine plant house used for preparing plants for display. They set to work on a rare collection of alpines bequeathed to the society, stripping a dozen or more valuable plants for cuttings, and taking one or two other compete plants. Mr Geoffrey Smith, superintendent of the garden, said yesterday that he had heard of gardenlifters boasting that they never visited an open garden without a polythene bag and a pair of scissors. At Harlow Carr, they 'went through the alpine house like vultures,' ruining many of the plants by taking cuttings as plunder for their own gardens. Some plants could not be replaced – a New Zealand grey cushion plant; a grey conifer which took 25 years to grow; and a clump of androsace from which someone had grabbed a handful of cuttings. 'Romantic' plants like gentians and mecanopsis (Himalayan poppy) were sometimes irresistible to garden lifters. He once planted 20 gentians on a Friday and found only three left on the Monday.

An official of the Royal Horticultural Society said that the problem at the society's garden at Wisley, Surrey, had not proved as serious as at Harrogate. But the RHS asked visitors not to take large bags with them into the gardens – 'probably,' said the official, 'as good a precaution as we are likely to get.'

Michael Parkin

Garden Godwottery
August 18 1969

Godwottery in gardens is something Peter Shepheard, the architect and writer, despises very much. By godwottery he means the attitude to gardens summed up by 'A garden is a lovesome thing, God wot.' Godwottery, the sentimental preconception of what a garden should be, results in a very strange collection of elements which have an outrageous incongruity with each other and with all modern situations, writes Mr Shepheard, and one can see him shudder. Cotswold stone retaining walls; vaguely Spanish wrought iron gates; crazy paving, nowadays often coloured yellow, green, and pink; plainly irregular ponds now usually of pale blue fibreglass, fed by streams of impossible source; gnomes, fairies, and animals, usually plastic, of vaguely Neapolitan colouring; dwarf cypress trees. All of which, Mr Shepheard says, proves the truth of the definition of sentimentality in art as 'having the idea of the feeling before the feeling.'

In a marvellously trenchant new Design Centre publication called *Gardens* he suggests that the remedy is to shun preconceptions, observe nature, and above all trust one's own feelings for the stuff of which the landscape is made. Forget about godwottery, and look at the wild landscape itself, and indeed much of the man-made landscape. The growth of plants, the movement of water, the structure of rocks and seashore all in some way have relevance to the design of gardens even if only as a part of an underlying comprehension of the way nature works. And look around the towns, villages, harbours, and canals of the country, especially those built in the age of craftsmen; examine the paving and steps, walls and fences, kerbs and gutters – examples of a thousand problems solved in permanent and beautiful forms.

Mr Shepheard is a wonderful comfort to the people neglected by most of the writers about gardens: those of us who like the idea of a garden but who find it very difficult to settle down to work at it. He tells you that a garden should never be a worry, advising you to plan it so that it only takes up the time you have to spare for it, even if this means reducing it to paving stones, one tree and some climbing plants. Here at last is someone with the heartening philosophy that men should rule the garden and not the garden man. Mr Shepheard – how I like him, and I greatly recommend him to others with rather unkempt gardens on their conscience – advises one against quite unattainable ideals like bowling green lawns, weedless beds or the highest dahlias in the world.

Fiona MacCarthy

A Perfect Year
November 1 1969

This is new year's day in the garden – the day good gardeners make their bad resolutions. Never again, we vow, will we sow and plant as if we thought our gardens were in Italy or Israel. When the seed catalogues are delivered, we will remember how our morning glory seedlings came up yellow, stood still for six weeks, raised a despairing tendril, and finally expired. We will leave melons and glasshouse tomatoes to the owners of heated glasshouses, eschew peaches unless we have a sheltered south-facing wall to spare, and firmly remind ourselves that zinnias need a Californian climate, onions a Spanish one, garlic a Provençal one.

Fortunately such resolutions are as seldom kept as those our weaker brethren make on January 1. So it is that when we do get a summer like the one that lasted until a few days ago, we enjoy its bounty to the full, even though we had planned for it with the washout of 1968 fresh in our memories. It has indeed been a perfect gardening year. Here in mid-Kent the winter was hard enough with a long spell of severe frost: my Thanet broccoli looked so moribund that only procrastination saved it from the compost heap, yet in late April it produced a succession of large immaculate gourds. There was no false spring to tempt us into premature sowing or planting, and when the soil did warm up it was kept nicely moist until my first pea crop (Sutton's Sweetness) had burgeoned hugely. Royal sovereign strawberries grew bigger, and hybrid sweet corn sweeter, than ever before in my experience. The first week of August brought peaches too melting to peel, followed by still more luscious Rochesters on my free-standing tree. Onions ripened hard and brown of their own accord, zinnias revelled in three months of almost continuous sunshine, morning glories, raised in a cold frame, festooned a tall yew hedge with sky blue saucers; and for the last six weeks we have been guzzling melons (Sutton's Sweetheart, charantais-type, also raised in a cold frame and planted out under Ganwick cloches) on which it would have been folly to sprinkle sugar. Maincrop potatoes have been lifted clean and dry. Even moneymaker tomatoes, planted outdoors with chutney in mind, have ripened all four of their permitted trusses!

Now it is time to look ahead: and an excellent prospect it is, for the new wood of flowering and fruiting bushes has also been ripening as never before. But exposed and unwatered rhododendrons are wilting, and clematis actually dying of thirst. August-planted strawberry runners, left to themselves, have shrivelled; irrigated, they are making splendid crowns. By the time this article is published we may have had torrential rains: but don't stop watering – it takes more than one cloudburst to make up the 6in. rainfall deficit we were suffering a week ago.

Derek Senior

Let's Do Up the Garden: 1970–1979

Christopher Lloyd's *The Well-Tempered Garden*, 1973 * Summer drought and hosepipe ban, 1976 * Barbara Hepworth's garden and studio opens, 1976 * RSPB's Big Garden Birdwatch established, 1979

The Damnable Tight Trousers
June 6 1970

Sir,– The party that abolishes the damnable tight trousers of today, by whatever means, gets my vote. Millions of man-hours must be wasted by men having to take their shoes off to change into old gardening trousers (do no politicians ever garden?). At the moment these are old enough to be wide enough to be taken off again while still wearing shoes; but well within the life of the next government today's tight trousers may well themselves become the old gardening trousers, so that twice as many man-hours will be wasted. Verb sap! – I have the honour to Be, sir, Your obedient Servant,

Neville Gringeley-Sale, Lt Col, The Red House, Etwas, Salop

Trees Putting Elbows on the Lawn
June 5 1971

We should alas sympathise with boys and girls who put their elbows on the table at meals: it shows they understand what tables are for. But how many gardeners are alive to the charms of trees that put their elbows on the lawn? With the season for visiting great country houses and their prodigal grounds now upon us again such oddities may give us ideas for the home garden. Living branches of trees cannot be made to languish graciously on the lawn overnight; but they are even less likely to get there if we prune or lop them every time they challenge the lawnmower's boorish progress. A principle may be involved here. It can best be described as gardening tolerance – the tolerance that knows how far to go in allowing perennials, shrubs and trees to pursue their wayward impulses without let or hindrance. In this sphere many of our large country gardens show themselves to be instructive models. They reveal lavender leaning unashamedly upon close-mown grass, St John's wort overhanging a path and a lusty oak threatening to enter bedroom windows. Loyally conservative in their politics, our august county families are yet well up with the permissive society when it comes to ideas about gardening – though the bedrooms darkened and made viewless by the obtrusive oak may turn out to be the servants quarters.

The casual beauty of plants, shrubs, and trees that are allowed to wander and trespass remains a bonus just so long as we have the firmness to draw the line somewhere. In my own garden a mature plant of spring-flowering heather that had gained a foot at the lawn's expense has lately taken a cut-back of an inch or two – no more. A summer-flowering companion is down for a similar clip in the autumn. It will be remembered that heather is a close-matting woody perennial, which means that it suppresses grass as it advances over the lawn with the same finality that it smothers weeds in the rockery. This is an important qualification for being allowed to overhang the lawn at ground level. Plants of open habit allow the grass to grow through them in ugly confusion as they advance, so they vote themselves out of this privilege. Annuals are also unsuitable except where they overhang paving or hard paths, for they leave half-bald patches upon the grass through the winter. For leaning out of flowerbeds and shrubberies in this way takes the severity out of straight edging. There are various close-twigged or thick-foliaged perennial evergreens that have the same smothering effect as heather. Here are a few examples: Cotoneaster congestus, Hebe Carl Teschner, H. pinguifolia pager, Lavandula spica Folgate, L. s. Hidcote, Santolina chamaecyparissus nana, S. virens, Sarcocca humilis and Senecio laxifolius. A useful prelude to cutting the grass close up to plants lying over the lawn is to run the handle of a rake or hoe beneath them; they can then be lifted up by hoisting the ends of the tool on top of a couple of empty flower pots. This leaves room to cut the grass with hand-shears without damaging the plant and I find the effect is fair enough if the job is repeated at alternative mowings only. Of course, if you mow with a Flymo there is no problem: the machine itself lifts the plants out of the way.

Trees of many species will put their elbows on the lawn, or more literally rest their lower arms at the point where gravity first pulls them to earth, if they are permitted this informal posture. They range from cypress to beech, and from cryptomeria to sweet chestnut – not forgetting horse chestnut, though these two are unrelated. If your garden includes a tree with a branch arching low, then sweeping upward again at the tip, this usually implies a lively continuing growth and increase in the branch's weight. So this is the type for leaving alone to see what happens. Once grounded, a recumbent bough makes the garden look just that bit more relaxed and mellowed. Tidiness and efficiency are put in their place.

Here are the locations of three outstanding examples of 'elbows-on-the-ground' trees accessible to the public: at Kew Gardens, an unusually long-armed Bhutan pine standing a short distance from the Victoria Gate; at Bodnant Gardens near Conway, a magnificent sweet chestnut not far from the visitor's entrance; at Whittingham village, East Lothian, a remarkable 700-year old yew which rests a host of gnarled limbs upon the ground in a grand circle – it was under this canopy, we are told, that the plot to murder Lord Darnley, husband of Mary Queen of Scots, was hatched in 1567.

Benington Marsh

A Place for Children
January 30 1972

One day, when I was working on my allotment, the peace was suddenly shattered by a sharp parental cry: 'Get off and keep off.' A few moments later a small boy, head lowered, arms hanging rigid, hurried for the exit gate, muttering to himself no doubt – since infants, I understand, now swear – 'You can keep your bloody allotment!' This made me wonder whether it is always original sin that makes older boys kick footballs into flower beds or ride bicycles over the begonias. Dad's short temper may be to blame; or his blinkered dedication.

Which is a pity; because, when you come to think of it, a garden is as good a place as any for children to be in. Setting aside boisterous play (as children sometimes do) where better to indulge their innate curiosity? They can observe the life-styles of growing-plants and insects; explore the pattern and structure of seeds, stems, leaves, and flowers; and submit themselves to a garden's natural discipline. Small children, fascinated by gardens, are always keen to 'help.' During the summer I had the company of two small children on my plot. It was a rejuvenating experience. I confess to some feeling of trepidation at the start, but when the holiday was over and those two bundles of energy had departed, a silent gloom pervaded my plot. It was a week or more before I had readjusted to a tortoise-slow pace and a close-like hush.

The presence of children in a garden can be both electric and charming. They talk incessantly, ask rapid-fire questions (which deserve honest, breathless answers), rush from one job to another, show a disfavour for using paths, plead to be allowed to water the rain-soaked lettuces, and insist on being shown how to use all tools and appliances – especially the garden rake, which is their favourite, and also the most difficult to use. It was on her first visit to the plot that my five-year-old granddaughter confronted me with two uplifted round blue eyes and, addressing me by my first name (to put us on level ground), delivered her ultimatum: 'Keep me busy, Michael, or I'll smack your bottom.' I was, as they say, nonplussed. Fortunately, however, her seven-year-old brother at my side was not at all taken aback. Quick as thought, he pulled out three weeds (real ones), offered them to her and said 'Look, Catherine; run down the path, right to the end, and put these weeds on the rubbish heap; and by the time you get back I'll have three more ready.' With whoops of joy she was off, starting a lengthy stint which kept her busy, freed me from the threatened sanction, and relieved the plot of some weed-infestation. What's more, my grandson and I were able to continue the 'men's work' on which we engaged. The moral is that children should be allowed to be busy in the garden, with a business suited to their age.

Ideally (repeat ideally) children would have their own small gardens, abutting on the main garden but partly secluded from it, with a tree to climb, shady corners in which to hide, a pool to play in, and a play-house large enough to hold a table at which to eat sandwiches prepared from their own home-grown lettuce, mustard and cress. All credit to the public parks who often make imaginative provision for children in play areas – though a private garden, however small, could, for most children, be something rather special. Miss Gertrude Jekyll, that great gardener at the turn of the century, understood children as well as gardens and wrote a book about both. It was her view that children should be given a garden ready made, and preferably in autumn. (There may be purists who claim that children should start their gardens from scratch, like the pioneers on virgin land; if so, they must be told by someone who calls a spade a spade that that sort of thing won't wash, for the children, with more choice than the backwoodsmen, would pull out before their backs and spirits were broken.) Given an autumn garden, the children should be allowed to alter its design to suit themselves, but it should be face-lifted and planted up (with the plants and bulbs of their choice) by the beginning of November. Then they can forget all about it during the cold months until early spring brings the garden – and the children – to renewed crocus-bright life.

Michael Hyde

Business is Blooming
June 5 1972

In spite of the rival attractions of motoring and boating, not to mention the zeal of architects and purblind government departments to make us learn to love high flats, gardening is now the Englishman's favourite leisure activity, as the government's own social survey recently attested. Not only that: more space for gardening is the Londoner's most felt want, and even in the new towns one man in seven puts it first on his list. The market for gardening supplies has now topped £125m a year (£40m of it for seeds and nursery stock) and is rising by about £15m a year. The seeds I bought in my youth from a long-established (but long-since-vanished) family business in central Manchester were measured out for me with a tiny scoop from a hollowed wooden drawer into a plain white paper packet, which was then sealed and labelled with a fountain pen. How long they had been in that drawer I could only guess. Today Suttons's seeds – many of them embedded in nutrient pellets – came sealed into moisture-proof packets of laminated foil and polythene, which even the exacting Ministry of Agriculture accepts as a sufficient guarantee of high germination for an indefinite period.

Similar transfusions are working wonders elsewhere. The Rothschilds, having converted one of the world's most extravagant private hobbies – the Exbury azalea plantation – into a wholesale supply business, recently put money and a manager into R & G Cuthbert, whose shares have doubled in value in the last few weeks. The dominant pattern, however, is of rationalisation within the nursery trade by way of takeovers, mergers, and consortia. Typical are such arrangements as that whereby Dobies of Chester include Carters' seed specialties in their mail order catalogue while Carters themselves now sell only through retailers, or that whereby Waterers of Twyford have joined forces with the Sunningdale nurseries at Windlesham: the former (whose mail-order catalogue was the most colourful in the business) now sells exclusively through seven garden centres, with a combined turnover of £1m a year, while the latter handles all the joint mail-order business and is thereby enabled to maintain its precious stock of rare plants – especially old shrub roses. The same trend is apparent among nursery men on the wholesale side of the business, supplying commercial growers and retailers. In East Anglia, for example, five firms specialising respectively in tree fruit, soft fruit, roses, flowering shrubs, and herbaceous plants, whose nurseries all lie within 40 miles of one another, have formed a joint marketing organisation, with considerable savings on overheads.

The mushrooming of garden centres is perhaps the most evident outward sign of the current revolution in the garden supply business. But there are garden centres and garden centres. Some, like Scott's of Merriott in Somerset, Notcutts of Woodbridge in Suffolk, and Jackman's of Woking in Surrey, are the cash-and-carry outlets of nurseries that have built up great reputations over the years as mail order firms, but now find they lose money on the average amateur's small mail order. These garden centres will be the salvation of irreplaceable stocks of the less commonly demanded species and varieties of garden plants. Others are lucrative sidelines for great gardens which are opened to the public as show places and visited by tens of thousands of keen gardeners every summer day. Bodnant in North Wales is the supreme example: all it needs is a greenhouse strategically placed beside the exit and continuously stocked with container-grown specimens of the exotic plants the visitors have been admiring, with a cash register at the check-out point.

Other garden centres, again, represent a diversification into the nursery business on the part of chain stores (like Cramphorn's) in the pet and garden sundries trade. And there are others which simply buy up plants raised in the open ground, stuff them into beds or pots of sand and sell then off to inexperienced, would-be creators of instant gardens. In an effort to prevent this category from discrediting the trade as a whole, the Horticultural Trades Association last spring launched an approved garden centres scheme, in which more than 100 of the 400-odd garden centre operators in the country have now enrolled; they may fly the authorised emblem so long as they are not found on inspection to fall short of the standards laid down.

As the motoring organisations have found, however, it is much easier to set standards for car-parking and lavatories than for the quality of meals served; and by the same token the HTA emblem is still a better guarantee of comfort and convenience for the whole family while father makes his purchases than of the health and pedigree of the plants he buys – but it is early days yet. The success of the garden centre proper depends on three basic factors: the convenience, for the motorised gardener, of an accessible out-of-town supermarket catering for all gardening needs, often with a restaurant and play park to distract chidren from the fun of switching plant labels; the economy, for the nurseryman, of the cash-and-carry principles; and above all the virtues for all concerned of plants grown in plastic or reinforced, paper containers. It is, indeed, fundamentally the packaging revolution that lies at the heart of the boom in the gardening business. This applies no less to the manufacture of sundries and to the mail-order trade than to the growing of plants in containers. What sells the new composts, fertilisers, and the like is not so much their intrinsic novelty or value as the well-designed handles on their plastic bags that make worthwhile quantities easy to carry home. What sells the new fungicides, herbicides, and pesticides is the handiness of a puffer-pack, an aerosol aphid gun, a pocket touchweeder, or a soluble sachet compared with the time-consuming messiness of weighing out ounces of powder, mixing it with water to the consistency of cream, stirring that into a bucketful, and pumping the results through a syringe. And what will rescue the mail order herbaceous plant trade from economic anaemia is the fact that specialist growers like Ken Muir of Clacton (strawberries) and Wyck Hill Nurseries of Stow-on-the-Wold (geraniums) are not only producing good plants, but packing them for postage so that they stay good.

All this is costing us gardeners more money, but we are paying it gladly; hence the boom.

Derek Senior

Great 'scape
June 22 1974

'God almighty first planted a garden,' wrote Francis Bacon, 'and, indeed, it is the purest of human pleasures.' The Hon Charles Hamilton did more. At Painshill near Cobham in Surrey from a flat and barren heath he created a landscape: a world of trees, plants, water and ruins set within undulating cultivated land, its contours etched with dark woods and merging into blue distances. Charles Hamilton was one of the earliest and probably the most original and influential of the 18th century's English landscape gardeners, the amateur precursor of the professional Capability Brown.

Charles Hamilton, son of an earl, Comptroller of the Green Cloth to Frederick Prince of Wales (now remembered as 'Poor Fred, who was alive and is dead'), leased Painshill in 1738. Landscaping of formal gardens was already a craze in the country; rocks, caverns, grottoes and waterfalls were fast replacing clipped hedges and geometric flowerbeds in the gardens of the *beau monde*. 'All the horrid graces of the *Wilderness* itself, as representing Nature more, will be more engaging, and appear with a Magnificence beyond the formal mockery of princely Gardens,' said Shaftesbury.

'Every Man now, be his fortune what it will, is to be *doing something at his Place*, as the fashionable Phrase is,' reported a contemporary voice, 'and you hardly meet with any Body, who, after the first Compliments, does not inform you that he is in *Mortar* and *moving of Earth*; the modest terms for Building and Gardening. *One large Room, a Serpentine River*, and a *Wood*, are become the most absolute necessaries of Life.'

Hamilton had nobler ideas. He had studied the work of Claude, Poussin and Salvator Rosa on his grand tours, and determined that he too would create idealised landscapes: but not in paint, bounded by the two dimensions of the framed picture. His scenes would be created with real trees, hills, lakes; appreciated with five senses instead of one; entered as magically as a later Alice was to step through her Looking Glass. In Painshill's 200 acres Charles Hamilton created the only completely artificial landscape in Europe. He moved earth to shape the land into contours gentle and dramatic (there is an Alpine area). He created a lake from the water of the river Mole by a device so ingenious as to merit an article in the *Gentleman's Magazine*, and raised islands on it. He made a vineyard which yielded 5,000 litres of wine a year (sold at 7s 6d a bottle). He planted trees rare, numerous and variegated (Horace Walpole called him a treemonger) separately and in woods, and the first rhododendrons and azealeas in England. He erected garden follies – gothic ruins, a Turkish tent, temples, a hermitage (a hired hermit unfortunately did not last long), and a grotto of marine rock whose caverns were encrusted with crystalline fragments like stalactites to glitter in the sunlight reflected from the lake. Hamilton 'directed and oversaw all the operations, both in the buildings and the gardens,' his neighbour Joseph Spence reported, 'and now he says he would not have the same to go through again for the world.'

Painshill made Charles Hamilton famous. The park was open to all, and pony carts stood at the White Lion in Cobham to take them there. And everybody came. 'I have been to see Mr Hamilton's near Cobham, where he has really made a fine place out of a most cursed hill,' wrote Horace Walpole in 1748. 'Painshill is all a new creation, and a boldness of design and a happiness of execution attend the wonderful efforts which art has there made to rival nature' (Thomas Whately, 1770). Hamilton's temple of Bacchus was the only piece of English architecture Thomas Jefferson found to praise on his trip to England in 1786. And John Wilkes wrote, 'I sauntered through the Elysium of Mr Hamilton's gardens till eight in the evening, like the first solitary man through Paradise.'

Paradise is the right word. Now we come to the present day. The paradisal park has been lost – split among private owners since the war, and sadly neglected. And yet, like a true Eden, it survives behind the private fences to tantalise anyone who has glimpsed or learned of it. Almost miraculously, Hamilton's landscape is still intact in spite of a jungle of overgrowth, ragged woods and uncultivated fields; and westward drivers along the A3 little realise what lies behind the border of trees on their left. Pains Hill (as it has become) has a band of anxious devotees, all of whom have recently expressed their support for its preservation and restoration. But the National Trust, the Georgian Group, the Garden History Society, the Institute of Landscape Architects, the Surrey Archaeological Society, the Esher History Society, the Cobham residents association and Preservation Society are as powerless as they are anxious. There is no legislation that protects historic gardens as the Town and Country Planning Act of 1971 protects historic buildings from demolition or alteration 'in a way that affects their character.' The owner of such a garden can make it into a tennis court if he likes. And there are no funds available for the preservation of historic gardens which do not belong to a house (Hamilton's own house has gone; its replacement is in separate multiple ownership). The National Trust has no funds of its own to purchase property; nor has the Georgian Group. Surrey county council has for years been interested in Pains Hill, but reluctant to acquire it by compulsory purchase: because, I was told, they already own more acres of open countryside than any other county. Then recently came the opportunity they had waited for. The owner of 43 acres of the park offered his land for sale. Surrey council was known to be considering its purchase; Elmbridge borough council cooperated by investigating the enthusiastic local support for the idea. Pains Hill devotees dared to hope.

They were wrong. The cuts in local government spending imposed by the last government came just in time to affect the meeting of Surrey's planning committee to discuss their possible acquisition of Pains Hill park, on March 14. The result – 'a reluctant decision' – was: no action. 'It would be different if the thing was under some threat, but it's protected by green belt regulations.' This time it's they who are wrong, say the devotees. Now Hamilton's Pains Hill is under a desperate and imminent threat, besides the possibility that its neglect will go beyond redemption. The area now for sale on the open market contains the crucial element of Charles Hamilton's grand design: the landscape that formed the backcloth to the garden of lake and woods. It is also the area that will contain the only access to that garden when the A3 is converted into a six-lane highway. The land is already on offer in two parts. If it is sold privately, it will inevitably further split up, and Hamilton's creation will be lost for ever.

'This is a very early English garden, the most influential of them all, created by a marvellous amateur,' says Mavis Batey of the Garden History Society. 'The English garden was the ideal combination of art and nature that inspired Rousseau, that has always been honoured and recognised on the continent, but never understood in England. These gardens are natural landscape pictures, which must be seen as total compositions – Pains Hill's temples may be protected as listed buildings, but they're nothing without the vistas which are their backcloth. The trouble is that the English don't understand English gardens: they think they're just part of the English countryside, and walk round them looking for flowerbeds. These gardens are part of our cultural heritage, as much as our art and architecture; and they're going to be lost for ever unless more is done to protect and preserve them.'

Help may be on the way, for gardens in general and Pains Hill in particular. Elmbridge borough council's recreation and amenities committee meets on Wednesday to discuss possible ways of raising the money to buy the 43 acres: they have also written to the Countryside Commission, which was recently empowered to make its own grants (instead of only making grant recommendations to the Treasury) and instructed to make country parks in Green Belts an area of high priority. Meantime Michael Shersby's Town and Country Amenities Bill, which empowers the Historic Buildings Council to make grants for the repair and maintenance (not the purchase) of historic gardens not adjacent to a house, moves towards its committee stage.

Pains Hill has survived for 200 years. But without help it cannot survive much longer. I went round it myself and saw the overgrown walks, the broken bridges, the fragments of stone pillars in the lake, the jungle of overgrowth that blocks Hamilton's vistas. But the place is still a paradise: even more beautiful than in Hamilton's own time, now the trees have grown massive and established and the contours mellow. The largest cedar in the country rises above the jungle into the quiet sky; the sunlight still shines into the crystalline grotto; new saplings shade the follies now so much more ruined than Charles Hamilton intended. Round the lake sit members of the Walton angling club, which rents fishing rights from the major owner (of 107 acres) of Pains Hill. They shouted angry challenges: they don't want their haven disturbed. But Pains Hill was once the delight and refreshment of many. Should it not be so again?

Janet Watts

Everything in the Garden's Lovely
August 13 1974

One of the smallest bodies affiliated to the National Union of Students is getting slightly restive. It wants a hostel in which nine students (approximately 18 per cent of its membership) can sleep. The other day, a deputation waited on Mr Fred Peart, Minister of Agriculture, Fisheries, and Food, to put its point of view. Mr

Peart? Yes; this is his territory. Vice-chancellors, the Department of Education, the committee of polytechnic directors have no powers here. The students in the case are government employees, and they are studying horticulture at Kew's Royal Botanic Gardens.

Their campus is an extraordinary place. Even in the depths of winter there is something to see (try the witch-hazels, say helpful noticeboards); right now, things are at their dizzying peak. At the same time, however, it is a vast outdoor laboratory, a collection of problems and challenges, a workshop where one of the byproducts happens to be beauty. There is a curious sense of double vision; and it's all a long way from Oxford and Essex. Kew students, members of NUS though they are, do not have much truck with the twice-yearly junketings at Margate and elsewhere. 'We don't do much,' says this year's union president, Ken Pearson. True, a student has occasionally gone to NUS conferences in the past, 'but so often they're debating grants and things.' For the Kew student body, grants are irrelevant. The students are already wage-earners – to the tune of £23 gross a week. And this is not the only irrelevancy. In the case of the hostel, for instance, militant attitudes would be pointless. The Kew authorities want the hostel as much as its would-be inmates. Half the gardens' establishment, it seems, studied here themselves; and know all too well the difficulties of finding digs in pricey Kew and Richmond.

The three-year training scheme leading to the Kew diploma (itself roughly equivalent to a higher national diploma, this can beat a degree in some quarters) is as extraordinary as the place in which it is run. In some ways it is a handover from the days of Gertrude Jekyll, if not of Capability Brown. In others, it is positively Utopian: a blueprint for the way higher education could – indeed, should – be managed. The first impression is one of stringency. The average university student would blanch at the time-keeping demanded. Three months of each year of the course are given over to lectures on subjects which include genetics, entomology, horticultural chemistry and physics, land surveying, management, and climatology. The rest, excluding 15 days' paid holiday, is spent working in the gardens themselves. The working day starts at 7.50 am, and Heaven help you if you're late. The pay, the argument goes, is there to be earned. 'A certain amount of overtime is compulsory,' the prospectus adds. You get paid for this, too, but can reckon on saying goodbye to about one weekend in six. There is also the question of entry qualifications. These, basically, are four O-levels or a technical qualification, along with at least two years' practical experience of garden work in parks, nurseries, or 'approved, horticultural establishments.'

Mr LA Pemberton, Kew's supervisor of studies, admits that there is something old-fashioned about the 'previous experience' demand. But, he says, it gives potential students the chance to change their minds before they start in earnest. 'We want them to get their basic skills, and also to realise what the rough is as well as the smooth.' Even at Kew, the rough is there. Chores exist that the most dedicated student would recognise as such. Hedge-clipping – in all weathers, naturally – and washing out glasshouses are two unfavourite jobs. ('But,' a first-year student claims, 'I don't regret it. It will give you an insight into how the gardeners feel.')

Above all, there are the rules governing dismissal. These are tough. 'Failure to show satisfactory progress or service may lead to discharge,' is only a preliminary. Later comes rule 13: 'Students are expected to conduct themselves in accordance with the accepted standards of behaviour and good taste as required by the rules and regulations. They are expected to make a sincere effort toward a good relationship with their supervisors and fellow students. Student gardeners misconducting themselves or breaking any of the rules will be liable to instant dismissal. The director reserves the right to terminate the engagement of any student at any moment should circumstances arise which, in the director's opinion, render such a course desirable.' Try writing 'Ban edges' on the lawns with weed killer, and you'd be out; what's more, they'd replace the turf overnight. In spite of all this – and it could be argued that it's because of all this – student morale is high. The students form only one-seventh of the garden's total labour force, and they seem to accept the implications. 'It's very difficult to give the student privileges,' says second-year Jonathan Rickards, 'so possibly it's better to cut them out.'

The size of the student body is an advantage. All 50 or so know each other to some extent; under a system of vertical grouping, third-years help their juniors, and the learners are on first-name terms with their garden bosses. But more potent is the allure of Kew itself. For the majority of students, it is mecca. And there are the financial considerations. The Kew diploma, along with membership of the Kew Guild, is an international passport to jobs abroad that can bring £5,000 to a 25-year-old. Such is the attraction that applications for the Kew course come in from all over the world. Formerly a nursery-gardener in South Australia, Richard Jones saved up the air fare and endured a miserable first few months in English digs to be on the Kew roll. Underlying this sense of purpose is another, subtler, morale-booster: a sense of being accepted. Many Kew students are often the ones whom their schools, if not God, forgot. Their O-levels are strange and unhandy mixtures: geography and art; geography, maths, art and woodwork; English literature and language, geography (again), and biology. In addition schools do not seem to lean over backwards to encourage any career interest in gardening among their pupils. To get into Kew is to get a whole new dose of self-respect.

Kew, then, has all the classic elements that make for a contented student body: small numbers, vocationally oriented work, highly motivated company. But, as cream on the cake, it also has two extras that are probably unparalleled in higher education. The first is summed up by the second-year student Brian Gornall. 'The important thing about the course is that it's for real. If it were simply demonstration exercises it wouldn't matter if you made a mistake. But here …' If an item in the Kew collection dies under a student's care, it's dead and stays dead, regardless of excuses and recriminations. Conversley, the sense of achievement at keeping that item alive and well and living in outer London is tremendous.

The second extra concerns research. All students have to do a special project. Brian is working on the hosta family, whose nomenclature, as they say, is somewhat confused. Brian aims to clarify it. Richard's subject is a nightmare plant from his homeland, dubbed the kangaroo paw, and third-year Robert Ivison is into the genus hoya, also known as the wax flower. ('I was working with them and somebody suggested doing a thesis. There was no information I could find, and so I thought that this was a good start: I could try and put together something people could read'). And this is the point. Frequently the research of a 23-year-old Kew student will be both original and useful – directly, immediately useful. Frequently, too, it could involve on-the-spot resources that a postgraduate might envy. Claire McCormack, a first-year student, has just conceived her research subject. The rarest plant in Kew is a primitive tropical – sago palm, called Encephalartos woodii, which is extinct in the wild. There are only four specimens known in the world – and they are all male. With the aid of Kew's super-sophisticated propagation techniques, Claire hopes to find some way of bypassing the sex problem and reproducing E. woodii vegetatively.

If the plan comes off, what a breakthrough. Breakthrough for Kew, breakthrough for women in horticulture, and breakthrough for Claire herself, who failed biology A-level by four marks.

Anna Sproule

Follies Bizarre
November 16 1974

'O folly!' said John Keats in contempt, lamenting the weakness of men. But the men he apostrophised so sadly may have repeated his words in delight when they caught sight of some temple or tower or grotto at the end of a lyrical vista. The visible sort of folly has figured in men's lives and landscapes for centuries, and nowhere more than in England. No other country has so many of these false, fragile, useless monuments of stone, shell and rubble: beautiful, ugly, frightening or absurd jeux d'esprit popping up on the soft slope of a peaceful prospect to give its visitor a jump, a shudder or a laugh.

Barbara Jones, an artist who publishes a book called *Follies and Grottoes* on Monday, had had a soft spot for them since she first saw Ralph Allen's sham castle façade on its hillside at Bath as a child. 'So much more interesting than a real castle – thin and surprising instead of solid and predictable: and so fragile – tenuous and ephemeral, only just there. I loved walking through a front door into grass instead of into a hall with furniture: instead of being inside, being outside again.' She considers herself no exception in the supposedly sensible race that produced these surprising things. 'I don't think the English are so stolid; I think they're a highly eccentric and fantastic race with an enormous taste for the gaudy and the exotic. The Dutch dye their cheese red exclusively for the English market; the English love their fairgrounds and the chromium plate on their cars. There's an element of fantasy that always finds an outlet: now it's shifted itself to pubs – those modern ones with everything fake, sham beams in glass fibre, carpets running up the walls – total fantasy that never really dies.' Follies began to appear in Englishmen's estates some 400 years ago. 'Follies come from money and security and peace': when the Tudor wars were over everyone branched out from their castles and fortified dwellings and had a new architect-designed house. Follies were a bonus, a luxury, an outlet for their own individuality. 'With follies they could do anything: instead of the architect telling them what to do, they could go out and play God.'

It became eccentric not to have an eccentricity in one's grounds. Follies were of two sorts, the purely fashionable commissioned by people trying to keep up with their neighbours, and 'follies of a different and purer eccentricity,' says Barbara Jones, unable to tuck her favourites out of sight. The first 'absolutely dinging, nutty thing' was Sir Thomas Tresham's Triangular Lodge (1593), 'a lovely essay in stone arithmetic' by a man very hung up about threes. It has three equal sides, three floors each with three windows in each side, three sets of three-by-three triangles along the walls, and triangular pinnacles crowning the top triangles of each façade. There was the old rum sort of folly, which Barbara Jones ascribes to ancestor worship; many of these builders were nouveau riche, and a collapsing ivy-clad ruin in their grounds suggested they'd been around a long time. Then there were the follies that went underground: the grottoes and underground chambers for which they burrowed as well as built. Perhaps a link with latter-day garden gnomes: 'They're all underground things, aren't they? Gnomes traditionally mined the earth's gold and silver. Gnomes always have little spades – perhaps there's a magical thing too: if you leave them there overnight they might do the digging. I'm sure it all comes from a desire to make one's mark on nature. We all do it don't we? I mean, my garden's only 26 feet long, but I've made three little seats and an arbour, put in one or two interesting boulders – one does have a real urge to beat the grass and trees.

'More mood and emotion are built into follies than into any other kind of architecture,' she writes. The earliest one seems to have been gloom. Jonathan Tyers, who bought Vauxhall Gardens in 1733, was driven by its incessant merrymaking to buy Denbighs in Surrey and create there a wood (designated Il Penseroso) with a temple loaded with solemn inscriptions, a hidden clock striking every minute that 'forcibly proclaimed the rapid Might of Time', and a valley of the shadow of death with an iron gate flanked by coffins and the skulls of a harlot and highwayman. 'Melancholy was very modish then,' says Barbara Jones. Other follies were charged with grandiloquence, terror, surrealism, megalomania ('the great I Am syndrome', like McCaig's colosseum dominating Oban). 'Follies vary very much in atmosphere: some are frightening, some are light-hearted: it's only the nutty ones that are absolutely terrifying.' Effects of drama and horror can improve with age: when Barbara Jones visited the labyrinth at Hawkestone, a friend scrabbling up a wall disturbed a great company of bats which combined with the dirt and darkness (lacking candles held by footmen) to give them a pleasure unknown in the 18th century.

Follies always had an element of surprise, 'though it always seemed strange to me to spend thousands of pounds on a surprise that was only a surprise once. You had to keep going round with lots of new guests obviously.' Follies acquire their own legends: Barbara Jones would sit drawing a crumbling tower or mystifying obelisk and be approached by locals with fiercely contradictory stories all dating from several centuries before the monument was built. In the follies' own time, there was a vogue for explaining their purpose and design in allegorical terms, the course through a park being seen as a microcosm of a man's progress through life. But Barbara Jones scorns such verbal justification of art: 'I'm very suspicious of assigning motives to creating a beautiful garden. I think the landscape gardeners thought up all those words afterwards to sell the design to a client. I know it from my own work.' An artist begins with an idea for a visual effect and ends by realising it: the words are only a necessary intermediary to sell the idea.

Barbara Jones did a smaller study of follies 20 years ago when people tended to deny or deprecate their follies. 'They'd say: "Well, they did some funny things in those days, didn't they? Though I suppose it's not as bad as seducing the serving wench." It was all very ha-ha, and distinctly ashamed.' One old lady gave her quite a talking-to about how her family had never built follies, and the miniature sham castle in her garden was only a memorial, with a tablet to prove it. People also got touchy at the idea that their follies had a melancholy effect, melancholy having lost its appeal and become mixed up with mental illness, so the suggestion seemed a slur on their ancestors. But this time round Barbara Jones found that all was interest and pride in family follies. Only two people refused her permission to see and draw the sight (one of them the ex-Beatle George Harrison), and one man sent his manservant to crack a bottle of champagne on being told her mission. At last, it seems, people are beginning to love their follies again. Very wise of them.

Janet Watts

A Well-Laid Plot
October 11 1975

For anyone new to vegetable growing five minutes at a demonstration plot is probably more rewarding than a whole Sunday with gardening books. The ideal thing, of course, is to visit Wisley in Surrey, and come away with a copy of *The Vegetable Garden Displayed* for future guidance. But for those to whom Wisley seems almost as remote as the South Pole there is now a model vegetable plot in the Northern Horticultural Society's increasingly splendid Harlow Carr gardens at Harrogate. Following enthusiastic requests the plot was started a year ago by the ever-practical and televisual Geoffrey Smith. It is now rounding off its first year, and preparing for the next, under the care of the new superintendent, Mr JD Main. Like the plot at Wisley, this one is also of the standard allotment-garden size, 30ft by 90ft. It is on a south-facing slope, set in a carpet of bowling green turf, and sheltered by six foot beech hedges on two sides and Paraweb fences on the other two. This plastic screen fencing is made of strong, horizontal two inch strips, spaced two inches apart and fastened to strong six foot posts. It is said to have a permeability of 58 per cent, and to give protection to leeward of up to 60 feet. Against invasion by rabbits there is a low length of strong, small-meshed, wire-netting extending round the edge of the plot, while trees farther back take the brunt of Pennine blasts from the directions of Pateley Bridge, Blubberhouses, the Brontë country, and Ilkley Moor.

A visitor looking for guidance will get instant ideas on the laying-out and planting-up of a plot. Clear labelling will enable him to see which varieties are chosen and how they shape up to northern conditions. He will also see at once the value of windbreaks as well as a certain necessary openness. A notice board on the plot provides information about yields of crops as they are harvested and their value at current market prices. The runnings total will probably by now have reached, or even surpassed, £200. In spite of cold winds and a late start the eventual arcadian summer at Harlow Carr produced some excellent crops. Duke of York early potatoes, though caught by frost, recovered to yield fourteen-fold. Hurst's Green Shaft peas had 10 to a pod of excellent flavour. Golden Acre cabbages grew to a five or six pound bulk, and the Sturon onion sets turned into true giants of their race.

When I last visited the plot in early September it was still being kept trim and attractive, free of pestilence and disease, and without weeds; and there remained rows of healthy, well-grown vegetables for autumn and winter. April-sown Swiss chard was handsome, and thriving, May-sown calabrese sturdy and producing, and July-sown Webb's Wonderful lettuce, carrots, beet, and onions were coming on apace. A 41lb harvest of courgettes (true French) was recorded and 38 cobs of sweet corn (First of All). The one row of runner beans was partly Best of All and staked, the other part Kelvedon Marvel, and dwarfed by nipping out the shoots: 58lb 8oz had been gathered by the end of August, with both still producing – and equally well, it seemed. For winter crops in northern climes, expert advice had suggested Pentland Brig kale; Monument leeks for direct sowing and self-blanching, Musselburghs for transplanting; Celtic Cross, Hollander Langendyke (extra late) and Ormskirk Rearguard cabbages; and Citadel and Peer Gynt sprouts. These last were already wisely earthed-up for greater support.

This new Harlow Carr venture is the adopted child of the society's recently formed Edible Plant Group. The group has a fair-sized membership with a current programme of useful talks by experts. It looks forward to expansion. Apart from the vegetables, there is a herb bed already established with plants from the Castle Howard gardens; and it is intended to have a demonstration fruit area before long. One would like to make a plea for a tiny plot in which a few selected individual vegetables would be allowed to live out their life span – thus showing us what they would do if we didn't eat them. Such items on my own allotment escaping execution, give pleasure. I am thinking of the flower and seed heads of leeks, globe artichokes and scorzonera and the sunny inflorescence of some brassicas. Even the radish blossoms.

Less active though no less enthusiastic people might think a half-size plot a good idea, especially now that land is scarce and the demand for gardens great. It would certainly be to the advantage of many if the two parent plots of Wisley and Harlow Carr could give rise to a proliferation of model plots, initiated by local horticultural societies throughout the country. Some progressive leisure garden sites, I believe, already have them; and organic gardeners will be interested to know that Lawrence D Hills of the Henry Doubleday Research Association has something much more like an organic gardener's Wisley under consideration at their Bocking trial grounds in Essex. Meanwhile we must be glad of those rare model plots produced and maintained by born gardeners to give themselves pleasure and the rest of us the opportunity to admire and emulate.

Michael Hyde

Who's a Clever Pansy, Then?
March 5 1976

Ever since *A Melon for Ecstasy*, the novel by John Wells and John Fortune about a man in love with a tree, our passionate and British relationship with gardens and plantlife has deteriorated shockingly. Yesterday, at the Royal Garden Hotel, London, this new and dreadful intimacy with plantlife was further encouraged and celebrated by the *Green Fingers* nationwide plant talk competition. Plant talk, a natural form of intimacy practised by a growing number of permissive gardeners, consists of talking to plants regularly in an effort to make them grow. Results are said to be impressive, though experts have time and time again said that this practice will not have the desired effect. But *Green Fingers*, a magazine which offers a week-by-week gardening course, had actually persuaded a panel of gardening experts to judge the champion plant talker, from a group of seven regional finalists. The winner was 63-year-old Mrs Frances George from Stoke-on-Trent.

'I think of them as children,' she said. 'Yes, they are. They start as seeds on the ground and grow. You've got to have faith. God was the first gardener. My first baby was named after a flower. I talk to them all day long. My neighbours must think I've a man in the house. I say to the weeds, "Hey, what are you doing?" I tell them you have to be cruel to be kind. I give them a cup of tea to drink. No, I won't grumble at them – not when they're doing so well.'

Frances Perry, the gardening writer, said: 'Speaking does not help. But I think vibrations do, and warmth. If people are talking to their plants they're interested. They handle them and three out of a hundred people have a sweat in their hands which has growth-promoting hormones in it.'

Percy Not Sacked, Says BBC
March 25 1976

The BBC regretfully parted company yesterday with its most famous gardener, Mr Percy Thrower, who from next month will move over to continue the battle against slugs, thrips, and aphids in commercials on the other channel. 'Don't use the word sacked,' said a BBC television spokesman. 'This has been under discussion for some weeks and the BBC and Percy Thrower have simply agreed to part company.'

The parting came because Mr Thrower told the BBC he would be making a series of commercials for ICI gardening products, to be broadcast on most commercial television channels some time after Easter. Because of this his BBC *Gardeners' World* programme, recorded this week in the garden of his Shropshire home, The Magnolias, for transmission on March 31, will be the last after years of radio and television broadcasting with the BBC. Mr Thrower, who is 62, has been presenting *Gardeners' World* since 1969 and many of the programmes have been filmed in his own garden. He also runs a nursery in Shrewsbury and his gardening books have a total sale of over a million copies. He retired in 1974 as head of Shrewsbury parks department. A spokesman for ICI said his departure from *Gardeners' World* had nothing to do with the company. Mr Thrower had been associated with ICI for 17 years, he said, giving technical advice and opening stores.

The successor to Percy Thrower in *Gardeners' World* will be 40-year-old Mr Peter Seabrook, who at present fills the gardening spot, *Dig This*, in the BBC's lunchtime Pebble Mill programme.

The Centenary of RNRS
May 19 1976

Kristin Rosenberg, one of Britain's leading painters of wild flowers, has designed four stamps to be issued by the Post Office on June 30 to mark the centenary of the Royal National Rose Society. The stamps are Kristin Rosenberg's first venture into stamp design. She produced the original artwork in miniature, creating the design in the actual size of the stamps. The 8.5p stamp depicts the rose Elizabeth of Glamis, a pink floribunda named after the Queen Mother, who is patron of the society. The hybrid tea rose, Grandpa Dickson, is featured on the 10p stamp. The 11p stamp shows the shrub rose Rosa Mundi, and Sweet Briar, a rose introduced at the end of the last century but still popular today, is shown on the 13p stamp. Kristin Rosenberg started painting wild flowers nine years ago and has won 18 medals for her watercolours in the Royal Horticultural Society flower show exhibition.

Green And Pleasant Land
July 26 1976

Children have come, two have gone, one still lingers, and now, at last, I am privy to the pangs of nurturing maternity, the sort of hovering, muffler-wrapping, lint-pickingy mother lover I have seen in other women and never before felt myself. Only this new and quivering emotion has been aroused not by last-go broodiness, not by a glimpse of a neighbour's baby with its downy head wound in shawls, but by the dear green flora of my newly acquired garden. Oochy kootchie poo, I murmur tenderly, over my unfolding beans. Bless oos cotton socks, I coo to my embryo tomatoes. Who's a good wee garlic then, I whisper to four green shoots. Mamma's ickle treasure, I croon to the aubretia. It is, I know, a disgusting and probably senile dementia and I count myself lucky that no one has yet sent for the men in white. No longer is my top of the TV pops *The Disappearing World* or some riveting and important analysis of foreign affairs in *World in Action* or *Panorama*. The authoritative voices of David Dimbleby or Robin Day are nowhere compared to the total command of all my faculties exerted by Peter Seabrook of *Gardeners' World* and the *Man from Clack's Farm*. When I hear P Seabrook expatiating about the Worcestershire asparagus knife I drop my saucepans and rush for the television set. Indeed, if I am to judge by my own reactions, no other programme on the whole nationwide network gets as much devoted scrutiny as *Gardeners' World*. On no other programme have I ever been so aware and so critical of the camera work. Get the lens in there, I yell, as Mr Seabrook fumbles with some flora just below vision. For heaven's sake dolly in, I shout as the man from Clack's Farm does something vital to his marrows. The every move of my two heroes is a revelation to me and Clack's Farm itself has become my nirvana, the place where all good gardeners go when they pass on.

I have even lost all understanding of those who profess to be bored by gardening talk. Sweetly falls the sound of voices discussing compost, revered are those who can tell me what to do about slugs. I am overcome with gratitude to those who bring me cuttings and teach me the mysteries of root hormone powder. A short time ago John Osborne and his wife Jill Bennett arrived back from California and said they couldn't live there, it was too boring, everyone kept talking about their gardens. I had to be restrained from emigrating.

But there is a silver lining to everything, even incipient madness. For a start, my new obsession has distanced my last child from me, thus enabling him to accomplish in double quick time all sorts of otherwise drearily long-term psychic things like resolving the Oedipal complex and overcoming separation-anxiety, which is no end of a relief. Children have a vestigial tolerance for gardens in which they may rush about kicking balls, beating each other up or attempting to shoot beetles with air guns, but your actual working garden, flower-laden and veg-lined, is not their cup of tea, particularly if their distaff parent has gone ga-ga about it and keeps dragging them out in the early morning to admire their dinner on the stalk. We have had the garden only months now and already they are bored silly as I sit at meals, frothing at each dish and saying over and over, like some besotted lover, these are our own beans or throwing a small tantrum because they are so insensitive as to leave a wedge of our own tomato on the plate and don't want a third helping of our own parsley sprinkled over our own potatoes.

And I have acquired a deep empathy with farmers because, as I see it, farming is only gardening gone ape; at last I understand the farmer's heretofore bewildering grumpiness, his bucolic moodiness, his refusal to be pleased by any climatic change that lasts for longer than four days. Because gardening (and therefore the more so farming) is out of doors housekeeping, the life-long state of being a house-proud housewife without a house or, more, accurately, without a roof. There we are, polishing the fields, flicking our dusters round the leaves, scrubbing the fences and lathering the maize. But an indoors housewife at least has some hours of relaxation afterwards, when she may sit and admire her gleaming handiwork before the enemy – any other inhabitant of the house – comes trooping in to pollute her floors and smear jammy fingers over her walls. The farmer is more vulnerable. After a hard day's work he must leave his territory completely unprotected, open to the skies and the Enemy therefrom. He must lie twitching in his bed while gales uproot his fences, rain flattens his wheat, and a million parasites crawl, burrow, and fly towards his fields to munch upon his crops.

Worse. I have discovered that what of God's earth can be fenced about and called, by law, your possession, your territory, then becomes an extension of yourself, whether it be house or house and garden. And the penalty to be paid for this capitalist annexation, this theft from the people, is high. My garden is all of 20ft x 10 and I myself have now enlarged to these dimensions like Alice after eating the mushroom. When the sun beats down week after week upon my soil, I feel great fissures split my skin, I wither and turn sere as does my cherry tree. When rain comes at last, my pores drink in the precious liquid along with the beans, When the wind howls I sit inside and tremble as my sunflowers do each time a gust hits them. Any damage outside and I am damaged within. Last week, when some mysterious power ripped off a set of tomato flowers, I felt a distinct sag on one side of my body, a small emphatic stroke.

Nor are my garden's boundaries, my own fleshy borders, vertical alone. For me, my 10 x 20 plot extends horizontally upwards like a blue tube zooming into outer space. If that tube, elongated into light years, happens to hit a 10 x 20 plot upon the perimeter of Betelgeuse 11, then I have no doubts at all that the dry dust of all that enigmatic star plus all its mineral rights clear through to the core are mine, all mine. Any wasp, fly, aphid, rodent, frog, or bird that crosses my blue tube rather lower down is also mine. That gull, swaying up there on its wide Persil-white wings, is, you may think, a free agent but I know better. While it hangs above, but between, my garden walls, I am its overlord.

Mind you, I am constantly aware that the ownership of land confers certain responsibilities and, being the conscientious person I am, I take them much to heart as would any good feudal mistress. When my starling nested in my roof I was extremely careful not to disturb her by looming too near, in spite of the irritating fact that starlings occupying space beside the sea believe themselves to be seagulls and shriek all day long in hopeful imitation. God knows, I tried to re-educate it. As it perched upon my tiles I wandered up and down below, tweeting melodiously to give it a more suitable example of birdsong. Tweetie tweetie warble warble, I warbled and shriek mew shriek it went against all nature. The stupid creature was obviously congenitally thick but I am still persevering, as one must if one knows what is best for one's peasants. I mean one's starlings.

And then an ornithological tragedy was played out upon my grass. The foolish starling underestimated the size of its nest and its starling chick descended too early. For two days it blundered about in my garden, beating its puny wings and once even hopping upon my arm. Its mother sat on the wall and yelled, dropping wodges of speared worm from its beak in a maternal frenzy. I rushed about below with bowls of water and tried to stuff soggy bread into the chick's wet yellow mouth. Neither of us succeeded. She took off at last, shouting abuse at us over her starling shoulder and, the next day, the poor wee chick was curled up under my nasturtiums, its pink claws upwards, its little breastbone sharp and boney, starved. I took the event hard, it being my chick dead under my nasturtiums, and gave it a funeral far above its station. Noblesse oblige.

These few short months of gardening obsession have helped me mentally prepare several penetrating monographs on the Garden and its Relation to the Formation of Class Structures in Society. These searing analyses are the result of a careful inner tabulation of my responses vis-a-vis my soil. If you do not have a garden, your children must play outside upon the street and they take their chances there, ebbing and flowing, acting and reacting with the other children who come and go. They are, willy nilly, outside parental territory and they take on the values of the street, of their peers. A garden gives parental control. Supervision can be exerted. Other children, if they are to come and play in another's garden, must submit themselves to a filtering, an examination, a winnowing as they flow through the funnel of the garden gate. The owner's values can come into play, No, not Johnny, we catch a whiff of anarchy there. Not Fred, for his snotty nose. Yes, Francis, for his pleases and his thank yous. Yes, Dorothy, for her ingratiating smiles and neat pink bows and acceptable accent. Through the medium of the garden, class values may be reinforced, class aspirations made more real. These elect you may play with, these discarded you may not.

Also, having a garden cuts its owner off from the hurly burly of vulgar public space. In a wood, in a field, on a beach, haphazard interaction (as we sociologists say) is inevitable. With the advent of the garden, such haphazardness ceases. Privacy is available, the concept of the intruder, the poacher, the trespasser, is made manifest. Four walls mean I am inside and you can be kept outside. The division means alienation, alienation breeds suspicion, suspicion breeds hostility. Ownership accustoms you to chosen faces and stamps all other faces strange and probably threatening. I buy land, I erect fences to preserve my land, I make laws to keep you out and the law keeps you out long enough for both of us to forget our common humanity. If I don't meet you I don't know you, we will develop different values, different customs, we will become different and soon I shall send in the gunboats. I have a door and you are the wolf at it. A garden may be a lovesome thing God wot but it beats the hell out of brotherly love.

And yet, paradoxically, a garden is the best practical argument I know for communal living. My garden is pathetically small, yet it could keep us quite nicely supplied with summer vegetables if only they didn't all pop at the same time. One cauliflower per week is our requirement and what do we get? Fifteen cauliflowers all at the same time, a mini glut. On the other hand, the space we have for asparagus is useless – each spear comes up a week later than its neighbour and you can't relish one asparagus spear, however amazingly fresh. Wastage is inherent. For each seed I need, I must buy anything from 30 to what looks like a trillion and throw the rest away. And while I am out buying tomato plants my neighbour with a greenhouse is discarding six in 10. The potato peelings and other vegetable refuse of three people produces enough compost to bury a small garden and that while a neighbour with a larger garden must supplement her own with chemical manure. It is obvious that 10 lettuce plants all maturing at the same time carry within them the seeds of the downfall of the nuclear family, so clearly do they wish themselves upon an extended family. Five flourishing courgettes, 10 bean plants, 20 potato plants demand an end to monogamy. Six spinach plants urge promiscuity upon the human race. Runner beans in any quantity at all undermine the worthiest family planning programme and challenge the concept of private property.

So all human life is there, enclosed in a garden, and a deal of inhuman life, too. Last week a strange little creature invaded my honeysuckle. It had a long slender beak, a little mole-grey face, a blur of sandy wings; and what looked like a large bee's backside. It was all of four inches long, it hung absolutely still above the trumpet of the honysuckle and darted from flower to flower. To me, it exactly resembled a humming bird. The expert at the zoo said no, humming birds were unknown here, have their being only in the Americas. The insect expert said no, it couldn't be a hummingbird hawk moth because that insect had a flickering tongue, not a beak. I am on my way to the Natural History Museum now, to try and identify my peculiar garden visitor. Mine.

Jill Tweedie

Green Fingers
May 24 1977

If you're a gardener you might occasionally have wondered why your gentle petunias refuse to flower. The answer is simple – they have been living under the dominant shadow of the aggressive masculine begonias for far too long. That, at any rate, is the kind of explanation that we could expect from Germaine Greer if she wrote about gardening.

Germaine Greer write about gardening? Don't be silly; that's just not the sort of thing you'd expect from the author of *The Female Eunuch* and determined defender of women's rights. Apart from arguing that women have as much right to potter about in the garden as men, what possible interest could she have? Well now, Germaine Greer is in fact writing a column about gardening for *Private Eye*, under the confidential pseudonym of Rose Blight. She is reported to be very keen to do the articles, so we can brace ourselves for endless articles about flowers not being able to flower as long as they are in the clutches of weeds.

The Artistry of Calling a Spade a Spade
May 26 1979

One of the Earls of Pembroke was described by a contemporary in 1623 as 'a true Adamist, toiling and tilling in his garden.' By 1923, PG Wodehouse had built several stories around fervent Adamists, befuddled old earls in corduroy trousers who would have sprayed their own grandmothers to death if they found them clinging to the underside of a rose-leaf. Gardens change but gardeners do not. To call gardening a leisure activity is to forget five centuries of warfare; real gardeners are not enthusiasts, they are madmen. From Henry VIII at Hampton Court to the old codger in the local allotment who refuses to return your ball, they have struggled against impossible odds, trying to turn this damp, cold island into the Garden of Eden.

And so it is hardly surprising that The Garden, at the Victoria and Albert Museum, is not only a documentary exhibition tracing this conquest of nature but also a place at which gardeners can worship. The entrance to the exhibition is crowned by a monumental pediment made up of rakes, shears, hoes and a pair of old gardening boots, painted white to resemble marble; like gardeners, the tools of the trade have undergone few alterations through the centuries. The museum's floors have been strewn with rushes or have disappeared beneath a carpet of synthetic grass; its air of scholars and art has been replaced by the smell of flowers and the taped, twittering of larks; its heavy columns and lofty ceilings have been hidden behind green trellising in the summer-house style.

But in trying to bring the garden indoors the organisers have reversed the process which took place when an Englishman picked up his spade. The garden as an extension of the house is encountered everywhere, but begins in Tudor times when Henry turned the grounds of Whitehall into a series of rooms, enclosed by walls and fulfilling specific functions. His privy garden even had its own Persian carpet, a complicated arrangement of patterns and knots made up of coloured soils and flowering herbs. Scattered at strategic points along the borders are the king's beasts, paying him heraldic homage from atop their wooden columns. Henry in his role of ruler of both house and garden can be seen in the first painting you come to in the show. The unknown artist takes time off from his meticulous observation of the costumes worn by the king and his family to look out through the windows which flank the group, and to submit the gardens to the same treatment. It is lucky for gardeners like Henry that artists like Jan Syberechts or Stanley Spencer have been on hand to record this most ephemeral of art forms. Just as an angler has to make do with snapshots of his catches, so the English gardener has had to rely almost exclusively on others to record his achievements. But the paintings and drawings with which the exhibition is so well stocked only add to its air of sadness as they mourn the demise of so many glorious achievements. The garden as the perpetual victim of progress is seen most clearly in the series of aerial photographs which appear in the conservation section. Flying above some of the country's most famous stately homes, it is often possible to glimpse layer upon layer of garden reduced to hazy shadows in the grass or strange configurations of snow drifts.

And so throughout most of the exhibition you find yourself looking at skeletons, tiny scraps of visual and written information which the newly instigated school of garden historians have tried to mould into a story. Nothing but descriptions from travelling Germans remain of the 120-foot tall giant which Soloman de Caus built on an island in Richmond in 1609–1612; his mechanical birds and singing gods, his barnacle-encrusted grottoes which doubled as aviaries, have all been swept away by Capability Brown and his precursors in the move away from obvious artifice towards an equally artificial naturalness. Brown, because of his 'disinterest in horticulture,' is made to play a distinctly minor role in this exhibition. A landscapist rather than a gardener, he dealt with masses where most of the heroes discovered here were concerned with details. None more so than the 18th and 19th century plant-hunters, a band of fanatical explorers who scoured the Empire for exotic blooms which they then submitted to scientific examination and the rigours of the English climate. The belated appearance of flowers in the English garden is one of the exhibition's major surprises.

Exactly why it has taken gardening so long to be recognised as an art form is never really explained. It is easy to assume that everybody loves them and to forget that the garden was as much a barometer of taste as painting or architecture, and that it could be put to just as many subtle uses. Under Elizabeth I it was an instrument of flattery and every leaf of sweet-smelling herb or carefully shaped shrub was involved in a complicated allusion to her greatness. The enclosed garden, a Christian symbol for the immaculate conception, was remodelled to accommodate the Virgin Queen. As medieval magic gave way to the era of the Royal Society, gardens were planted in which the vegetation was made to repeat the orbits of the pre-Copernican universe with the mound of earth at its centre. The late 17th century melancholic could not sigh convincingly if surrounded by rigid parterres and neat paths, so he commisssioned his gardener to create dark forest glades and rushing streams. The Victorian male, riding on a crest of prosperity, treated the garden as he treated everything from his artist to his wife: put it into a straitjacket and then on display. By the time you get to the V & A's 19th century refreshment rooms, stuffed with ferns in glass cases, the garden has been stripped of all its former innocence.

Waldemar Januszczak

Chelsea Rules: 1980–1989

Chelsea Physic Garden opens to the public, 1983 * Geoff Hamilton's Barnsdale Gardens TV success * Hurricane, October 1987 * National Centre for Organic Gardening opened, 1986 * Percy Thrower dies, 1988

The Female Garden
May 26 1982

Do women make better or worse gardeners than men or is there a difference? In any garden history the names of male botanists, gardeners and designers over the centuries far outnumber the female. But it is also true that in this century many of the most influential gardeners – most of them self-taught amateurs – have been women. 'Above all, Phyllis gardened like a man,' said Marjory Fish of her neighbour and friend Phyllis Reiss, who had over 30 years from 1933 created the enchanted garden of Tintinhull in Somerset. Mrs Fish did not mean this as either a compliment or a criticism; more a description of a method and overall approach which to her was foreign. Phyllis 'was quite ruthless about plants, throwing out anything that did not conform to her ideas. She never allowed sentimental feelings for individual plants to interfere with the overall scheme.'

Meanwhile, almost down the road, Marjory Fish was perfecting over a similar span of time a cottagey garden at East Lambrook Manor which I, for one, have only to look at to know it is the work of a woman. The scale is human and intimate. The garden is very much an extension of the house. Although there is a structure – paths laid down by Mr Fish – the feel is of a riotous but soft mixture of textures and smells. Many herbs grow alongside old cottage garden plants. Marjory Fish became famous for reviving numerous old English garden plants which she made popular in her writings for magazines and in books.

The work of both these women and a host of others is described in *Down-to-Earth Women*, by Dawn MacLeod. It is the story of women gardeners in this country, and it set me wondering: is there justification for such a theme? The three modern gardens I love most – that of Rosemary Verey near Cirencester, of Eve Molesworth at Iver, and Joyce Robinson at Arundel – are all creations of women who are gifted and knowledgeable amateurs. It is not just that I enjoy them visually. It is the surprise element, the eccentricity and daring, you might say – odd plants and colours juxtaposed and intertwined regardless of rules – that makes them thrilling. They are also happy gardens with nothing rigid about them.

Women became serious gardeners comparatively recently. But back in 1840 Jane Loudon in her charming *Gardening for Ladies* suggested we should venture out. 'Whatever doubts may be entertained as to the practicability of a lady attending to the culture of culinary vegetables and fruit trees,' she writes, 'none can exist respecting her management of the flower garden. This is pre-eminently a woman's department.' So the tradition of the veg being 'his' and the flowers 'hers' began early. Unlike her contemporary, Louisa Johnson, author of *Every Lady Her Own Flower Gardener*, Jane Loudon did not suggest gardening should be taken up by single women 'as a distraction from the disappointments of life.' Mrs Loudon was more positive and highly influential.

Many prominent women gardeners have also been painters or much involved with applied arts. Gertrude Jekyll is the classic example. Born in 1843, she attended the Kensington College of Art – now the Royal College. Marvellous examples of her handiwork, particularly needlework, still exist, and it was only when she was 50 and her doctors insisted that such work could ruin her eyes that she turned more exclusively to gardening from her home at Munstead Wood in Surrey. Thus began a stream of wonderful books and her famous partnership with architect Edwin Lutyens which created so many enchanted gardens. Penelope Hobhouse, an authority on Gertrude Jekyll, feels that she needed Lutyens as much as he needed her. For only an architect (and only a man?) could make that bold framework – the incredible stone-work, the pergolas, vistas, inverted steps etc – and only she could soften it with the brilliant use of billowing plants and shrubs. In so many cases, Vita Sackville-West and Harold Nicholson being the most familiar example, gardens are created by partnerships: the man rigorously lays out the structure – the broad sweeps, the vistas, the geometry – while the woman has complemented this, softening those lines with plants. Vita wanted and achieved 'the strictest formality of design with the maximum informality of planting.'

'I'm sure,' says Penelope Hobhouse, 'that men feel much more strongly about straight lines. With women it's much more like embroidery – interweaving colours and textures.' Eve Molesworth agrees. She thinks women generally make better gardeners than men, 'because the men are too precise. Women prefer to interpret nature and go along with the rhythm of a garden which is so wonderful.' The one male gardener they all agree is an exception to this rule is Christopher Lloyd and he, interestingly enough, is also a considerable embroiderer. To Miss Jekyll we also owe the idea of the lady of the house arranging the flowers, previously work for the under gardener. She felt – and I agree – that flower arranging was 'a branch of gardening.'

In *The Obstacle Race* Germaine Greer suggests that one of the reasons that women have historically been less successful painters than men is that painting required systematic training (thought unsuitable for women). It also was immensely competitive and required considerable patronage. The same could be said for music. Gardening, however, like novel writing – both arts which women do well – is essentially a domestic, uncompetitive and solitary art which can be pursued at home. It also requires great patience and of that most women agree we have much more. It is notable how many women, like Rosemary Verey, turn to gardening once their children have grown. For a garden is always a fragile achievement, easily destroyed. Penelope Hobhouse points out that historically much of the differences in approach between men and women can be explained because women were rarely trained and so approached gardening from an instinctive interest in flowers rather than as trained designers.

Horticultural training for women started slowly. Kew's first lady gardeners caused a stir in 1895. Swanley college was opened to women in 1902. In 1932 Beatrix Havergal founded the Waterperry horticultural school for women which spawned such famous pupils as Sylvia Crowe and Brenda Colvin and the two excellent ladies Sybille Kreutzberger and Pam Schwedt who now tend Sissinghurst. Today women are trained in garden design and horticulture alongside men on equal footing. So perhaps in the next generation we may detect no difference. But I wonder.

Felicity Bryan

Come Into the Secret Garden ...
February 19 1983

Lotus bertolotii is extinct. Everywhere, that is, except in four acres near World's End. This floral dodo is but one odd inmate of London's best-kept botanic secret – the Chelsea Physic Garden, which will be revealed to the public on April 20 after 300 years of privacy. Until now this secret garden, a high-walled paradise, founded in 1673 by the Worshipful Society of Apothecaries, has been a living laboratory for bona fide students of botany, medicine, homeopathy, herbalism and scientific research. Custodians, including the trustees of the past 84 years, the City Parochial Foundation, have always closely guarded the garden's academic status. Only last year official word was: 'The garden cannot be opened to the public without restriction since the resulting pressures on a research and educational establishment would make its work impossible.'

In 1982 there were eight public open days, and written permission had to be obtained to attend. This rule is being swept away by the eleven new trustees, all horticultural celebrities under the chairmanship of arboretum expert Dr David Jamison. At the moment students from Chelsea College are researching the plant feverfew as a potential cure for migraine; the biochemistry department of Imperial college are working on ergot alkaloids; and the British Museum natural history department is studying the cytology of ferns and pelargoniums. The students will still have this lovely place, a walnut's throw from Chelsea Reach, to themselves for most of the week.

But in a wider educational context, on Wednesdays and Sundays from 2-5pm, there is to be an entrance fee of £1; children – must be accompanied – (50p). The garden curator, P R Briant, speaks wistfully of a small postcard shop, a lecture theatre, covenanted friends of the garden even. Portakabin toilets might be subtly introduced with the aid of creeper camouflage, he suggests. Here is the second oldest botanic garden in England (the elder by 50 years is in Oxford). A century ahead of the Royal Botanic Gardens at Kew, and much more accessible, the four most intensively cultivated acres in London sit snug in their triangular boundary. The 5,000 plant species, the weird, the wonderful, and the homely, are arranged in formal geometric designs.

Not just medicinal plants either, as the word 'physic' would suggest, for back in 1673 the Paracelsian idea that every plant was a potential remedy for human ailments resulted in more than 100 plant families (many from the new worlds) fanning out around the garden like an evolutionary family tree. At the green vortex stands Michael Rysbrack's statue (1732) of Sir Hans Sloane. Garden moulds seem to be devouring him utterly: an appropriate licheness of the man, who, having in 1712 bought the manor of Chelsea from Charles Cheyne, became owner of the garden freehold, and thus its saviour, the Worshipful Apothecaries being hard up at the time.

Heptopyrum rumariodies (Siberia) may not need this sheltered micro-climate; but some queer green-petalled flowers and purple blotches of crocii have shot up through the basaltic lava brought back by Joseph Banks from Iceland in the 18th century. It is winter; but a mad swath of honey-suckle is in bloom, and an orgy of small birds is mating on the Rackhamesque boughs of a tree with crown gall – or is it neurofibromatosis? The biggest olive tree in Britain is here. It is 30ft tall and daft as a brush – its fruit ripens in December. In April there will be a chance to see the flowering of New Zealand's national flower the kowhai, reputedly the offspring of seeds brought back by Banks from Captain Cook's first *Endeavour* voyage. There was cannabis too, until last year, when enterprising amateur botanists climbed the wall in the dead of night and whipped it away for potting. It is precisely this spirit of horticultural privateering that Briant fears when the garden's little black door admits the public hordes. He hopes to forestall secateur troubles with a cutting booth.

Beverly Pagram

No Fairies at the Bottom of the Organic Gardens
March 3 1984

Professor Alan Gemmell last Saturday defended the use of artificial fertilisers and garden chemicals – with due regard for all proper safety precautions. As he had anticipated, not everyone would agree.

Alan Gemmell misunderstands organic gardening. I don't know any organic gardeners who believe in fairies. We do believe that if we put poisonous chemicals in the soil in which we grow food, or on the plants themselves, they may well be taken up by the plants and finish up, with deleterious effects, in anybody who then consumes them. Is he sure this cannot be proved? And how can acting on our beliefs hold up 'probable progress'? Is progress only possible by using chemicals? Since we don't go in for monoculture, but rather for variety, we are not flying in the face of nature, and do not get things massively wiped out by pests or diseases attacking isolated crops. My cabbages are, indeed, planted in rows, but with lots of other things, vegetables, flowers, herbs, even some weeds, growing between the rows and all around them.

We note, as Alan Gemmell does, an absence of worms in soils deficient in humus or poisoned, and we see that the presence of worms indicates unpoisoned soils rich in humus. We know plants can be grown, without earthworms, in hydroponic solutions, as I grow my indoor hyacinths, but, if growing vegetables in this way (does anyone want to?), we should be careful about the composition of the solutions. We've all heard of poisoned watercress.

Was not the Irish potato famine disease due rather to monoculture and lack of rotation of crops than to lack of the services of the agrichemical firms? Poisons used on pests also kill or drive away the creatures which are predators on those pests, such as anthacoris on aphis and the small parasitic flies that attack carrot fly. I know that large scale organic growers have certain difficulties. Might these not be overcome if influential people like Alan Gemmell encouraged research in this kind of growing? With variety in planting, plenty of compost, plenty of flowers to attract pollinators, rotation of crops, well-rotted animal manure if available, small scale gardeners should have no significant difficulties.

No romanticism! From both a practical and a hedonist point of view, I find my organic gardening pays. I enjoy, at minimum cost, a varied assortment of excellent fruit and vegetables, and flowers, too.

Pests and diseases? Few and usually dealt with, often only with soapy water and extra compost.

MF Drinkwater,
Bird in Hand, Whiteshill
Strand, Gloucestershire

Ha-Ha: Neither Funny Nor Peculiar
July 9 1983

To be a successful landscape designer you have to be something of a seer, a visionary, capable of imagining how trees, shrubs, and indeed all the components of horticulture will have matured in 50 or even 100 years' time. Capability Brown had that gift and now, 200 years after his death, his landscapes seem so inevitable as to appear untrammelled by human artifice; which is how he would have wished it.

He started with an advantage, of course, in that Kirkharle, the Northumberland village 25 miles north of Newcastle in which he was born, is surrounded by the kind of countryside – Capability Brown landscape in embryo – which was later to emerge as his own invention. His first job, in fact, was as a gardener on Sir William Loraine's Kirkharle estate, where he helped convert the landscape into 'a woody theatre of stateliest view.' Within 10 years though, the 16-year-old Lancelot Brown of Kirkharle was well on the way to becoming 'The famous Mr Brown', nicknamed Capability. The derivation of the nickname is familiar enough; it came from his habit of assessing a landscape in terms of its potential or capability. But it is apt in another sense in that this early meritocrat who taught himself architecture and who eventually became master gardener to George III, was nothing if not capable.

To advance in his profession he had to move south, and in 1741 he was appointed gardener to Viscount Cobham at Stowe in Buckinghamshire. He was 24 and responsible for a team of 40 men.

His success at Stowe made his reputation and enabled his projects of the next 20 years – Syon, Chatsworth, Burghley, and Longleat, for example – a rollcall of some of the finest achievements of English landscape design. He claimed, fairly enough, to create landscape 'with a poet's feeling and a painter's eye,' and in a way his conception was founded upon painting. Brown's patrons were aristocrats, men who had made the Grand Tour of Italy and Greece as part of their classical education. Their taste in painting and landscape was formed by the work of Claude and Poussin, French artists who had transformed the Italian campagna into a sunlit arcadia, a 'woody theatre' punctuated with lakes, temples and grottos. Turner's great painting of Petworth Park, which Brown had designed in 1751, illustrates the conception perfectly; one of rolling unbroken parkland, a natural paradise fit for gods and goddesses and, of course, the English aristocracy.

To achieve this Brown had ruthlessly to erase the inherited tradition of the formal garden with its rows of shrubs and plants arranged in geometric, military order. And he was ruthless. Not only did he tear out the formal geometries and replace them with the flowing contours of nature but at Alnwick, for example, he changed the course of the river Aln, and at Blenheim converted a stream into an imposing lake. Water, clumps of trees, and unbroken sweeps of grassland are in fact the characteristic ingredients of Brown's designs. He called himself a place-marker and one of the inventions crucial to his designs was the ha-ha, the ditch which prevented cattle escaping while leaving the landscape uninterrupted by walls or fences. This sense of practicality, which included his care to conceal the unsightly, was, like his expertise as a horticulturalist, one of his strengths. His achievement consisted of far more than the implementation of a new, picturesque aesthetic; it owed much to his sturdy pragmatism.

The Newcastle exhibition which commemorates the bicentenary of his death focuses upon his lesser known northern compositions for Temple Newsam and Alnwick, for instance – and is laid out in the form of linked gazebos. Wandering through them, we can examine his drawings and maps and see the realisation of his plans in the paintings of Zoffany and Richard Wilson. This, however, is not quite the same as wandering through one of his landscapes, and a slide show or a video giving us some feeling of being within one of his idylls might have helped.

Still, for most of us the great estates which bear his invisible presence are within easy reach and they contain his true memorial. He looks out at us from the Nathaniel Dance portrait, quizzical, shrewd, and forthright, a canny Northumbrian if ever there was one.

William Varley

Call of the Wild
March 16 1985

There is a wide-awakening enthusiasm for growing wild flowers in our gardens. Partly this is a sentimental harking back to a lost state of innocence (although that state, in its way, was one of hardship not at all relished by its involuntary participants); partly a gut reaction to the all too evident loss of flora and fauna in a countryside where farming is being streamlined to monocultures, and herbicides are all too efficient in eliminating the flowers that we, not financially involved, consider to be our birthright.

Hence the drive to grow native plants, each of us in our own garden, no matter the size. I (and my mother before me) have been doing this for many years in the form of meadow gardening, though I must say at once that I do not see the point of deliberately restricting ourselves to native wild flowers. Because, for geological reasons, this country is out on a limb of Europe and lost a large part of its flora in the last ice age, never to regain it, our tally of wild flowers is small compared with other European countries.

As well as our own wild daffodil or Lent lily, Narcissus pseudonarcissus, of which both seed and bulbs can be purchased from one of the most comprehensive distributors in this line, John

Chambers, I should not hesitate to try also to establish the hoop petticoat daffodil, N. bulbocodium, and the cyclamen-shaped N. cyclamineus, which can be seen at Wisley in their alpine meadow and in the Savill Gardens of Windsor Great Park. Another bulb that makes itself most agreeably at home in my meadow is the quamash, Camassia esculenta, which resembles a bluebell except that its flowers open out into stars. The fact that it is a North American native seems no reason to me for not including it. In gardens, as opposed to the countryside, purism has no place.

So all the wild flower seed mixtures that you can buy have this inbuilt limitation. Another possible snag to those who have not already made a study of the subject is that some of the seeds offered (though usually in separate packets rather than in mixtures) can become quite fiendish weeds even by a weed lover's standards. There is no warning from Mr Chambers – who, to be fair, has not the space for descriptions and dissertations in his highly compressed catalogue – about which seeds will be suitable only in very specialised circumstances and should otherwise be avoided. Ground elder, the despair of many a gardener, is dreadfully invasive. Common sorrel is innocent enough; you can make soup from its leaves and the flowers and ripening seeds impart a beautiful red haze in a meadow. But sheep's sorrel, equally pretty at a lower level, is the devil of a spreader on acid soils, with a running rootstock. Agrimony, with its slender spikes of yellow stars, is comparatively innocuous but I should never recommend it to anyone owning a long haired cat or dog. Its burrs are a penance to extract.

One of the easiest and most successful ways of starting an area of meadow is by ceasing to mow your lawn. It will still need cutting, but only twice a year: the first time in late July or August (you can hire a power scythe to cope with this one), when all the flowers have had the chance to run to seed; the second in October-November, to keep the sward from developing tussocks of coarse grass. Lawns have the great advantage that they encourage fine grasses like fescues and bents but discourage the coarse ones like cocksfoot. So that when you allow your lawn to run up, it will already have the basic composition that you desire.

If, as I often hear from correspondents to be their case, you have an area of very rough grass containing predominantly docks, nettles, and cow parsley, the chances are that the ground is excessively rich. Never add any sort of fertiliser to a meadow; starvation conditions (and an open, sunny, site), encourage the widest assortment of wild flowers, so that on the two or three annual occasions that you do cut the grass, this should be carried and composted. One way to bring order to an area of very rough grass would be to treat it like a lawn with frequent mowing for the first couple of years. By the time you changed over to a meadow treatment, the coarse elements, which cannot stand tight mowing, would have gone. In other cases it may be preferable to start with a clean sheet by applying a total weedkiller based on glyphosate. Tumbleweed is the best known product, or Roundup, which is the equivalent available to farmers and horticulturists. Then you can sow with a suitable mixture of wild flowers and fine grasses. Spring is a good time to do this. Coarse weeds and grasses will try to muscle in, in the first year. The best way will be to pull them out by hand (yes, there is work involved). Your first cut, in late summer, will dispose of later infiltrations of the fat hen and groundsel persuasion.

Planting wild flowers into your meadow will be the most successful way of establishing many of those you want, and most can be raised from seed. Either sow them in pots or boxes and line out the seedlings subsequently to be grown on; then plant into your turf in the autumn. Or you can drill your seeds in a row at the outset, as you would carrots or parsley. But where the precious seeds of such as cowslips or snakeshead fritillaries or snowdrops were in question, the first method would be the least wasteful. A plot of wild flowers without the grasses is another sort of proposition and exceedingly colourful where poppies, cornflowers, corn marigolds, and suchlike are included. But these are weeds of cultivated land. After they have scattered their seeds you will need to disturb the ground so as to prevent perennials from taking over and to make a seed bed for the next generation of annuals. Mixtures that include, as some of John Chambers's do, shrubs like gorse, broom, and heather, offer yet another possibility. In the first years there'll be colour from annuals and biennials, but you'll not want to disturb the ground and subsequently the shrubs will take over.

Most seed houses offer wild flower mixtures these days. If they include elements you do not fancy (black medick would be one of mine – it drags all the other vegetation down into a tangled mass), either consult the seedsman or make up your own mixture from separate packets.

Christopher Lloyd

A Chemical-Free Zone Starts Here
July 26 1986

Thirteen years ago Alan and Jackie answered an advertisement for a young couple to work at an organic research station with full board and no pay. 'No one applied except us, so we got the job,' says Alan. They managed to negotiate a salary of £5 a week each, suffering a combined drop in income from £5,000 to £500 a year. This excessively modest project grew into the Henry Doubleday Research Association of which Alan is now executive director and Jackie assistant manager, and which has just opened the country's first national centre for organic gardening at Ryton, near Coventry. It has 22 acres of vegetable, herb, rose, and bee gardens, a research area, wild flower meadow, a cafe with organically grown food, including wine from France, a shop selling organic garden products, and a library of vegetable seeds outlawed by government legislation and supplied free to association members. It's a place where people can go all the year round and see how organic gardening – using no artificial fertilisers or chemical sprays – actually works.

The Henry Doubleday Research Association was created by Lawrence Hills to investigate ways of improving organic agriculture and horticulture at a time when he and the few others like him were regarded somewhat as cranks. 'Now,' says Jackie, 'the interest is phenomenal.' Today the association has 8,000 members. It was this interest that inspired the move from a 1.5 acre site in Essex to larger and more accessible grounds in the Midlands. 'Setting up the new centre has cost us a third of a million pounds and used all the association's reserves,' says Alan, 'but we felt it was time to reach out to a much larger public and the only way to do so was to have premises this size.' The money was raised by membership fees and donations. Jasper Carrot gave the £4,000 proceeds from one of his concerts, and David Bellamy is launching a £150,000 appeal. In the past year they've planted 5,000 trees and shrubs, converted an old farm house into offices and built the coffee shop and a bungalow for Lawrence Hills, now president, and very much a father figure of the HDRA. There's a full-time staff of eight, with 20 part-time workers and 15 on the MSC scheme.

'But you can't create an organic garden overnight,' says Jackie. 'The trees and shrubs are all very young and we don't want visitors to feel disappointed when they come this year. We hope they'll get the flavour of the place and come back again next year.'

There's already a lot to see: luxuriantly healthy vegetables; 100 different varieties of herbs; demonstration 'no dig' and raised bed gardens; an area of unusual vegetables; another showing how to deal with pests, diseases, and weeds without resorting to chemical sprays. The bee garden is planted with sweet clover, oriental poppies, and blue borage; and there are green manure and compost displays. Members all over the country are encouraged to take part in seed growing tests (they're sent the seeds and all the necessary equipment).

Research plays an important part and they're initiating work at several universities and polytechnics. 'We're making contact with like minded individuals in institutions who can supply the resources while we supply the land,' says Alan. To find out whether vegetables grown in central London are affected by pollution, for example, they chose 10 London members, got in touch with Imperial College scientists who visited the gardens and did the analysis. At Coventry Polytechnic, a research entymologist is trying to come up with organic methods of slug control, using slugs found at the centre (he collects them each morning from under a bit of old carpet), and growing plants which he hopes will have slugicidal properties.

'You don't get a lot of problems if organic methods of gardening are used,' says Pauline Pears, the centre's co-ordinator. 'But you do have to change people's ways of looking at things and persuade them that daisies in the grass and the hole in the cabbage leaf don't matter. If you killed every pest in existence it wouldn't help because you'd kill the beneficial ones too. What we're trying to do here is show how you can get the balance weighted in our direction so you end up with something to eat.'

At the moment, says Alan, nature is beating the farmer at his own game. 'In the 1930s there were seven or eight insects worldwide that were resistant to sprays. Now there are nearly 500, so you can see who's winning. British agriculture is in a mess and tax-payers' money is being poured into supporting a system in which massive chemical inputs are producing surpluses of food we can't use. It can't go on much longer, and all it needs is for the organic movement to present a viable alternative and to be heard above the siren voices of the petrochemical companies who have snapped up so many of the seed companies and can now breed varieties that will only do well if given large doses of their own artificial fertilisers. But if food can be grown successfully without chemicals, why take the risk?'

The Henry Doubleday Research Association actually began some 30 years ago when Lawrence Hills became fascinated by the plant comfrey. He discovered it had been brought to this country by Henry Doubleday, a 19th-century Quaker who was looking for ways to produce natural gum for putting on the back of the recently introduced 1d postage stamp and had written to St Petersburg botanical gardens for suggestions. Back had come a supply of comfrey which turned out to be no good for stamps, but gave a colossal yield (about 100 tons an acre) for animal and human food. Lawrence Hills began to grow the plant experimentally in 1954, and in response to hundreds of letters (he was gardening correspondent of the Observer at the time), started his own newsletter and, four years later, the association which he named in honour of Doubleday.

Angela Wigglesworth

A Growing Concern
September 3 1986

For more than a century, those uniquely British institutions – the Settlements – have pioneered new ways of living in the city. It is no surprise to find them getting greener, for they are used to innovation, to making new links between the environment and social need. Birmingham's settlement is celebrating the first year of its urban ecology centre: the beginnings of a practical demonstration of what green can mean for the inner city – not just trees and wild flowers and rooftop gardens but a transformation of the meanest wasteland to produce more of what is needed – food.

The potential, thinks Gerald Dawe, director of the centre, is surprising: perhaps £3,000 worth of vegetables from a half-acre site. The city's climate favours growth, and techniques of land reclamation are well developed. Pollution can be a problem: one study, in Walsall, showed some vegetable-growing families exceeded the World Health Organisation limit on intake of Cadmium – a metal as toxic as lead. But soils can be tested (the Urban Ecology Centre plans soon to offer this service), and the dangers are reduced by soil replacement, by choosing vegetables with care and washing them well.

Talk alone though, says Dawe, will not convince people of what is possible; they have to do it for themselves. And tucked away, behind a row of Victorian houses is Sparkbrook – not two miles from the

Bull Ring – is an unexpected experiment that does just that. Ashram Acres began five years ago when a few neglected back gardens were reclaimed to grow vegetables for a multi-racial community hard hit by the recession. Two thirds of its workforce are jobless. Bad housing and poor services compound the poverty. But when the Ashram community service project began to work out with local people what was needed most, it looked not just at the problems, but to the hidden resources of a seemingly hopeless neighbourhood.

'We worked on the assets; land and people,' says Gill Cressey, one of the project's pioneers. 'Most of the jobless here are registered as unskilled yet from their farming backgrounds in Pakistan, Ireland or the West Indies, they come equipped from childhood with countless skills that go unrecognised in British job centres. And the neighbourhood abounds in vacant sites – large and under-used back gardens, the wasteland of demolished property. Ten gardens now make up Ashram Acres: most growing a rich variety of vegetables, the rest grazed by goats for milk and cheese. Asian vegetables – okra, mooli, karella and others – are a speciality and all are organically grown. Experiments that work here – companion planting, home-made frames from window panes, or tubs from tyres – are soon adopted on other gardens in the neighbourhood. For this is a working model of resourcefulness, showing what is possible on city land, seeding new initiatives.

But Ashram Acres offers much more than ecological success: it is a model for community living. Grants have been neither sought nor given. Its workers are volunteers, with a core membership of 15 who pay £2.70 a week and labour in the gardens for all the vegetables they need. Other families in the neighbourhood come to grow and buy and share the frequent celebrations. For Mukhta Khan, with ill health and six young children, gardening is therapeutic as well as economic: 'It feels good to be here, there is a job for everyone.' His children come with others after school to work and play with the goats and rabbits. Women prepare and preserve the produce, and even those who keep strict purdah can tend a goat in their own back yards.

So much of what is 'green' is cosy, idealistic and exclusive. Ashram Acres is none of these. But it is hard work. 'The gardens set their own demanding agenda,' says Ute Jaekel, another pioneer, 'even watering is an almost impossible task some days.' But the work has meaning for local people: food is a major item of their budget; fresh vegetables are a vital source of vitamins and minerals in generally impoverished diets. For Birmingham City Council, the experiment is persuasive: a local response to local needs. This month sees the start of a new venture in neighbouring Small Heath, which will train 80 of the district's long-term unemployed to grow and market Asian and Caribbean vegetables on five of the city's many wasted acres. The project aims to work with local 'caring' institutions – hospitals, schools and children's centres – offering, in the first year, not only free vegetables, but training in how to cook them properly.

The City Council is investing £87,000 in the scheme: 'The scope is there for creating new markets and new business to fill them in horticulture, management and catering,' says Jim Cocker of the economic development unit. 'If we can show the way, perhaps commercial farmers will see the opportunities.'

Joan Davidson

Gardeners Scale the Heights in Prison
September 5 1986

Gardening inside prison walls has its special problems, but they can be overcome, as prison officer Paul Bamber has discovered at the award-winning Preston prison. What was once a dusty cinder exercise yard has for the second time in three years won the Windlesham trophy, which Preston received again yesterday, for the best prison garden in the country. Mr Bamber, who directs a team of 10 prisoners, spoke about his difficulties. 'We have a shade problem – high walls mean long shadows and damp areas,' he said. 'And we have to work within prison security: we can't put large trees or creepers near the walls.' Members of Mr Bamber's team come and go – one was discharged on Tuesday, another leaves today. He said: 'None of them is a professional gardener. But they all do a wonderful job.'

Awards also went to the regional winners: Lincoln Prison, Kingston Prison in Portsmouth, and Leyhill Prison in Bristol. The gardens were judged by the Royal Horticultural Society.

Tom Sharratt

Cottesbrooke
October 16 1987

There was a team in muddy wellies scrubbing the carrots and another in starched linen trimming and dicing them before, briefly steamed, they were brought to table. But such perfect symmetry of cultivation and consumption is no more. Cottesbrooke was a miraculous anachronism, preserved for us now in a remarkable book by Susan Campbell, *Cottesbrooke: an English Kitchen Garden*, which gives us a picture of how food was grown for the hall or squire's estate. That such a kitchen garden remained intact in full working order up to earlier this year is astonishing and the detailed picture of its working life throughout the year reverberates with historical echoes from the ancient Greeks to John Evelyn, interspersed with tips for jobbing gardeners and accounts of the produce at its mouth watering prime.

Blenheim, Welbeck, Holkham, all our great walled kitchen gardens have disappeared. Some of the largest have been turned into garden centres, others make Christmas tree nurseries, their huge brick walls protecting the young plants. Susan Campbell first heard of Cottesbrooke, in the East Midlands, from a local museum which informed her that grape bottles were still in use there. The grape bottle with its echoes of distant vintage led her to this thriving and compact horticultural complex of more than two acres, which included two walled gardens, an orchard, frames, hothouses, stores for fruit and roots, with Doug, the head gardener, and his staff of six all looking after one woman, Lady Macdonald-Buchanan. Nothing in the running of the gardens or the house had changed much since she took up residence in 1935. Not a lot, it seems, had changed before that either. As a chunk of social history Cottesbrooke is invaluable.

The book traces the manor from its mention in Domesday. The present hall was built around 1700 by a member of the Langham family, who owned the estate for nearly 300 years. Though major changes were made to the gardens by the new owners before the first world war, and the hothouses, frames and buildings date from this time, the rest of the kitchen garden remained much the same and predates the hall itself. It has been in constant cultivation since 1628.

What staggers the contemporary gardener with a lean-to shack, a postage stamp lawn and a clump of dahlias, is the amount of architecture. There is a peach house, a mushroom house and a vinery. There is also a propagation house, a palm house, a carnation house, a stove house, a fruit room, a boiler and a mess room, a potting shed, a box store and a vegetable washing room. The garden buildings served an enormous range of produce. In January in the mess room they are blanching chicory, forcing rhubarb, asparagus and sea kale. This room is a copy of the mushroom shed built in St Petersburg for the tsar. There, shelves of compost – fresh horse dung and straw beaten closely together – lined the shed, then the mushroom spawn was inserted and fresh dung placed on top.

In February, Doug's wife Joy pricks out the seedlings, an exceedingly finicky chore which she says she enjoys. Over 160 different types of seed are sown. In April, the Miranda and Mayfair lettuces are three times the size of the ones in the supermarkets. Doug has been selling some of his to the local greengrocer for 12p each and is astonished when the author tells him that iceberg lettuces cost 70p in Marks & Spencer. These giant lettuces obviously benefit from Doug's own brand of liquid fertiliser, he soaks a bag of soot and sheep dung in a barrel of rain water. Everything in this garden arrives early, in May the strawberries are ripening, the dwarf broad beans are flowering, the peas bushing out around their sticks. Potatoes were forced in tubs in the vinery and, because her ladyship was staying in Sussex in May, all the produce, the carrots, beetroots, parsnips, onions, leeks, asparagus, barb, as well as fresh herbs, mint, parsley, thyme, sage and chives, were all neatly packed in a box with a few pot plants. In May too, the peach and the apricot fruit are setting but the morello cherry has yet to flower; Joy is still in the potting shed, potting up seedlings.

How we all want to live like her ladyship, with a team in muddy wellies scrubbing the carrots and another in starched linen trimming and dicing them before, briefly steamed, they are brought to table. How we would all like 500 pot plants brought to the house early every Monday morning and arranged in the jardinieres before we are truly awake. But as most of us cannot live like this, the book enables us to smell and taste a little of what it might have been like and even to feel sad that such perfect symmetry of cultivation and consumption was created, lasted so long and is now no longer in existence.

My only gripe is that there is no index. What is a grape bottle? Difficult to find in the text, it was a method of preserving bunches of grapes through the winter by placing them in bottles of soft water with a piece of charcoal to keep the water fresh, the bottles kept in the cool darkened fruit room. The method was popularised in France in the 19th century. Like Cottesbrooke itself, grape bottles no longer exist.

Colin Spencer

15 Years' Normal Tree Loss at Kew
October 20 1987

An alianthus, the tree of heaven, has fallen across the roof of King William IV's temple at Kew Gardens, in London, cracking the interior. The sapling was taken from northern China and planted in 1837, the same year the temple was built to honour the king that Victoria succeeded. Now it is part of the overnight storm ruin of 1,000 trees at the world's oldest and most famous arboretum. Nearby, a Victorian bronze plaque displays an etched plan of the gardens as they were first laid out by Princess Augusta in a then royal estate in 1759. Near that lies an elm-like zelkovia from the Caucasus and two turkey oaks. They were 200 years old, among the last links with the first zest of the creation of Kew. So were the plane trees which have been toppled or stripped of main branches. No one knows how long a plane tree can live in Britain, according to Mr John Simmonds, the gardens' curator. In the Mediterranean they have been known to last 2,000 years, but at Kew the question was rendered academic early last Friday.

The remains were on view yesterday when the gardens were opened to show the press what the hurricane did to the mightiest and most long-lived of all the organic works of nature. It destroyed an eleventh of Kew's 11,000 trees. Among the victims was an avenue of 30-year-old tulip trees which were just coming into flower. Mr Simmonds said: 'It is like looking at time-lapse photography. We have suffered 15 years' normal tree loss in just a few hours.'

First reports of the damage at Kew caused worldwide shock and solicitude. Yesterday a hundred cheques arrived in the post, Venezuela offered saplings, and a man from Oregon rang offering to bring his chainsaw to help. Other Americans have offered technology to try to replant some of the fallen trees, but Kew staff don't think this would be safe. Safer areas of the gardens will be reopened to the public as soon as possible. Kew counts itself lucky because it did not lose entire vistas or greenhouses. Its country offshoot, Wakehurst Place, in Sussex, has lost about half its trees. 'Native oaks 200 years old were pushed over, one after the other,' said Mr John Lonsdale, assistant curator. 'Damage is serious and extensive, but everyone is totally committed to keeping going and to recovery.' A woman member of staff recalled: 'Someone was saying only last week that the weather conditions were right for producing fabulous autumn colours. We shan't see those now.'

John Ezard

Reinstatement for the Garden Gnome
November 21 1987

As a means of adding value to your property garden gnomes stand, sit or squat somewhere between lean-to sheds and swampy ponds, viz, entirely gratuitous additions that attract or repel buyers in equal measure. Indeed, they properly belong on the list of great divides, for they arouse passions as instantly as any politician, leaving little room for don't knows and much scope for the shadowy league against garden gnomes. These anonymous gnomeknappers are apt to spirit the relentlessly grinning figures away, then send their owners gleeful 'wish you were here' cards from foreign resorts. Even suppliers tend to chuckle like sprites at the mere mention of the word gnome. Like all endangered species, however, they have their supporters; and these take gnomes as seriously as did Alpine garden pioneer Sir Charles Isham, credited with introducing the little people to Britain 140 years ago. His gnomery at Lamport Hall, Northamptonshire, lasted until the second world war, when soldiers used the ceramic inhabitants for target practice. Had the collection survived, it would probably now be priceles. Others continued the slaughter for the next 30 years, covertly dumping anything remotely Mabel Lucy Attwell (gnome teapots, pixie ashtrays, etc) into dustbins at dead of night.

Such kitsch became okay again only when museums, notably the Victoria and Albert, began declaring their interest; older, terracotta gnomes are now extremely sought after. Sotheby's retains an expert in gnomery, alias miniature garden statuary. Further evidence of revived interest is the gnome reserve at West Putford, Devon, started in 1979 and still run by Ann Atkin, with assistance from her husband

Ron and their son Richard. Up to 25,000 visitors come every year to see the 1,000 or so gnomes in settings that evoke worlds tangible and intangible. Some pretty down-to-earth business is being done by leisure entrepreneurs keen to provide ideal gnomes – anything from the ubiquitous little fellow with the fishing-rod to Disneyesque dwarfs – at prices from £1 to £30.

There has been a definite trend away from the bright coloured plastic cheapie to more upmarket stoneware gnomes, says an official of the Cadbury garden centre, near Bristol, which knocks out about 1,000 a year. They are especially popular with children, old people and patio man; but not with owners of what the trade calls luxury gardens. To them, there is no such thing as a gnome of distinction; instead, they incline to animal statuary – otters, owls, and crouching cats are particular favourites. You'll know when the time comes to improve your terrace with Noddy, Big Ears and Co: it will be when the sporadic complaint, 'why don't you stock gnomes?' becomes an insistent roar and Homebase finally surrenders.

Charles Kersley

Golden Balls and Bloody Bastards
November 26 1987

You may not be aware that the apple that fell on Newton's head was a flower of Kent. I doubt very much if a golden delicious would have had the same effect. There is, or was, an apple called improved hang-me-down, and pears called golden balls and bloody bastard. Life was altogether more colourful and confident in the kitchen garden 100 years ago. For some time I have kept the most serene and dreamlike programme on television, *The Victorian Kitchen Garden* (BBC2), to myself like the blackcurrant pastille in a tube of fruit gums and given you the lemon. But today I will not write about brain damage in Glasgow (*Coma*, BBC1) or Aids in Africa (*Antenna*, BBC2). I will comfort you with apples: Prince Albert, 'a good cooker and good looker'; Gladstone, 'which some gentlemen would not have in their gardens'; beauty of Bath, 'a good scrumping apple'; and Ashmead's colonel, 'which is still winning tasting competitions'. That's Harry Dodson talking. He was the head gardener at Chilton, near Hungerford, in its heyday. On the husk remaining, a derelict acre surrounded by a tall, rosy wall, he and the BBC have created this splendid tribute to the Victorian stomach, a great kitchen garden.

Great Victorian houses grew their own supermarkets, and expected plums, nectarines, pineapples, melons, and grapes to be available on demand. When this garden was a going concern Harry grew 40 kinds of pears so, whenever pears were required, pears were available and at the point of perfect ripeness. Thomas Rivers, the nurseryman whom even Charles Darwin approached humbly ('My name may possibly be known to you. I am working on a book on the variation of animals and plants'), sold a thousand different pears. His son, by the way, bred conference, almost the sole survivor of the frightful modern massacre of fruit.

Harry, who ran the garden with 14 men under him, has revived it in his old age with one young girl, Alison, to help. His green and gold melons hang plumply again in nets like udders, his pink and gold peaches are unmistakably buttocks. Grapes are the only thing he has not been able to recreate in a year; they used to overwinter in their own house, each bunch drawing rainwater from its own patented grape bottle. The invigorating bounce of the Victorian mind was never more apparent than in the patent cucumber tube. 'An enthusiastic cucumber grower,' explained Harry, 'was very disappointed because he couldn't grow them straight.' After a lengthy tussle with recalcitrant cucumbers, he invented a sort of milk bottle open at both ends. Harry tried this out in the garden and the frustrated cucumbers grew straight, they had very little option. There was a slight flaw in the idea or the enthusiastic cucumber grower's name would now be on a par with Newton and Darwin. Unless you stood there, wound up and ready to pounce, the growing cucumber filled the tube and stuck like a ship in a bottle.

Glorious Victorian assurance booms in the names of the plants Harry has grown again. Magnum bonum, a potato; ne plus ultra, a pea; best of all, a tomato. It is remarkably restful. There seems all the time in the world to watch the pears taking on the rosy glow of the wall, the cardoon, like a green peacock, growing vaster than empires and more slow. Time to keep your seed in your waistcoat pocket from one year to the next. A time to sing, 'O, thank the Lord,' without being altogether certain which lord you were singing about.

'Enjoy the summer innocently while it lasts,' said the Shilling Kitchen Garden in 1859. 'Treat your master well if you happen to be a servant. Treat your servant well if providence has made you a master. Be thankful to Heaven.' The summer didn't last, of course. The big house went or the big money went. The kitchen garden with its 40 sorts of pears went, and the nurseryman with his thousand. The chauffeurs and the grooms and the gatekeepers went. Only the shell of the kitchen garden, the wall, remained.

And Harry of course. And a packet of peas which the father of the presenter, Peter Thoday, had given him and he had thrown in a drawer for years. They were ne plus ultra and they germinated. I find that cheerful.

Nancy Banks-Smith

The Inspirational Testament of a Grand Old Green Victorian
February 13 1988

Our much rained-on allotments have been unpleasantly aqueous and the soil slabby (as they used to say) and clarty (as we still say in these parts). It seemed sensible, therefore, to cultivate the mind instead. A little learning is not necessarily a dangerous thing in these days of exploding technology.

Myself, however, I prefer with advancing age to look back rather than forward: to pick up overlooked or forgotten knowledge of past times. After reading Susan Campbell's attractive publication,

Cottesbrooke: An English Kitchen Garden, and after viewing television's *The Victorian Kitchen Garden* – now being repeated – I was inspired to investigate what or who might have brought about this flowering of Victorian gardening.

It seems that John Claudius Loudon (b. 1783) and his young wife and amanuensis, Jane, must be given much of the credit. Loudon seems to have been the inspirer of much of that Victorian gardening enterprise and inventiveness. The son of a Scottish farmer, he came to London at the age of 20 to join the circle of enthusiastic botanists and gardeners around Sir Joseph Banks. He exhibited landscape paintings at the Royal Academy, farmed, started an agricultural school for young men, advised about the introduction of plane trees to London's smoke-polluted streets and squares, designed, with characteristic restraint and elegance, botanic gardens, park lands, and cemeteries, compiled eight volumes of trees and shrubs, native and imported, produced in 1821 a 1,000-page *Encyclopaedia of Gardening*, and brought out the first gardener's magazine.

He became temporarily rich, married the charming non-gardening novelist, Jane Webb; went to live in Porchester Terrace in semi-rural Bayswater; and travelled extensively, looking at agricultural and gardening innovations of good taste. He went to Moscow over battlefields just vacated by the retreating Napoleon, and met British gardeners surprisingly employed by Russians. Later he went through France and Italy, noticing such details as the use by gardeners in Monza of square plant pots to save greenhouse space. In Venice he secured a specimen aquatic plant, then unknown in England, named after the Italian botanist A Vallisneri. The flowers of Vallisneria spiralis had the curious habit of rising to the water surface for fertilisation, then spiralling back below. He carried his specimen in a can, on muleback through the Simplon to Paris, where he put it on his bedroom window ledge. Next morning, alas, it was gone, consumed by voracious sparrows. In this and other ways he was beaten, but his dedication and drive continued undiminished.

It was while working on his *Arboretum et Fruticetum Britannicum* that he is said to have sought permission to inspect the Duke of Wellington's famous beeches. But a hurried reading of his letter led to the Bishop of London – not Loudon – receiving a parcel containing the duke's breeches, as worn at Waterloo. Loudon never overlooks the plot-holders and cottage gardeners, saying it is a sin to put away tools uncleaned; not carry a garden knife; drop a hoe with blade uppermost; or stride across crop rows; and garden in a hurry. And always know your plants' names. He advocated growing elders in cottage gardens for their valuable flowers and berries, a state we should return to now that hedgerow elderberries are non-existent or tainted. He suggested raising them at no cost from whips or cuttings, and training them three to five feet high. Indeed there were elderberry orchards in Kent: bark, leaves, flowers, and berries all had their uses. Loudon describes the blackcurrant as a humble shrub found in alder swamps, wet hedges, and sometimes in woods. The name gooseberry, he suggests, was a corruption of groseberry because it resembled that prickly bush. And he wrote a book on growing pineapples.

The tireless energy and drive of John Claudius Loudon – he was said not to sit down or to eat between 7 am and 8 pm – resulted in his becoming disabled. When surgeons arrived at his home to amputate his right arm, they found him in his garden to which, he said, he intended to return immediately after the operation. He died while dictating to Jane his last book, *Self Instruction to Young Gardeners*. She completed it, reissued other of his works, and wrote books of her own. No full biography of Loudon has appeared – perhaps it is too colossal a task – but Geoffrey Taylor has praised him in his book, *Some Nineteenth Century Gardens* (Skeffington, 1951).

Michael Hyde

Obituary Of Percy Thrower: The Complete Gardener
March 19 1988

Percy Thrower, who died in hospital yesterday, aged 74, was one of the more memorable characters to emerge as television developed its repertory. After the war the BBC looked around for someone of recognised ability as a gardener who was able to communicate his knowledge, enjoyment and understanding of gardening to the wider British public. They lighted on Percy, who was then parks director at Shrewsbury, and who had attracted wide attention by his work in restoring gardens in Germany after the war. He quickly caught the public's fancy; that rich earthy voice and rather slow, deliberate speech embodying much of what they felt was right.

Most performers have a gimmick of some kind, and very often they hardly realise themselves what they are doing. Percy's was simple. When he walked into his greenhouse in the studio he would take off his jacket and hang it up on a handy nail. This revealed all: there was Percy, sleeves rolled, ready for work – and the meticulous Thrower tidily hanging up his jacket. His material was always very good, his explanations simple but accurate, and for the first time the public could see a master craftsman doing routine garden jobs in a way they could copy with advantage. He earned a place with such old masters of BBC gardening as CH Middleton and Fred Streeter. But he was more than a broadcaster. Percy was a very good administrator; the great success of the Shrewsbury flower show every August is very much a consequence of his judgment and ability.

He helped in every way he could to promote gardening, lecturing widely over the country and taking part in brains trusts and gardeners' question times. His own private garden was a beautiful example of his craft. His contribution was recognised with many honours, and his place in horticultural education (a phrase he would never have used) is that of a great craftsmen and teacher who talked to people in terms they could understand, appreciate and enjoy. Percy Thrower, the prototype of all TV gardeners, projected a sense of quiet reassurance a Harley Street specialist would envy. Peace and calm and quiet breathing. However fast the little webbed feet were going, everything above the waterline was gentle and restful. TV gardeners are not like that any more. They are much younger, more excitable. They leap about a bit in jeans. They may even be women. But Percy was Percy Thrower of the Magnolias, whose gardens were open to the public. Magnolias, now there's a shrub that likes to take its time. When you plant a magnolia you plant a masterpiece.

Percy John Thrower, MBE, gardener, born January 1913; died March 18 1988.

Alan Gemmell

Hunter Gatherers! How We Could Pay Tribute to the Men Who Scoured the World to Brighten Our Back Yards
June 4 1988

It has become a hackneyed comment on our forebears to say, 'They don't make them like that any more,' but I almost found myself repeating it aloud while re-reading JD Hooker's *Himalayan Journals*. Of course, the plant hunters of the 18th and 19th centuries had a great deal in their favour. They were often venturing into genuinely uncharted territories and would therefore inevitably find new things. But as we admire and appreciate the plants that they brought or sent back, I wonder how often we realise the hardships they had to endure. Several met tragic ends in foreign lands; none more sadly than David Douglas who fell into a trap set for wild bulls in Hawaii.

I have thought a good deal about plant collectors this spring, partly because I have never seen the genus Berberis showing off its splendour so magnificently. If I had been given the chance to discover one new plant for horticulture, it would have to have been Berberis darwinii, first found growing in Chile in 1835 by Charles Darwin while he was on his circumnavigation in the *Beagle*. But Darwin himself didn't bring it home; I doubt if even so hardy a plant could have survived the remaining year of the Beagle's voyage. Berberis darwinii actually reached Britain in 1849 thanks to a man who played one of the greatest though generally unappreciated parts in shaping our gardens: William Lobb. While looking through a list of his astonishing introductions, I pondered the idea of a plant collectors' garden. Given a fairly small modern garden, what few plants would I grow to commemorate each of the finest of all the collectors? To do proper justice to William Lobb himself, I would need a mildly acidic garden (in Lobb's native Cornwall perhaps) where I would add to Berberis darwinii, the Chilean bell flower Lapageria rosea, the fire bush Embothrium coccineum, and the gloriously crimson-and-yellow-flowered evergreen with holly leaves, Desfontainea spinosa. Sadly, given a small garden, I couldn't really grow the plant that was literally Lobb's greatest introduction, the wellingtonia, Sequoiadendron giganteum.

A real memorial to Robert Fortune would take several acres, because he was the first to collect in China after the end of the opium wars. His greatest contribution was not in collecting wild species but in bringing out plants that had long been cultivated by the Chinese: tea, for example. In my English garden, I would have his Anemone japonica, winter jasmine, weigela, and Dicentra spectabilis. Reginald Farrer was the rock gardener par excellence and a great mentor of alpine gardening, although this month is the time of year to pay tribute to his most splendid plant introduction. I have Buddleia alternifolia trained as a weeping standard in a long mixed border where it is an ideal contributor of height: its fine tracery of branches gives little shade to the herbaceous plants below. How can any one garden pay proper tribute to Ernest Wilson who single-handedly introduced more than 1,200 species of tree and shrub alone? But even in making a token gesture, your garden will be so much the richer. For thanks to Wilson, my garden is imbued with a rich, heady perfume for several weeks in midsummer. Its source is elusive. But those who know, make a bee line for large terracotta pots stationed strategically at path corners and close by the woodland seat. There they find Lilium regale, surely the most appropriately named of all lilies and quite simply a joy. And a tree to commemorate Wilson? Sadly my garden is not large enough for his wonderful dove tree, Davidia, so I shall settle for Acer griseum, the paperbark maple; if I can find a respectable specimen.

As far as I know, there is only one garden in Britain devoted specifically to the exploits of one collector: the fairly new Ernest Wilson memorial garden in his birthplace, Chipping Campden, Gloucestershire. It is well worth a visit although the plants are inevitably still young. What a pity that Stratford-upon-Avon doesn't see fit to commemorate its son, Charles Maries (Hamamelis mollis and Abies mariesii among others); or the ancient Scottish royal seat of Scone, David Douglas (Douglas fir and almost too many other conifers to mention); or Falkirk, George Forrest (rhododendrons by the score); or Manchester, Frank Kingdon Ward (the rhododendrons that Forrest left behind). Perhaps there are garden memorials to these and other collectors. If so, I shall be pleased to spread the word.

But if you are within striking distance of the exquisite little Cotswold town of Chipping Campden on June 18 or 19, you will visit the Wilson garden. Many residents also open their own gardens to the public in support of charity. The gardens are well signposted, teas are served at strategic points, and maps are available in the town. I know of no other place of comparable size with such a wealth of good horticultural things to see.

Stefan Buczacki

Hacking Away the Verbiage
December 17 1988

A great deal of hidden meaning lies behind many of the stock phrases we use. Sometimes we remain totally unaware of these meanings ourselves. For instance, if I stand with you in front of that area in your garden which makes you purr with greatest pride and innocently ask, 'What changes are you planning here?' you'll immediately be put on the defensive. Naturally, I'd only be as nasty as that to a very close friend. Were you so incautious as to ask, 'How do you like this?' of some carefully-planned planting, such as the magenta bloody cranesbill in front of the mustard yellow yarrow coronation gold; or of your latest mawkish acquisition in statuary, my tactful reply would be, 'I like it there,' i.e., 'You could trample over my dead body before I'd have anything like it in my own place.'

If I should spot a plant in your garden of which I have a low opinion and lash out against it, I'll know I have you on the run when your reply that it's 'useful.' That immediately puts it on the lowest level of reasons for growing anything. Don't tell me that 'nothing else will grow there.' If you'll take the initiative of improving the vile conditions that you've been prepared to accept till now, all kinds of plants will grow there. There are even ways to get rid of an obsessive tree under which nothing worthwhile will grow but which has a preservation order on it.

'Plants for the connoisseur', or 'a connoisseur's plant', is something more often written about by the aspiring horticulturist than used in actual conversation, where its pretensions might raise a laugh. The implication is that here is a plant which has been greatly enhanced by my knowing it and describing it to you. You may join me on my dizzy platform if you please. If not, you are an outcast, your destiny henceforth to wallow among the rabble that grows marigolds for colour. The connoisseur's plant will either have green flowers – 'so deliciously cool' – or it will require a magnifying glass to detect any way in which it has differentiated from chaos. The connoisseur himself may help here, by showing you a seemingly endless series of photographic close-ups, in which the flower's private parts are minutely exposed. This will open up whole new vistas that your eye never previously detected. 'Isn't Nature wonderful?' you'll be bound to exclaim, but with a lurking suspicion that none of this has anything to do with gardening.

'When is the right time to plant?' Anything you like to name, from an alpine treasure to a forest tree. This is one of the questions a nurseryman or any guru whose free advice is being sought, will be most frequently asked. The unkindest reply (and therefore, of course, the one that I most gleefully and helpfully supply) is 'Now.' The questioner was hoping to be able to put off the need for decisive action or, indeed, for making a decision of any sort. How familiar one is with the procrastinator's garden. Trees overgrown ('When should I have my trees thinned?'), shrubs unpruned ('What is the right time to prune my philadelphus?'), plantains dominating the lawn ('When should I apply weedkiller?'), old plants that should long since have made room for new.

'I don't know where I should put it,' is likewise a refuge from taking action. A surprising number of gardens could easily accommodate twice as many plants, both of kind and in numbers, without the slightest overcrowding. Snowdrops, violets, winter aconites, and crocuses tucked in under a deciduous shrub is just one example of a continuing momentum where plants are taking turn and turn about through the seasons. Similarly, clematis can grow over shrubs or up a pole instead of special wall space.

Often the most sensible way to make room for new plantings is to get rid of old, worn out ones. If the plants themselves are not worn out, your enjoyment of them may well be. Good gardeners don't stand still.

Christopher Lloyd

Show Stopper – The Chelsea Flower Show is no Longer an Occasion to be Relished
May 25 1989

It is something of a surprise to discover that the Chelsea Flower Show appears in *Harpers & Queen* still comically listed as one of Jennifer's social dates for the year. You can find it sandwiched in between the Berkeley Dress Show, Glyndebourne and Henley although it would be hard to spot a debutante doing the season (how exactly do you recognise one these days?) among the seething crowds who have fought their way up and down the marquee for the last few years. Worst of all was 1987 when 240,000 eager gardeners surged amid the bonsai, delphiniums and gladioli. That year proved too much for everyone. The Royal Horticultural Society took action to prevent overcrowding and RHS members (£19 a year) are now supposed to book their tickets in advance (£8 extra). They seem strangely reluctant to do so. As a result there are still thousands of unsold public tickets for today and tomorrow. For £14 (£10 tomorrow when the show ends early) you too can turn up at the gates of the Royal Hospital and join the tramping hordes.

The Chelsea Flower Show is one of the few annual events where it is better to be one of the lowly proletariat than a member. Although all four show days used to be for RHS members only – you had to join at the gate to get in – the first Tuesday was reserved for the holders of the sacred pink (or green, or yellow) tickets who had paid their dues at the start of the year. It sounds entirely civilised, a chance to see the best of British horticultural expertise in the company of like-minded fellow gardeners. The reality was desperate. So many people joined at Wisley, the RHS's show garden in Surrey, now transformed by entrepreneurial fever into a giant, horticultural cash register, that members' day became a positive scrummage, a heaving battle ground of surging, thrusting humanity. No more the thoughtful stroll past the clematis stand, the close study of the alpine garden in the company of mossy old men and cheerful Jekyllite women; instead, the heaving masses of the bargain basement. The yobs (including me) had been let in.

These days it is hard to persuade yourself that Chelsea is still an occasion. Once it was compulsory to attend in a hat while your escort buttoned himself up into suit and tie; occasionally you might take your gardener along with you too. There is, I suppose, still a certain amusement to be had from turning up at Sloane Square underground just before eight on the first morning and seeing all those formidable lady gardeners marching from the train with an air of determination. These are the serious cultivators, fitted out in stout brogues, tweed skirts and plastic macs, fully armed with note-book and pencil with which to compare and criticise. Here are women who have stepped straight from the pages of Barbara Pym. But for most of us the occasion no longer demands a certain dress, a certain style. It is just a heaving throng of thrusting, poking and prodding people. More like the sales than the season.

Inside the marquee it is almost impossible to stop and look at anything. The gangways are marked out with large, vulgar traffic signs indicating no-entry and one-way only which most people ignore. This means that at popular stands there is a vast, stationary mass, into which you must plunge in order to contemplate Notcutt's wistaria or Blooms of Bressingham's astilbes. Once you have forced your way into Hillier's 150th anniversary monument you may just have room to scribble excitedly on the back of your catalogue. Never have roses looked so delicate; never has a Malus floribunda reached such fragile perfection. Look at the white, foamy tiers of the Viburnum plicatum, the lace-like tracery of the Exochorda macrantha. Why didn't you think of planting Geranium sanguineum with Teucrium fruticans, a delicate pale blue climber? Just breathe the scent of that fragrant Mexican orange blossom.

If you are rash and inexperienced, you will immediately place orders for an inordinate number of choice shrubs (more than your garden can possibly hold) and rush home, determined to create just such a breathtaking arbour as you saw on Stand 50. If a sour and jaded gardening friend accompanies you, she will begin a speech that goes like this: 'Of course, you know they grow them in the dark at 50 degrees justs to get them all to flower together like this. You didn't actually think that Clematis macropetala flowered at the same time as Daphne burkwoodii did you? And that Rosa chinensis is never out with Spirea nipponica. By the way, you do know that its flowers only last two days, don't you? And they drop off completely if you get any rain. Yes, that Viburnum globosum is quite nice, but it does grow 10 feet high so I'd forget it for your little back patch. Oh, and as for your dreadful soil, you've no chance of growing that Eucryphia .'

Stunned with disappointment, you retreat into the melee and press on round the tent. A crowd has gathered in the corner. What are they admiring? Something special? To your dismay, you discover that the things which attract the most attention are invariably the nastiest examples of the grafter and pollinator's art, quite unnecessary and unattractive experiments with size and colour. What, for example, is the point of a pink (or worse, yellow) delphinium, a plant designed by nature to be perfect blue. What is the point of the pink flowering strawberry plant, or – strangest of all this year – the columnar apple tree, designed to grow entirely without branches: 'now even the smallest garden can have an orchard'? Of course, there are oases of inspiration. There is the unfailing delight of Peter Beales and his marvellous old roses, things of delicacy and fragrance, putting the garish modern hybrid teas to shame. It is easy to fall victim to the charm of these currently fashionable species and fill up your garden with them only to find yourself next summer staring at black spot, mildew, balled flowers and curious deformed buds.

Outside, it is equally depressing. After abandoning your 40 minute queue for coffee (there is a seafood and champagne tent which seems to be permanently full from eight in the morning) you can always wander round the Victorian-style conservatories and orangeries wishing you could afford one. Or you could take a stroll round huge stands of intimidating machinery. These stands are invariably frequented by elderly men in tweeds who occupy prosperous acres in the Home Counties, the sort of people to throw gallons of noxious chemicals over their gardens once a week. Every year the garden experts deliver their verdict that this year's flower show is the best ever. But for many of us, such a claim rings hollow. After years of battling round the marquee, I have given up Chelsea. Out in the real world of scorched lawns and aphid plague, there is far more pleasure to be had from visiting real gardens, other people's green and private worlds where mildew and the odd canker can still be seen. Armed with the famous *Yellow Book*, published by the National Gardens Scheme, you can find enough private gardens to visit to last all summer. The entrance fee is small and donated to charity. The crowds do not threaten. And the proud gardener usually gives you a cup of tea.

Jane Ellison

Growing Native:
1990–1999

Richard Mabey's *Flora Britannica*, 1996 * Sylvia Crowe dies, 1997 * Beth Chatto begins her gravel garden, 1991 * Heritage Seed Library established, 1995

Garden of Earthy Delights
March 8 1990

Fighting Like The Flowers: An Autobiography, by Lawrence D Hills (Green Books, £12.95)

This book is many things, all of them good for us. Essentially it is the story of one man's part in the laying-down of the seedbed of today's ecology movement. What no politician now dare leave off his agenda was something once only promulgated by dotty farmers like (the late) Lady Eve Balfour, and eccentric nurserymen like Lawrence Hills. The latter's role in making us all 'organic' was a crucial one. The origins of what is now an international awareness of what must and must not be done to preserve the natural order were, in his case, the horticultural equivalent of the wireless receiver made from cotton-reels. Like this homely gadget, Hills's modest experiments worked. His correct discoveries were so thickly scattered all over the gardening magazines and in so many popularly written books about growing flowers and vegetables that a case could be made for the British allotment holder being in the van of those who, a generation or so ago, set in motion the practices which alone can save the world.

Hills belongs to that top rank entrepreneurial class which includes inventors (his father), social geniuses (his cousin is Dame Cicely Saunders) and plantsmen, people who achieve vast results from, metaphorically speaking, a packet of seeds. Almost totally uninterested in money, except for the tiny amounts required for their work, they simply put us right. In the process all kinds of so-called great matters are robbed of their false claims. Hills joined the Soil Association in 1948 and 20 years later founded its subsidiary, the Henry Doubleday Research Association, named after an Essex Quaker whose ecological discoveries would have hastened our current concern for the environment had not his family put a match to all his papers. Hills's initial pursuit of Doubleday was because they were both devoted to comfrey, 'the plant that was to change my life'. His account of his chase after this homely fodder is as enchanting as that of any orchid-seeking botanist.

As a victim of the then unknown condition which required a gluten-free diet (coeliac disease) Hills had a rough time for more than 50 years and his autobiography, a tale whose infectious happiness makes one very self-questioning, uses a comic philosophy to deal with chronic illness of various sorts. But what is likely most to enthrall the reader is its meticulous pricing, right down to the last halfpenny, of this cheerful, useful, and witty existence. Wages, bedsitter rents, sheds, a table on which to write on alpines (bestsellers), fees for being a publisher's reader, funds to start the *Ecologist*, the organ of the Soil Association, the cost of a bike, a complete debit and credit page of how things were before all the noughts began to be added to the most insignificant purchase, cost-accounts this admirable life.

The world crashes on its foolish way beyond the compost and the planting. The war makes him appreciative of small treats, 'offal today

– the most beautiful words in the English language'. He marries, late, a lady as bright and as sick as himself, a doctor with Menière's disease, and long a convert to the teachings of the Soil Association. The gospel as taught on a little farm in Suffolk and from a tiny market garden in Essex, cranky stuff until recently, is now recognised as the truth. Hills sees us all on the road from *Silent Spring*, along which we have to go, there being no other way. He describes the devastating effect of Rachel Carson and her abuse by the chemical industry. Ironically she was dying of cancer when her great book appeared. It strengthened the hand of pioneers like Hills. *Fighting Like The Flowers* is an unashamed exposure of the nuttiness of the truly sane.

Ronald Blythe

Cutting Attack on Peat
March 27 1990

A boycott of gardening peat was launched yesterday by 10 naturalists' groups, led by two royal societies and Friends of the Earth, worried about the effect on wildlife of extraction methods. The conservationist, David Bellamy, and the presenter of BBC television's *Gardeners' World*, Geoff Hamilton, called on gardeners, councils, and the horticultural industry to buy alternative mulches and potting composts, to save unique wetlands and their fauna. In reply, the Peat Producers' Association, comprising 38 companies, is leafleting stores, defending extraction methods. 'There are no satisfactory alternatives to peat,' said Mr Robert Stockdale, of Fisons, the largest producer.

The company admitted that it had broken planning law by harvesting peat on 62 acres of Thorne Waste, near Doncaster, the type of habitat at the heart of the new campaign. Mr Stockdale said that confusion over boundaries had led to the work, which had now stopped. 'We are negotiating over adding a similar-sized area to a Nature Conservancy Council reserve on a much more interesting part of the moor,' he added.

The boycott campaign is led by the Friends, the Royal Society for Nature Conservation, the Royal Society for the Protection of Birds, and the Worldwide Fund for Nature.

Martin Wainwright

The Greenest Fingers of the Century
April 7 1992

Harold Nicolson and Vita Sackville-West are often presented as a great horticultural collaboration, in which the method and symmetrical inclination of Nicolson's personality are combined with the knowledge and romantic exuberance of his wife's. This is wrong: the genius of Sissinghurst Castle in Kent belongs entirely to Vita Sackville-West. Her husband was the benevolent and plodding enabler to her remarkable talent. She is the greatest British gardener of the century and her garden one of the most splendid achievements in the history of horticulture. Of course there is always a chance that she may be pipped at the centenniel post by someone like Penelope Hobhouse, the inspiration behind the gardens at Hadspen and Tintinhull, but gardening is a slow business and I think the award may be safely conferred on Vita now.

She had many abilities. She could match plants and situations like nobody else, she allowed the wilderness to invade and inspire her husband's considered designs and she was sensitive to the character of individual plants, their need for shade, dry soil, a warm brick wall or the supporting company of other plants. She had green fingers but it is her taste that separates her from other early 20th century contenders like Major Lawrence Johnston, creator of the garden at Hidcote in Gloucestershire.

Vita Sackville-West was blessed with an eye that operated in the quiet ranges of colour in shades of ochre, russets, dull pinks, off whites and pastel subtleties. A sentence from one of her journals just after the second world war, when the garden was being revived after years of neglect, shows the level at which she operated: 'I cannot help hoping that the grey ghostly barn owl will sweep silently across a pale garden, next summer in the twilight – the pale garden that I am now planting under the first flakes of snow.'

In a period when horticultural taste seems to be represented by the lone specimen conifer isolated in a patch of weedless soil, and by the perfectly mown lawn, devoid of moss, daisies and speedwell, it is important to remember that gardening is about poetry and fantasy. It is as much an activity of the imagination as of the hands. Regiments of marigolds and petunias were not for Sissinghurst, nor the dark masses of leylandii bushes. What is remarkable was how quickly she established her garden. After the Nicolsons bought the broken down Elizabethan manor house for £12,000 in 1930, it took just seven years for the plan and basic planting to be completed. They had little money after the purchase but set to work building walls and mapping the divisions of the garden into 'rooms', an idea which had probably come from Johnston at Hidcote. They planted avenues of limes where Nicolson was allowed his garish spring garden, dug out the ancient moat and excavated a new lake. In the designs Nicolson made his major contribution and was often seen with a ball of string and long ruler mapping out the lines which would soon be blurred by his wife's palette. This she set about by planting mauve borders, yellow walks, the white garden, the herb garden and the nuttery, where primulas form a carpet under hazelnut trees.

By the war Sissinghurst was firmly established and within another seven or eight years Vita had become one of the celebrated gardeners of her time. She was often photographed in hacking jacket, breeches and calf length lace up boots stalking about her property with a cigarette holder. She had a rather forbidding appearance but anyone who read the gardening column in the *Observer* newspaper or her occasional contribution to the *New Statesman* would know that she was a woman of exceptional sensibility, her refined taste always leavened by practical experience.

For my own taste it is a white garden conceived and planted just after the war that wins Vita her award. Irises, lupins, lilac, roses, campanulas, tree peonies – every plant that you can imagine represented in its pure form. If you do not believe me spend an hour or so this summer in the first week of June at Sissinghurst. Vita's garden is preserved and the house and gardens are open though they do sensibly limit numbers. Vita Sackville-West died in 1962. In her funeral service someone had the sense to quote her own poem, 'The Land'.

> *She Walks among the loveliness*
>   *she made,*
> *Between the apple-blossom and*
>   *the water*
> *She walks among the patterned*
>   *pied brocade*
> *Each flower her son and every*
>   *tree her daughter.*

Centipede

Not So Lovely in the Garden
October 10 1992

Do not, in an incautious moment, invite Sir Roy Strong round to admire your gaily painted gnomes and polypropylene pergola. The Queen made that mistake and even for a woman accustomed to being nipped around the ankles, it must cost her a twinge or two. 'Look at these excruciating whimsy topiary figures! And whatever is this?' cries Sir Roy, his voice rising steeply until it went out of the top of the screen. This was a statue of a slightly adipose child in a bath hat with its nappy round its ankles. It was rather difficult to grasp the concept from the back, but the kid seemed to be inspecting a dove. 'The less said about that the better,' said Sir Roy, shuddering like a dove that has had a nasty shock.

He is an elegant figure in gold polo-neck, black pants and sweet slippers with twinkling gold buttons on them. How different from the home life of Geoff Hamilton and his hardworking trousers which Sir

Roy and *Royal Gardens* (BBC2) temporarily displace. The norm in a gardening programme is for the presenter to admire the goods on offer. He may, if pressed, offer a little kindly advice on carrot fly but, in general, 'Oh, what a beauty! I've never seen one as big as that before!' is the tone expected. Not Sir Roy. He reminds me in some ways of Dr Magnus Pyke whom I remember working his way along a greengrocer's display, commenting in a carrying voice on the benzole cyanide in cress, the oxalic acid in rhubarb and the frightful results of over indulgence in brassicas. How many men, you wondered, were sitting on the greengrocer to stop him felling the doctor with a cling-filmed cucumber.

The burden of Sir Roy's song was that the queen has Let Hampton Court Go. She is not green fingered. At a royal garden party for, appropriately enough, gardeners in *Elizabeth R*, she described herself as 'a weeder'. Weeders are mutinous drudges. They are pressed into service, pleading incapacitating tennis elbow and dizzy spells, and then get ticked off for pulling up flowers by mistake. It tends to sour them. Hampton Court was in its great geometric glory under William and Mary. Even by royal standards, they were a bizarrely ill-matched couple but in matters of taste they were in perfect accord with each other and their age. Everything in their garden at Hampton Court was as regimented as trooping the colour. Thirteen synchronised fountains, 758 lime trees standing to attention along a mile of unwavering water, clipped trees with clipped accents and small military moustaches, dwarf box hedges wheeling into complicated patterns. And, of course, the famous maze. Virtually no flowers except a few regimental tulips and tall fritillaria imperalis, standing to attention with their topknot of leaves blowing like the feathers on a helmet. It is ironic that William should have been killed by that enemy of the tidy minded, a mole.

Of all this nothing remains but the maze. Oh, and a fountain. 'Only one and it hasn't even got a decent jet,' grumbled Sir Roy in the disparaging tone of Mr Ramsbottom, who found fault with Blackpool's waves because they were small. He added – Sir Roy, not Mr Ramsbottom – that the park benches were drab, the litter bins ugly and the King's privy garden was simply terrible. 'It wouldn't surprise me if Tarzan swung by on a rope. None of the statues or the Tijou screen can be seen from the palace, ruining the original concept. It's enough to make William and Mary, let alone poor Wren, turn in their graves.' The director of Hampton Court turned out to be a slim, young chap with a nervous laugh, as well he might. He agreed there was scope for limited restoration, 'but clearly the fountain garden would be enormously difficult to restore.' 'Well,' said Sir Roy, who does not smile at all, 'I would restore the lot. It would mean axing those 300-year-old yew trees. I for one can't wait to start.'

It is an education and an entertainment to go for a stroll in the garden with Sir Roy and, on the matter of restoring Hampton Court, I stand shoulder to shoulder with him. I think it is the safest place.

Nancy Banks-Smith

A Well-earned Wreath of Laurels
September 2 1993

Gardening stands as the greatest of British bastions – well, perhaps it's shared with dogs and horses. As a nation we have left our green-fingered mark from Vancouver to Van Dieman's Land, Kandy to Cape Town and, true to our colonial past, our own gardens bear testimony to botanical pillaging of the four corners of the world. However, we have to distinguish between plantsmen and women, and mere gardeners.

What sets a plantsman – of course, the term plantsman must be seen in this context as asexual, particularly as most of the greatest in this field were women – apart from the rest of the greenfingered world, is a collector's zeal to possess plants in great numbers, a botanist's desire to examine their individual characteristics and a detective's curiosity for seeking their identity. No true plantsman, when given a nameless cutting from a friend's garden, will simply plant it and watch it grow. A plantsman must trace it – genus, species and cultivar – and find out where it comes from, what it does and where it does it best. Nor will he or she shrug off the miserable decline of some ailing rarity, but will fight for its survival. The true plantsman will go out at midnight to protect it from frost, move it tenderly to kindlier surroundings like some convalescing consumptive and finally grieve over its death – at the same time determining, however unreasonably, to replace it.

Most landscape designers in the early years of the 20th century, like the Italian revivalists, the concrete-loving modernists and the philosophical Japanese pebble and moss gardeners – would only tolerate plants insofar as they complemented the grand design. It is a tribute to the great gardener Gertrude Jekyll that her views on plants withstood the plantless years and have left their mark so firmly on British gardens at the end of the century. Miss Jekyll is chiefly remembered as a garden designer. However, her knowledge of plants was encyclopaedic and the great beauty of her elongated drifts of colour in a mixed border were a strong influence on the generation of plantsmen that followed her.

There was Miss Jekyll's friend Ellen Willmott, who sponsored EH Wilson's plant-hunting trips to China, and was a great Victorian plantsman, still raising plants – many of which bear her name – well into this century. The garden at Sissinghurst Castle in Kent is one of the finest and best loved in England. Vita Sackville-West made it with her husband Harold Nicholson, who regarded its creation as his most significant achievement, though most people nowadays tend to give all the planting credit to his wife. It was Vita's passion for collecting plants at every Royal Horticultural Show that made her into the true plantsman of the family. She collected old roses and forgotten pinks, grew 24 different varieties of thyme – never cooking with any of them – and made a wildflower meadow in her orchard. Her famous white garden, inspired by falling snowflakes and a white barn owl, completed one of the most romantic and fascinating gardens ever made.

Major Lawrence Johnstone, who made the garden at Hidcote Manor in Gloucestershire, did not write a word about his gardening pursuits, but his garden remains as a monument to his skill. He studied architecture before laying it out with such sensitivity to the needs of plants that he was able to create conditions which allowed tender and rare specimens to survive. He was also a plant hunter, going on botanical expeditions to Kenya and China with the legendary plant-hunter George Forrest. His planting schemes were aided and influenced by Norah Lindsay, who made her own beautiful garden at the Old Manor House in Sutton Courtenay and helped in the planting at Port Lympne and Trent Park, the famous gardens of Philip Sassoon. She was a considerable plantsman with a fascination for wildflowers, which, she wrote, 'give and give and give, rushing in and out of the real garden with a reckless joy and dancing grace.' This passion for self-sown wild flowers, which the tougher-minded gardener would root out as weeds, is another characteristic of the true plantsman.

I have mentioned only some of the most notable plantsmen and women, but the list could run on to include many others – Beth Chatto, Rosemary Verey, Christopher Lloyd, Robert Burle Marx, Lanning Roper, Susan Jellicoe, the late Lord Aberconway, and even Queen Alexandra – who have all proved that however charming gardens can be when viewed as functional outdoor rooms adorned with statues and urns, it is really the plants that count.

Centipede must now award the laurel – sorry, Laurus nobilis – to the greatest plantsman of the century, Margery Fish. Her first book, *We Made a Garden*, was largely about the battles she had with her husband whose fondness for order in the garden did much to keep the great plantswoman down. After his death she blossomed into an obsessive collector and passionate lover of plants. Her struggles with capricious floral prima donnas to perform for her, and her uncritical, almost maternal, affection for the unshowy oddities are chronicled in her books about her garden at East Lambrook manor in Sussex. These books, once read, leave every gardener intoxicated with her plantaholic's craving to study botany, learn Latin and, above all, to know and possess every plant on earth.

Centipede

Question Time Gets in on the Ground Floor
March 4 1994

The new chairman of *Gardeners' Question Time* cheerfully led his panel into an urban wasteland devoid of vegetation. 'An awful lot of palaver has been talked about us abandoning the village hall,' volunteered Eric Robson, who had some success bringing the world of allotments to the television screen in a 1980s series. 'They're lovely things with a marvellous ambience, these halls, but it's a bit rough on people in the inner city who've aspired to have a garden for many years.'

For the first outside broadcast that most can remember in the 46-year-old history of the programme, the new-look team plodded from a Methodist hall – reserve venue in the event of rain – past derelict flats and mounds of rubble towards a muddy building site in the Manchester suburb of Hulme. The 50-strong audience went to a small patio where the BBC sound recordists had set up shop. With workmen thumping, and police sirens occasionally screaming, the chairman launched into a brief social commentary. 'In many ways it is a monument to the stupidities of the 60s – big high-rise blocks, grey depressing crescents and peeling maisonettes.'

But a new Hulme was rising from the rubble, with new houses and gardens. First question. 'Mary Maloney, what are the problems you're going to face?'

'Well, what to do with the garden when there is only soil there.'

Eric was puzzled. 'Well, you haven't actually got soil yet have you? We've got bricks, broken paving stones, the usual builders' rubble.'

The North British Housing Association, which is building 180 houses and flats around courtyards it hopes will be sprouting with flowers and veg, had explained earlier that horticultural matters had not been high on the agenda. According to Hilary Saltburn, a housing official, many residents had experimented with window boxes but little else. Only a few had allotments. 'Most are really beginners, but they're enthusiastic.'

Amanda Mares, who was producing her last *Gardeners' Question Time* before the BBC hands over the programme to an independent company, saw no reason to apologise to a largely middle-class audience which has been displaying signs of restlessness at crossing the class divide. 'I don't think anyone wants to get rid of the listeners we have, but we are reaching out to people who might be intimidated by Radio 4.' But increasingly they were getting letters from listeners in urban areas, and on new housing estates. 'They have a piece of earth and often don't have the slightest idea what to do. They often make expensive mistakes and have to dig things up and start again. We are getting there beforehand.'

While he was preparing his question for the broadcast, Colin Rowan, who lived in one of the notorious Hulme deck access flats, recalled that some went to extraordinary lengths to cultivate gardens in the sky. Clutching a seed catalogue along with a book on *Gardening in a Cold Climate*, Lily Moore, who has lived in the area for 25 years, was more concerned about her weeping fig plants. 'They go all right for two or three years then pop their clogs for some reason.' For half an hour the team of three was bombarded with questions about creating gardens from mounds of rubble. Geoff Hamilton, one of the panellists, had a quick answer: 'Get them to take the rubble away and break up the bottom and put a lot of topsoil over it. One of the nice things about this development is that they are going to co-operate with the tenants and do something at the beginning.' He didn't minimise the task. 'You've only got to look around here. Lots of builders' rubble, lots of water, compacted soil.'

Elizabeth Morris, who had brought her withered cactus for expert attention, spoke enthusiastically of plans for a garden tool and plant collective to share the common resources of the neighbourhood. 'A wonderful idea,' said Geoff Hamilton. 'See what resourceful people these gardeners are.'

Peter Hetherington

Parks: Who Needs Them?
July 1 1994

London was offered two rare chances this week to create high-profile public urban space. The first was pretty modest – turning the traffic island in front of Buckingham Palace into a partly pedestrianised area. It was the leftover from the royal parks review body's ambitious notion to make a vast piazza of the Mall, something considered far too revolutionary and unworkable earlier this year.

Even so, the scaled-down vision – which would have mightily benefited the million people who each year risk injury dodging the four lanes of traffic to get closer to the palace – received short thrift from Lord St John of Fawsley, chairman of the Royal Fine Arts Commission. 'It might be appropriate to Paris, possibly,' he said, 'but not to London.'

Lord Fawsley is thought to have been talking in loco the royal family, who might prefer to look out on foreign cars rather than foreign people, and he made the good, if minimalist, point that the 'integrity' of St James Park, on to which Buck House looks, would be lost. Perhaps, but critics would argue that his is a sclerotic view of a modern city's needs. 'It neglects totally the importance of open space in a city and the very reason why the parks were created in the first place,' says Martin Hoyles, author of a new Demos/Comedia report on the future of urban open spaces. The second plan, courtesy of a royal parks competition, was to disinter Marble Arch from its polluted tomb of traffic, to extend Hyde park fractionally and make it far easier to reach Speakers' Corner. Between them the two modest proposals show how London – it could be Birmingham, Leeds, Sheffield or any one of our cities – is half-inching towards rethinking the needs of its citizens. Neither scheme dares to even cut back on traffic, but somewhere a new heart is beating.

Or is it? Lord Fawsley's scotching of the Buck House scheme and the hostility towards the piazza plan spoke eloquently for the times. Public space throughout Britain is in decline, private space is paramount and parks and open areas have not been so culturally devalued for at least 150 years. There is, says Hoyles, a crisis of confidence as to what parks and open spaces are now for. 'They are often perceived as places of fear, where violence, rape and theft take place. There are particular threats to women, children and racial minorities.' 'Little but litter bins and the toilets of dogs,' said a splenetic woman this week in Finsbury Park. Full surveys on the use of parks in the 1990s are rare but Hoyles' assertions, based on studies of parks in Bromley, Bristol, Leicester, Greenwich, Hounslow, Sheffield and six other cities with more than 70,000 people, are supported at least by straw polls and vists to London spaces. 'The murder of Rachel Nickell on Wimbledon Common really shook me,' says Maud Stringer of Richmond. 'I began to see things that probably weren't there; I love parks, but these things are important.'

One of a bunch of lads skipping school: 'We hang out here. It's the best place. There's no police'.

A harassed mother in Battersea: 'No, I wouldn't let my children here on their own. God, they need to get out, but who can they turn to?'

We've come a long way. Open space in Victorian times was hallowed ground. Parks were an essential part of municipal development, the green lungs of the industrial revolution, galleries of colour, showpieces of horticulture. They were the preferred meeting place of all classes and ages and the sites of circuses, sports, political debate, and dances. Victoria Park in the East End, apart from attracting the likes of Bernard Shaw and William Morris and mass meetings of dockers and sufragettes, attracted up to 25,000 (male, nude) swimmers a day to its outdoor pool. While not totally free from vandalism, crime or provocative behaviour – there were great debates as to whether 'amorous' couples should be allowed into Kew Gardens and if so what positions they should be allowed to adopt on the grass – they linked a newly industralised society to its rural roots, were regularly held up as the paragons of civilisation and, by the by, they perfectly expressed man's control of nature. More than that they were considered to have social and educational benefit. Macclesfield council thought its newly-created open spaces 'would lead to a decrease in crime and a fall in the death rate'; drunkenness was said to have decreased and 'manners improved' after the Leeds Botanical Gardens were opened; Derby Arboretum aimed 'to give people an opportunity … to enjoy the pure air as an alternative to the brutalising pleasure of drinking and cock-fighting.'

There may have been a hidden motive to raise land values in some cities, but the primary aim of Victorian park-makers was to 'make people virtuous and happy' (Birkenhead) or to 'cure drunkenness' (Edinburgh). Four years after Derby opened its arboretum a parliamentary commissioner declared it 'has already produced a perceptible effect in improving the appearance of the working classes and it has, doubtless, conferred an equal benefit upon their health.'

As shared public spaces, parks help to define cities and the people who live there. Today they reflect the divided times – perfectly restored Victoriana mixing with shabby, desolate areas, shiny sports facilities jarring uneasily with limp rows of tulips. When Hoyles visited a Manchester park he found himself alone with abandoned cars. Short walks around several less popular inner-city open spaces this week reveal similar, if less extreme, problems. Most evident is the closing off of space to people. Everywhere there is evidence of borders having been dug up and turned to (seldom mown) grass; the public is enjoined to pay for sports facilities (another form of privatisation), sections of parks are being fenced off. 'It's all right if you're young and fit, in work and a man,' says Mary Chaldwell, 67, of Waterloo, 'but otherwise it's so depressing. Nothing like it was. I prefer to stay in my little garden, really.'

There is irony here. Mass interest in gardening and the environment – partly provoked by the wondrous colours, the perfect lawns and well-tended walkways of the best parks – has never been higher. Gardening is now the country's most popular outdoor leisure activity with people spending on average one hour a day on their patches. Britain has 2,500 horticultural societies and a reported 10 million keen gardeners spending £2.5bn a year. So why do we no longer appreciate the public demonstration of horticulture? Why the emerging gap between the private and the public? Money is one thing, says Hoyles. Local authorities have been endlessly squeezed and the decrease in park wardens, poor lighting and attendant vandalism have contributed to a spiral of neglect and less regular use, he suggests. 'The more places are neglected, the more dangerous they become, the less people go.'

Local authorities have no duty to provide or maintain their open spaces which are left to compete with the statutory needs of education, social services and housing. Usually they come off worst. Park police and gardeners have been pruned throughout Britain. Compulsory competitive tendering (part of the privatisation of council services) has meant contractors now do much of the gardening – breaking the link between council and people.

'Competitive tendering has saved £40m a year in the provision of open spaces and parks,' says Nick Reeves of the Institute of Leisure Management, 'but none of that money has been reinvested in open spaces. If it could be, it might go a long way to refurbishing them.' Reeves is convinced that investment in quality-of-life is central to crime prevention and societal good. Hoyles is more resolutely political: 'The Conservatives' emphasis on the private sphere has led to a growing ethos of selfishness and a frequent abandonment of open space.' The public perception is that parks are now devalued by their guardians. More than 200 urban leisure spaces in Britain are now under threat – to supermarkets and housing developers, sports consortia or roads. More than 300 school playing fields are similarly threatened. 'Local councils,' says one landscape designer (who asks to be nameless), 'are often glad to have them off their back. They don't have the resources to keep them up to scratch, they're always getting flak about them, or they think they can make a quick buck.' He alleges that some local authorities deliberately allow parks to run down so they can persuade the community that they should be sold off.

The abuse of Britain's lesser open spaces can provoke extreme reactions. Bournemouth council recently spent £40,000 ripping out all the mature trees and shrubs from a small patch that once even had a bandstand, says parks officer Susan Smith. Why? 'Because winos gathered there. The shrubbery provided them shelter. Now more people use the area for a few minutes each day.' The image is compelling. But people's needs and relationship with nature are changing, too, and the authorities in many cases may have been slow to adapt, says Hoyles. Instead of Victorians flocking from up to 60 miles away to enjoy urban parks, many urbanites now prefer to escape the city by private car for the countryside.

'There is a need to feminise public space,' says Hoyles, 'to make it safer and less aggressive … It would be naive to think that vandalism is not a major problem. Some way of breaking the vicious circle of neglect is needed. The initial effort needs resources, though these could be mobilised on a community basis, to clean them up and to maintain and develop them. If people start coming back part of the problem will be solved. It's their abandonment that often leads to their destruction. The interest in private gardening could be harnessed to more public, communal activities. Many gardeners need advice, plants could be labelled, there could be plant exchanges, garden waste recycling …' Hoyles is a fount of ideas.

And it is by no means all gloom. There are many initiatives to rethink the role of open space and bring the countryside into the city in a less regimented way than the Victorian park provided. There are 20 city farms in the London area and many others in provincial cities. There are moves to create allotments (notoriously under threat) in park areas, school gardens, herb gardens, environmental gardens, community gardens, wild gardens, 'multicultural' gardens, walkways across cities linking them all, and many specialist spaces – for the handicapped, the old, toddlers and sportsmen. Hoyles calls them 'intermediate areas' bridging the gap between the increasingly separated world of private and public life.

Whether this fragmentation of open space heralds a brave new future or is the despairing last stand of Britain's parks is debatable. Above all people must want their parks, and the lesson, everywhere, is that jazzy ideas dumped on people from town halls seldom live long. In New York a group called the Green Guerrillas helps people reclaim unused space to provide gardens or allotments. 'Man, they're really blossoming. We're winning,' said a spokesman this week. Lord Fawsley and Buckingham Palace, please note.

John Vidal

Hardy Perennial Still Blooming on BBC
July 30 1994

The colour cameras were heavy and unfamiliar. As the cameraman swung round to capture a picture of a punt on the River Isis, Oxford, he hit a tree and toppled into the water. It was one of the first shots *Gardeners' World* tried to take, but the film has since been lost, gone to the television equivalent of the compost heap. The early days of gardening on the small screen were restricted by the cumbersome technology, but the programme, with Percy Thrower fronting it, gradually took root to develop into one of BBC2's hardiest perennials – and next week it celebrates its 25th anniversary.

In the early years, when microphones were put in flower beds, Thrower once gave the plants a healthy sprinkling with a water can, there was a minor explosion underground and he inadvertently took himself off the air. Thrower, who died in 1988, became a national institution. He presented the programme from his immaculate garden – The Magnolias, in his home town of Shrewsbury, where he had been the park's superintendent – and appeared on the Morecambe and Wise Show with deadpan aplomb. He had already featured in *Gardening Club*, the black-and-white forerunner of *Gardeners' World* which ran for 12 years.

The row that led to his departure from the BBC – he had taken part in a television commercial for ICI Garden Plus fertiliser – prompted an array of headline gardening puns. 'Percy Thrower pruned by BBC', 'Percy Thrower finds himself in the fertiliser', 'Percy rakes it in,' they chortled. He was succeeded by Peter Seabrook, who teamed up with the veteran Arthur Billitt, as locations including Clacks Farm and Barnsdale became synonymous with the programme. *Gardeners' World* underwent another root and branch transformation in 1991 when it was farmed out to independent producers as part of the BBC's 25 per cent quota of programmes to be made externally. There were fears, expressed most vocally by Dr Stefan Buczacki, dropped as one of the presenters when Catalyst TV took over, that it would head downmarket. Geoff Hamilton, the only survivor of the clear-out, who presents the programme from the BBC's five and a half-acre site at Barnsdale, Rutland, said: 'We have a loyal audience, but our viewers are getting considerably younger. The programme has swung more towards providing inspiration than information.'

Andrew Culf

Proud to be Vulgar
September 24 1994

Political correctness is as rife in gardening as it is in other walks of our lives. Follow the fashion and you'll be listened to. Most such fashions, as it happens, are playing safe. Individuality has always been frowned on as crankiness. Let us examine the qualities that go to making the play-safe, PC gardener.

He – or, as often, she – loves to hark back. A haze of nostalgia, a whiff of stale potpourri is spot on. Hence the vogue for herb gardens (which ties in nicely with any natural propensity to slovenliness, most herbs being weeds at heart). Modern medicine is clinical, heartless, un-understanding. Just go back to those old remedies that great-granny knew and practised. Ah, they knew a thing or two in those days (but overlooked that many died in infancy, or giving birth, or of some now rare but then common disease). I grow herbs for the kitchen. I don't grow them all together in one patch, as that is inconvenient, some being annual, some perennial, some large (like our vast bay tree), some quite tiny. Herbs should be grown either because they are beautiful plants and also happen to be herbs, like henbane, or because they are in regular use, like lavender to scent our drawers or flat-leaved parsley to flavour every sort of savoury dish.

Further nostalgia, together with a reluctance to make the best of the present or to plan excitingly for the future, is evidenced in historicism in the re-creation of old gardens using their original plans and, if traceable in records, the same plants as were used when they were made. If not traceable, then plants that were in use then. This is a safe game in which nobody can lose. Praise for sensitivity and diligence with loads of mutual back-slapping is the order of the day. The National Trust excels in this and English Heritage is catching up, as it acquires more historic gardens. Well, there is something to be said for preserving or re-creating examples from our past, but the danger lurks of a terminal paralysis setting in. Copying becomes a substitute for original thought and creativity. The original owners of the gardens we seek to preserve were passionately keen to try out every new plant introduction, yet we insist on an act of fossilisation.

Going native with wild flower gardens or gardens consisting entirely of indigenous plants, is another fad that comes and goes. It tends to be linked with a kind of pseudo-patriotic jingoism. You don't find this so much in Britain as in Australia or California, for instance. Through accidents of our geological history, Britain's genuinely native flora is exceedingly poor, while our climate is ideal for growing a wider range of plants than is practical in almost any other country in the world. So we're not too crazy about sticking to our own flora, though wildlife gardens are enjoying a great boom. They are another good excuse for indulging a natural bias to untidiness. As long as you appreciate this and don't try to append highfalutin moral motives, the exercise is harmless, though 'ecological correctness' can become a wearisome way of trying to make plants obey your rules.

No subject is more beset with rules and taboos in gardening than the use of colour. This has social connotations and is closely linked with class. No one cares to be thought conscious of lower or upper classes these days, but everyone acts as though they existed. Thus, the lower classes, the owners of ex-council houses with front gardens, are portrayed as loving bright colours, red with yellow tulips, followed by a gaudy display of orange marigolds. Therefore, the upper classes are distressed by all this. No orange for them; it is the one colour they cannot abide. Nor any of those dreadful marigolds, either. Violent (the adjective would be theirs) colour contrasts are in bad taste. Colour harmony is the thing, especially in pastel shades, soft and soothing. Silver and grey is best of all. It is all stiflingly self-conscious.

Readers will surely have met something called the colour wheel. I'd never heard of it until after my official education was at an end, but Gertrude Jekyll believed in its efficacy, which automatically confers the seal of upper-class approval. But just how are we supposed to use the colour wheel? I can well see that diametrically opposed colours are as different as colours can be and that adjacent colours have much in common, but what then? Are there colours that we must not use together? I think not. Well handled (ie handled by me), any two colours can be pleasingly juxtaposed. (I'm still talking about plants, though I believe that much the same is true of fabrics). Or any three colours, come to that.

Your novice to upper-class, or upper middle-class, or yuppy-class gardener will be terrified of doing the wrong thing, of growing the wrong plants, of combining them stridently and, worst of all, of being commented on adversely by 'friends' and acquaintances whom they regard as important. Hence the asphixiating boredom born of the good-taste gardener, who hasn't a fresh idea in his/her head (well, we all have to start from scratch at some point) or any desire to develop one (we are even more painfully aware of this among flower-arranging groups). They'll all be growing old roses, all have a white garden and the Lutyens-designed Sissinghurst seat. All will yearn for a potager (rather than a vegetable plot). White-painted trellises and arbours will be in vogue. The entire paraphernalia of upper-class fad-fashion, in fact.

With more self-confidence and self-reliance there would come, perhaps will come, a wonderful sense of release. What all those other people are thinking and saying really doesn't matter, so long as you are making yourself and, perhaps, one or two other close friends, happy; as long as you are enjoying yourself and your plants in your very own garden. (Even if you are a paid worker in someone else's garden, you really have to identify with it as your own). And the more different colours and kinds of plants with their varying arrangement you can enjoy, the happier you will be in pushing out your frontiers of experience. Never stay still or you'll slip backwards. Never stop experimenting.

It is important not to accept received ideas automatically. Most advice would recommend against the use together of orange and pink flowers. And yet if you look at certain tulips, like the parrot, Orange Favourite, there is a pink flush overlying the orange on the outside of the three outer petals, and it is quite magical. I have a group, in my big mixed border, of a tall orange poker, Kniphofia uvaria Nobilis, behind a large quilt of pink (though not a pale pink) phlox. The wind blew the pokers so that some of them leaned directly over the phlox, giving it a nudge. And you'll have to take my word for it: it didn't look bad.

All colours can be mixed if you don't get too busy and over excited. Areas of rest will also be necessary. That is why I think scarlet oriental poppies look so good, during their early season, in a border that is otherwise nearly all foliage, the foliage of plants whose flowering is later than the poppy. The big innovation in my garden over the past 18 months has been in the conversion of the rose garden into a garden that gives you the feel of high summer (extending well into autumn) with more than a touch of the subtropical thrown in.

Roses arouse strong feelings. Many people identify in themselves an affinity for roses. Criticise the rose and you are criticising them. Like many other flowers, roses have their charm, but have been artificially elevated in status. It is time their faults (many of them of man's own making) should be recognised as well as their virtues. Our rose garden was designed by Lutyens and has remained more or less static for 80 years. Replant disease means roses can't be replaced on a piecemeal basis, which is my preferred method when a rose that has become weakly or one I no longer like is growing next to another that's strong and I do like – without also replacing a large volume of soil where it grew. This is extremely inconvenient and, anyway, the soil that has become tainted for roses is excellent for any other plant. With the help of my energetic friend and co-gardener, Fergus Garrett, a complete change has been made. The new garden already looks fully established and it enthrals us and many visitors, too. There are cannas, with their splendid leaves and flaunting, silken flowers; dahlias – why are dahlias unfashionable with the elite? (I could tell you) – for brilliant, clean colours; wonderful foliage plants, including a hardy banana; leaves of a stooled specimen of paulownia, three feet across; the Egyptian papyrus; castor oil plants, purple and green – I could run on.

With a great many plants we are experimenting, as no books can give us the answers. For instance, I planted out my streptocarpus, Cape violets, usually regarded in this country entirely as indoor pot plants. How would they, in a shady place, like to be treated as bedding plants instead? They've loved it.

And so it has gone on, the tender mixed with the hardy, but always with a sense of exoticism and lush flamboyance. It has been and continues to be exciting – and it isn't fashionable.

Christopher Lloyd

Glories of the Garden
May 30 1995

'Miss, this needs pruning,' observes Kelly, a year 10 pupil at Clapham Park school in Lambeth, as she runs her hands along the sleek leaves of a bamboo plant. 'I like this the best because it's long and sharp.' For Kelly, this is no everyday experience, and this is no ordinary garden. She is visually-impaired and the Clapham school's recently opened sensory garden has given her a new enthusiasm for life. 'She used to be quite introverted,' explains the headteacher, Barbara Raybould, 'but now with this interest it's really bringing her out of herself and giving her confidence. It has been very special for her.'

For all of the 35 blind and visually-impaired children aged between two and 16 at the Clapham school, the innovative courtyard garden is a thrilling, multi-sensory experience. Guided by textured pavements they are able to explore confidently among the shrubs and plants, such as myrtle, wormwood, curry plant and many herbs, all of which have been chosen for their strong scent. Each of the plants has a different texture, some rough, some smooth, others sticky, while the deep-red wallflowers and bright yellow lilies have been planted for their bold colours.

The seeds of the idea were sown when Bebb Burchell, former director of education in Lambeth, spotted a lavender bush in the grounds of the school during a visit. 'The children were really interested,' says the head, who then asked them what they would want from a sensory garden. 'They wanted sound, touch, smell – they also wanted water. They wanted something they could plant things in, which they could use for art and environmental studies.' They have got all this, and more. Underneath the Moroccan broom, which produces flowers that smell of pineapple, there are bricks embossed with braille letters. 'It's all part of the fun of learning to read braille,' says Barbara. The children can use them to spell out the names of the plants, which all have braille labels.

Toks and Zebiba, both year eight pupils with little sight, use the bricks to spell out 'water' which, as the children had requested, is one of the garden's main features. Along the length of one wall, a constant stream cascades down bamboo pipes and around big red wheels, producing a clink-clank sound as it falls. On the ground, spanning the length of the water wall, is a braille inscription taken from a book on dinosaurs, one of the children's favourites – an ingenious device to warn the children to stop. The inscription, Barbara reveals, also conceals a hidden message: 'If you can read this you can go to the office and get a pound.'

The first pound is yet to be claimed, but the treasures of the garden have enriched the lives of the pupils at the school in many other ways. 'We have a number of severely visually-impaired children with considerable learning difficulties, overlaid with behavourial problems,' says the head. 'They find it really calming to sit out here, putting their hands in the water, listening to the wind chimes, touching the plants. It's nice for time out if they are getting stressed in the classroom.'

The year two group has planted sunflowers as part of a project on growing, and the children enjoy painting in the garden. 'Art is a medium for self-expression and a leisure activity too,' says Eileen Clifford, the teacher in charge of art. 'You can explore and make decisions. Most of the children here have never done that.'

Clearly, the seven months of planning have been well worth the effort. The school was advised by the Royal National Institute for the Blind and the Royal London Society for the Blind, and the garden was designed by the consultant architect John Starling. 'It's all about being tactile,' says Starling, whose idea to carve the names of all the children in the garden walls was 'my grafitti on their behalf.' And it gives them a sense of ownership. Finance came from Lambeth Education Authority, and a £5,000 donation from James Burrough, Allied Domecq's Beefeater gin sales and marketing division which is based a few miles from Clapham Park, in Kennington. 'We decided to give our charity money locally, within the community,' says Audrey Coventry, James Burrough's personnel and services administrator. 'When the sensory garden came up, we thought it was good use for our charity money.'

For these inner-city children it is money well spent. Apart from the numerous learning benefits, the garden is an added bonus to those who live in flats without gardens. 'We only have a balcony,' says Kelly, who has made her own unique contribution. 'I brought in a scallop for the fish pond,' she proclaims. 'I gave him a brick with some algae on it and he changes colour – from orange to grey, and purple when he's hot. I looked that up in a book.'

Kelly's blossoming self-esteem – she now wants to go on to study horticulture at college – is just one example of the achievements of Clapham Park, which as far as possible aims to integrate the children into mainstream education. 'We try to equip them with self-confidence,' says Barbara. 'We have very strong links with our local primary school and colleges and try to ensure we're not in a closed community. We are looking outwards and giving the children the widest range of opportunities.' The sensory garden is proving to be a broadening and enriching experience to help with this aim. 'We plan to use it to the full – it's glorious.'

Julie Reid

Stranger Than Paradise
June 16 1995

Derek Jarman's Garden. Photographs by Howard Sooley
(Thames and Hudson, £14.95)

Gardens emit their own peculiar spirit, compounded of places and the creative energies we bring to them. Bleakness and light were the qualities that first drew Jarman to the blasted Kent coastline at Dungeness, under the shadow of the nuclear power station, the 'fifth quarter' at the edge of the globe where 'the wet shingle glistens like pearls of Vermeer light'. Hostile territory for paradise, you might think. But Jarman's garden started by accident, with the 'planting' of a dragon's-tooth flint in a rockery of bricks and concrete, followed by a dog rose staked with driftwood and a necklace of holey stones. Chance had anyway brought him to Prospect Cottage, on a bluebell hunt with Tilda Swinton and friends. He bought the fisherman's cottage for £750, after letters from Lord Sainsbury and Grey Gowrie had speeded up the purchase.

Through his careful construct of memory and daily life – valerian in the bomb-damaged house where he went with his first love, the airman Johnny; sea cadets singing shanties as they pass his door – Jarman's idea of the garden takes shape: a place of wonder and surprise, both Gethsemane and Eden, a shaggy and bewitching paradise full of magical stones and rusting metal, tufty mounds of santolina, purple sage, cistus and lavender slashed with hot poppy reds, where driftwood sculptures stand guard like aliens, and daffodils become surreal. Christopher Lloyd, Beth Chatto and Gertrude Jekyll give inspiration; his bêtes noires are equally predictable: Roxhill lawns, National Trust nurseries and Hidcote Manor, 'known to us as Hideouscote, which is so manicured that not one plant seems to touch its neighbour'. The oddest garden he ever saw was built by an old power worker amid the polluting oilfields of Baku, Azerbaijan: a hundred concrete animals, 'exquisite leaping deer, leopards and lions, as well as leafy bowers and a ziggurat with a spiral staircase.' Concentration is Jarman's greatest gift, an ability to focus on rainbeads in the sea kale and then to lift his eyes to the 'wonderment' of the nuclear power station, blazing away like a luxury liner, surrounded by 'a mysterious shadow that makes it possible for the stars still to glow in a clear summer sky.'

Howard Sooley rightly shares the credit with Jarman; text and image resonate to an unusual degree. Without descending into cliche, Sooley's photographs reveal the miniaturist beauty of even the most commonplace plants. He captures, too (often in black and white), the other-worldliness of the Dungeness coast and Jarman's junk-metal moonscape. Sooley himself crosses over into the narrative, Phostrogening the herbs; dressed in mauve, looking like a giraffe that has stared long and hard at a photograph of Virginia Woolf; hunting for secateurs on their trip to Monet's garden at Giverny, where Jarman is photographed, red artist's beret in hand, beneath the white wisteria of the water-lily bridge. 'He is one of the most distinguished Englishman that I have met,' writes Jarman of Sooley, 'and his portraits of me have changed the way I look.' Only rarely do the portraits strike a jarring note: Jarman in spangly kaftan seated like King Canute on the shingle; and later, collecting stones with American plumber's bag and winsome smile.

Jarman's impending Aids-related death adds an emotional intensity that is kept skilfully in check. Meditations on his garden, on garden tools and on the flora and fauna of Dungeness, give way to defiant poems commemorating the many dead friends of his 'frosted generation,' poems written on a cold grey day as the rain beats against the panes through which Sooley photographs the landscape.

Released temporarily from Bart's hospital, Jarman returns to Prospect Cottage for a last visit, driving down the lanes 'in the shimmering green of May.' The tasks he leaves to his friends look forward to the future while to us he bequeaths the honeyed scents of the Ness, of gorse and Crambe maritima, the resinous smell of sage after rain, the kick of the dog rose, and the faintest memory of native plants that have no scent at all.

Jennifer Potter

Save the Lazy Housewife
August 12 1995

Will you adopt a vegetable? I'm not kidding! If you go to the zoo you can adopt a tiger, a panda, or even a snail. So why not the red elephant, one of our carrots? The Henry Doubleday Research Association has 700 vegetable varieties that need adopting if they are not to disappear from cultivation. You probably won't be surprised to hear that European legislation is at the root of the problem. Vegetable seeds can't be legally traded unless they are first registered on a national or EU list. To do that costs several thousand pounds, because you have to pay for field trials. Then there's an annual registration fee running to hundreds of pounds. Only those varieties which are likely to sell in large quantities can possibly justify such costs; the more interesting and unusual types don't make it on to the list, or are forced off.

Ne Plus Ultra was top of the pops in the pea stakes in the 1860s. Like many peas of its generation it grew to more than 6ft and was one of the first hardy, wrinkled peas which ousted the older round-seeded types. What makes it especially good for gardeners is its fabulously sweet flavour and long cropping period – you sow it in late April and harvest from July to September. Alas, it is no more. It has been replaced by varieties bred specifically to satisfy the requirements of the frozen pea industry, which demands that peas be dwarf so that they can be picked by machine, and that they ripen all at once. Other tall peas that have met the same fate included Prince Albert dating to 1856, and Magnum Bonum, which grows to 8ft.

Then there's the crimson-flowered broad bean. All that we know about this variety is that we were given some seed by a Miss Cutbush of Kent, back in 1978. She was 73 at the time and said that it had been given to her many years before by her father. We can only guess at its age, but crimson-flowered broad beans were recorded as long ago as 1778. It is a striking plant, particularly alongside conventional black and white-flowered broad beans.

Another old variety which deserves a better fate is asparagus kale. This is listed in Vilmorin's *The Vegetable Garden*, published in 1885, and is reckoned to be one of the tastiest, and hardiest, of the kales. It's a kale that you can treat like broccoli: young leaves can be picked over the winter, and then the flower shoots broken out in the spring and simply blanched.

But it's not just old varieties that fall foul of the regulations. Ivory egg is a curious, drooping, plum-shaped tomato with a fine flavour and a pale golden-yellow skin. It's unusual in that, unlike red tomatoes, it contains no lycopeine and may, therefore, be acceptable to those people who are allergic to this fruit. We got our seed from America, where it is still grown, but it's unlikely that sales over here would be sufficient to justify the registration costs. HDRA has tried to get around this madness by setting up the Heritage Seed Library – a scheme whereby old-fashioned, tasty, and downright unusual vegetable varieties are given free to library members in return for an annual fee of £16.

This cannot be a long-term solution, and so we have persistently lobbied Brussels for a change in the law. Parliament recently passed a bill, largely framed by us, that would have solved the problem, but it was thrown out by the European Commission. In its place is proposed a directive which would allow for small quantities of seed to be sold without going through the full registration process, but unfortunately it treats 2kg of lettuce seed as identical to 2kg of seed potatoes. Does nobody behind a desk in Brussels know that one is probably enough to plant the whole of southern England, while the other would barely fill a couple of rows on an allotment? Unfortunately HDRA has been a victim of its own success. The Heritage Seed Library has proved so popular – it now has 4,500 members – that more polytunnels, refrigeration, packing and seed storage facilities are needed to cope with the demand. Hence the adopt-a-veg appeal. For £12.50 a year, you can adopt any of 700 varieties listed. In return you will receive a personal adoption certificate and have the satisfaction of knowing you have helped conserve threatened vegetables.

Anyone for Uncle Bert's purple kale, the Boothby Blond cucumber, or the Lazy Housewife climbing French bean?

Alan Gear

A Garden of Software for All Seasons
May 16 1996

In our household spring is the season of misses and melancholic fulminations. It's when we wander through our 1.5 acres brooding on why the shrub we planted with such care last autumn is now missing, why that modest ground cover seems to have eaten everything in its path (including a four-foot garden pump) and what possessed us to put that tree just there. I suspect we may have created a wholly new breed of shrub which has learned to stop putting down roots in the certain knowledge that it will be moved within the year – and the year after that, and the year after that. By the time it gets to its permanent site it will probably have grown wheels.

Enter the Garden Designer CD-Rom, offered by Global Software Publishing. Had it been available when we first set out we would both be about 15 years younger. It comes with the imprimatur of the television gardener Geoff Hamilton and allows you not only to prepare a layout of your garden on screen but to consult a mammoth plant encyclopedia as you do it. If you want something to start you off, there's a choice of pre-packaged layouts but the tools are also available to draw a precise plan of your own plot. The program lets you include schematic buildings, fences, furniture, paths and other objects. Paths can be shown with a wide variety of surfaces, and fencing can be anything from stone walls to log borders. Doodling around with the package suggests indeed that it can encompass just about anything from Chatsworth down.

But the real benefit emerges when you start the detailed planning. The tool bar allows you to place a new flowerbed in more or less any shape you want. Another click invokes an encyclopedia containing detailed references to 1,100 plant species, from Acer griseum to Zinnia elegans. From this you can start building your patch. The program lets you impose criteria with considerable precision. You want a moderately hardy, fragrant, border annual to grow in sandy soil? Set the filters and you get a list of three. So what's Euphorbia marginata when it's at home? Click on another button and it's instantly translated into Snow-on-the-Mountain, complete with a detailed colour picture of the flower, a silhouette outline of the whole plant, and a diagram of its seasons. Click on another icon and a full menu appears of the year's treatment: when to plant, thin, water and weed it. There's also a scratch pad for notes of the 'present from Auntie Lil' variety, just to make sure that the old dear is trolled past the appropriate bed on her annual state visit.

Probably the most useful option so far as we are concerned is the program's ability to run you through the seasons, giving you some notion of what will be on show in any given month. It sounds a bit gimmicky until you've sat for hours with about fifteen reference books trying to work out more or less what the beds will be like in, say, September. The sunflowers will just be starting to turn, for instance, but what on earth will the snapdragons be doing? At the top of your plan you can click on a small display panel which shows the state of all your plants month by month. If you highlight one in particular you can bring in a close up and trawl through its own annual cycle. That's worth £20 alone.

There are some odd omissions, particularly among the tree references, though I think I understand at least one of them. Nothing warns the unwary, for instance, that poplar roots have a habit of ranging over distances of 30 yards, which can provoke a spirited correspondence with your insurance company. Nor is there any mention of oaks. Or figs. We enjoy fresh figs and, having successfully left our potted tree in the garden over the winter, decided the time had come for its permanent home. Who could be expected to know it will only deign to fruit if housed in the equivalent of a small nuclear bunker? Excuse me while I lie on my other side for a while.

Harold Jackson

Bad Housekeeping: Cornish Patsy
November 16 1996

'Go to Trebah,' says James Campbell on hearing I'm off to Cornwall. Unfurl Ordnance Survey map of Cornwall. Names of villages sound like Staffordshire bull terriers quarrelling over a tennis ball. Harrowbarrow! Pencarrow! Locate also Trebah. A garden of note, apparently. Sounds like a Mississippi floosie. Resume journey in howling gale. November is so bracing. Drive to Trebah, to humour James Campbell. Gardeners so damned evangelical. Will give it five minutes and then find pub. Notice at entrance sign that it's a 25-acre sub-tropical ravine. Okay, will give it 10 minutes.

Enter, and am dumbstruck. Towering palms, primeval tree ferns, clouds of rhododendrons, a frothing lake of hydrangeas. Expect at any moment to meet a dinosaur, or perhaps Adam and Eve. Wander alone and enchanted through rainforest smell. Small river drops in series of cascades and pools down to private beach. Great leaves as big as dining tables. Mists, shafts of light, calls of birds – parrots, humming-birds – no, sorry, got a bit carried away there. But certainly buzzards and wrens. Sit on bench, contemplate this paradise and reel, dizzy with joy. Wonder if I could reproduce the effect in a windowbox. Want to stay here forever. Apparently, Trebah is open every day of the year. Wish I lived next door.

Dulcie Domum

The Last Refuge for Britain's Wildlife
July 18 1998

Jennifer Owen's garden looks much like other gardens in suburban Leicester. It's about 80 feet long and 40 feet wide, and features a small pond, a clipped lawn, a couple of ash trees, a row of runner beans, and a clothes line. It is home for Flower, the pet rabbit, and a guinea pig. But the garden beside the busy main road is airport, motorway, roundabout, home and motel for a lot of unexpected guests. Dr Owen, a retired botanist, has been keeping a meticulous wildlife record of the garden since she returned from Africa and moved to Leicester 28 years ago. In that time, she and her husband have identified and recorded 23 species of butterfly, 343 of moth, 93 kinds of hoverfly, 347 different beetles, 83 kinds of sawfly, 533 species of parasitic wasp, 53 of bee and 70 species of spider. Apart from the 1,851 insect species, 49 species of bird regularly sing their hearts out to the delight or dismay of 17 species of slug and dozens of invertebrates and amphibians. Foxes, squirrels, bats, woodmice, voles, newts, toads and frogs, too, all live in or visit the 24 sorts of grass, the 384 species of cultivated plants and weeds, the fungi and the trees. To the great surpise of scientists and the astonishment of amateur gardeners everywhere, something like 3,000 species, or 10 per cent of all Britain's known natural life, come to her quarter-acre patch.

Dr Owen's garden was cited in a parliamentary debate by Angela Eagle, junior environment minister, as an example of the richness of nature to be found in British suburban gardens. But Dr Owen, who lectured until two years ago at Leicester and De Montfort universities, does not think her garden is particularly special. 'The remarkable thing is that it is not remarkable,' she says. 'This is no jungle. It's an everyday family garden. The only difference between it and others is that it is more densely planted. There's no bare soil and there are lots of habitats for wildlife, but there must be many other gardens just as rich. The difference is that I have not tried to dominate it or interfere. Most people have an obsession with tidiness that ruins biodiversity.'

Her work is growing proof that suburban gardens might be the last refuge of British nature. There is more natural diversity in much of suburbia, she says, than in great swaths of the countryside, which for 50 years has been systematically denuded of life with pesticides and chemicals and the ploughing-up of hedgerows and habitats. 'Modern farming has depleted the countryside. It is so barren now.' Fifteen years ago, she estimated there were one million acres of suburban garden in Britain, a figure that is now far higher and set to rise dramatically if government plans to build 4.4 million homes in the next 25 years go ahead. Unnoticed and seldom celebrated, the British garden is now an important conservation and wildlife resource, she says. In a message that might dismay environmentalists battling on ecological grounds to stop green fields being built on, she says: 'Suburbia is becoming increasingly vital for nature. More and more gardeners do not use pesticides or chemicals. It's becoming like a great green belt. This garden is not an oasis. Much of its richness is dependent on other gardens and the insects and other life in it range across the whole.'

Her garden is one of the most studied in Britain, appearing in much scientific literature. It is also the subject of her own book that charted its ecology over 15 years. When she moved in, she says, it was 'a bit spartan and orthodox,' with roses and chrysanthemums. She and her husband, who died two years ago, cut out the weedkillers and did little more than encourage nature, providing habitats, different levels, and a rich mix of plants. Half the plants, she estimates, are now 'weeds' blown in on the wind. She spends less than £50 a year on seeds and plants. It also proves, she says, that the botanical purists who argue that native British plants are best for insect and other wildlife are wrong. Alien, introduced plants are proving excellent attractors, she says.

Today, the only evidence of Dr Owen's scientific work is a tent-like Malaise trap set deep in the undergrowth. Using no bait, it collects insects and pickles them in alcohol. She sorts them once a week and, if they are not immediately identifiable, sends them to specialists around the world. Every year new species turn up. Thirteen wasps that are new to Britain have been found and one is new to science. It is probably named after her, she says, but she does not know because the American specialist who identified it died recently.

Her records are not kept on computer but in 16 box files. They tell the remarkable tale of every visitor to the garden: in 1971, for example, Pargus haemorrhous meigen, a hoverfly, was recorded just once. The next year it jumped to 189. Last year there was only one observation. 'Yes, I am astonished how much there is here,' she says. 'It shows that, with the help of specialists, when you look closely at something, you will turn up all kinds of things. The more you look, the more you find.'

But does she use pesticides? 'I say I don't, but I have to say that I do get frustrated with slugs and snails so I admit there is some occasional, judicious use of slug pellets.'

Dr Owen hasn't a clue how the minister knew of her garden or why she picked on it, except that she and her husband once applied, tongue in cheek, to have it listed as a site of special scientific interest, the highest protection of the state. She never received a reply.

Dr Owen's tips to attract wildlife:

Plant your garden with as many flowers as you can to attract insects. Birds like berries and fruit.

Avoid bare soil and concrete. Plant everything. Don't worry about the weeds.

Give your garden as much physical variety as possible, with different heights and habitats for birds, insects and other life to live in. Ponds attract all kinds of wildlife.

Provide a mixture of open space and shade in your garden.

Prolong the flowering season of plants. Dead-head them.

Avoid chemicals and pesticides.

John Vidal

Got the Plot
September 25 1998

The Cable Street community gardens are a pocket handkerchief of green, encircled by a forest of Wapping council blocks and dwarfed by the great, blank tower of Hawksmoor's St George-in-the-East, which looms over its parish like a fortress. The garden, split up into 41 allotment plots and bisected by the Docklands Light Railway (which drums and hisses overhead, breaking the silence), is a confusion of vegetable beds, sheds built anyhow, enormous, swaying sunflowers, fences made with leavings from the railway, a bower constructed from half a rowing boat, shading a bench flanked by pots of pelargoniums.

'It's quiet – you're lost – though you're in central London, it's like being in the country,' says Iris Shaw, a retired school meals supervisor, who has tended her plot with her husband John for eight years. They grow 'all the veg, roses, glads – the only thing we don't grow is potatoes; we're not potato lovers.' Like the other plot holders, the Shaws don't have a garden, or much of one; Bill Wren, who's lived in Wapping for 27 years, honed his horticultural skills on friends' gardens before acquiring an allotment. 'I live in a concrete jungle – but as soon as I step through that gate I'm in the country,' he says.

Even for those not born and bred in the capital, the distinctly urban landscape around Cable Street melts into a bucolic idyll once they get weeding (true to their rustic origins, allotments remain conceptually closer to rural agriculture than urban horticulture). Sheila McQuaid, a housing adviser for Camden council, who grew up in Cornwall, says 'it's a lovely oasis of green, a place to go and have a picnic and not be hassled.' McQuaid has dug out a pond which is now 'full of frogs. And we saw a newt there the other day.' She grows organic vegetables which would be expensive to buy: chard, rocket and sprouting broccoli.

Over the way, Anwara Begum adapts skills from farming in Bangladesh – she grows a medley of British and subcontinental vegetables from plantain and rhubarb to coriander and radishes. 'It's a very small plot,' she says, 'not enough for me. My family is very large. I have four children and I am on income support. Growing vegetables helps me to save money.' Mary Laurencin cultivates her plot equally energetically; she is this year's Cable Street gardening champion ('I was so happy, really, when I won that prize'). Nearby is the plot of another gardening pro, John Stokes, now retired from his job with London Transport. He comes to the garden most days; he has transformed his plot from 'a forest' to a neat array of tomatoes, onions, runner beans, lettuce and beetroot. 'I was brought up on a farm in Ireland,' he says. 'I was glad to get away from it then, but now all the knowledge has come flooding back.' John is something of a

Cable Street elder statesman, always on hand to impart advice to fellow gardeners.

This mosaic of people represents the condition of today's allotments. There are those who get involved to save money, those who do it for leisure, or for stress relief, those who do it to avoid shop-bought produce sprayed with a cocktail of pesticides. The myth of the Arthur Fowler figure, the working-class, horny-handed son of toil who contemplates his potatoes safe from the gaze of the wife, is long dead.

Such a picture was a simplification, anyway. Although we think of allotments as being an urban phenomenon (Charles Tomlinson wrote of 'a paradise/where you may smell/the cinders/of quotidian hell beneath you'), they can be traced back to the beginning of the 19th century, when small plots of land were 'allotted' to the rural 'labouring poor' to compensate for the enclosure of common land. Allotments moved city-wards with the industrial revolution, and land owned by railways and pits was let to employees (in a strange twist, the coalfields communities campaign in 1995 won the right for allotment holders to retain their plots after British Coal was privatised, so that miners would have the right to dig up onions, if not coal). Both world wars saw allotment booms: at the height of the Dig for Victory campaign there were 1.5 million plots; in 1916 even the Queen Victoria Memorial flowerbeds outside Buckingham Palace were turned over to the cultivation of cabbages and potatoes.

Allotments have always, too, been deeply political, from the time of the wealthy Chartist sympathisers who donated land to struggling labourers in the 19th century to the allotment holders who formed a union in the 30s. They reflect our economic anxieties: their popularity is relative to our poverty. The boom years of the 50s and 60s were a slow time for allotments. A report commissioned by the Wilson government in 1969 advised that they should become 'leisure gardens' with asphalt paths, car parks and (shudder at the thought) planning permission required for sheds. But when the bubble burst in the early 70s allotments were once again in demand, with 40,000 on waiting lists by 1975. A Friends of the Earth campaign, in a drive for self-sufficiency, encouraged groups to take over and cultivate derelict land. The campaign – as a result of which the Cable Street gardens were founded – saw what the *Times* in 1976 referred to as an 'assortment of hippies, ecologists, squatters and community workers' investigating alternative lifestyles.

Now the debate has moved on again, and allotment holders anxiously watch a government which appears to hold contradictory positions on the matter. A Commons select committee report, published this summer, commended the health benefits to be gained from gardening allotments (there are thought now to be about 250,000, half as many as there were 20 years ago). On the other hand, John Prescott has done nothing to stop the selling off of council-owned plots; about 50 sites have been sold since May 1997. After all, it doesn't take much of a leap of imagination to redefine allotments as brownfield sites. And, as John Stokes says, 'I would go stark raving mad if my plot wasn't there. It's a godsend. And anyone at Cable Street will tell you the same thing.'

Call your local council for details of how to rent a local-authority allotment. A typical annual rent is £20. The National Society of Allotment and Leisure Gardeners (01536 266576) provides a legal service, a regular magazine and cheap seeds. The National Association of City Farms promotes community gardens. For details of local projects, or help with setting up your own community garden, call 0117-923 1800.

Charlotte Higgins

Down to Earth:
2000–2009

Rosemary Verey dies, 2001 * Eden Project opens, 2001 *
Christopher Lloyd dies, 2006 * 100-year-old Manor Gardens
Allotments bulldozed by Olympic Development Authority,
2007 * Kew celebrates its 250th anniversary, 2009

Art and Artifice, Illusion and Fantasy
May 24 2000

Here's how to spend a quarter of a million quid or so on a garden.
Call up Charles Funke Associates of Goldalming and ask for a
'garden of the night' as commissioned by his highness, the Shaikh
Zayed Bin Sultan Al-Nahyan for this year's Chelsea Flower Show.
Very nice it is too, with its canopy, scented flowers, marble and
lighting effects. Chelsea is also the place to be if you've only got
£25,000. For that you can buy a bronze of a bloke with a limp willy
and a sick-looking cat on his shoulders. It's also where you will find a
garden to represent (in the words of its designers) 'an allegorical
journey from beginning to a higher goal representing someone

embarking upon a new business venture with the scenes of mentoring and guiding, risk-taking innovation and energy.' Or a garden 'symbolising the chaotic activity of the heart following a cardiac arrest.' Pillars of rose quartz, instant labyrinth, rain forests, alpine pastures and even a zen-inspired, dot.com-sponsored garden 'with an English twist.' Such is Chelsea and the British garden industry today: art and artifice, illusion and fantasy combined with the terrific skill of the world's greatest horticulturists. Or the most preposterous show on earth brought to you by stylists, makeover artists, designers, horticultural snobs and corporations trying to flog instant tranquillity, fashion and effect to an ever-more pressed and grotesque society.

Chelsea this year is noticeably different. Gone is the famous old marquee, redolent of garden parties and flower shows up and down the country. In its place are two massive white sheds – or pavilions, as Sir Simon Hornby, president of the Royal Horticultural Society, likes to call them. The old marquee, he says, was 'discoloured and full of timber poles.'

'You could be anywhere now,' says Lucia, a designer and plantswoman surveying the site last week, and dodging the lorry-loads of ceramic waterfalls, woven hazel fences, Victorian lighting, obelisks, parasols, penstemons, petunias and 100,000 other blooms. 'It looks like a Channel tunnel terminal or factory outlet,' she says. 'The RHS used to be a great institution. Now it's all whizz kids and computers, spotty faces running the show who haven't a clue about plants. But if that's the way it's going – and some would say bloody good riddance to the past – then so be it.'

It is the way it's going. Gardening is now one of the fastest growing leisure industries in Britain, an essentially middle-class occupation serviced by up to 60,000 people. It is growing at a rate of 20 per cent a year and in 1999 the public is estimated to have spent almost £3bn on plants, a further £8bn on decking, irrigation systems, ponds, pesticides, conservatories and all the extras of modern gardening – as well as an astonishing £80m on garden gnomes and their upper-class equivalent, statuary. Three in four of us – a higher percentage than any other industrialised country – have a garden or some sort of outdoor space, even if only a window sill. Two out of three people, say the pollsters, garden as a hobby, making it the most popular British pastime. One in four women are said to enjoy gardening more than sex. More of us visit garden centres now than all the National Trust properties and theme parks combined.

Meanwhile, superstores such as B&Q and Homebase are getting in on the act, spotting a whole new profit line. Walmart, the huge US retail group which owns Asda, is expected to move in shortly. Television can't get enough of it and the celebrities, the politicians and the wannabes will all be at Chelsea this week. 'Gardening used to be full of mystique and mystery,' says Jennifer Adams, head of the Royal Parks and a leading horticulturist. In the old days, she says, gardeners used to look up plants in catalogues, order months in advance and exchange specimens. No more. What was once a close-knit world with little money to spend has turned into a consumer-led phenomenon and an industry that is increasingly hi-tech. It draws much more on high fashion, art and design than on the qualities of plants.

We may be buying more flowers than ever to beautify our homes or workspaces, but Britain, which has an international reputation for the most knowledgeable horticulturists in the world, is training ever fewer people with practical knowledge of plants. A combination of the end of the apprentice schemes run by local authorities and education policies which have denied grants to people wanting to study in horticultural centres of excellence, means that we are churning out each year many hundreds of garden designers and managers with academic qualifications but few of them prepared to get their hands dirty. Most degree courses need little or no practical experience. The problem is partly perception and fashion. Gardening is no longer on school curricula. Careers officers don't promote it and horticulture has been linked closely with agriculture which is seen to be in perpetual crisis.

'People are getting horticultural degrees without knowing the difference between hebes and sedges,' says Pete Weston, editor of

Horticulture Week. 'Nobody is going to college to learn how to propagate plants.'

The situation is so bad that companies are looking abroad for trained horticulturists – in Germany, Australia and Czechoslovakia, says John Richardson, chairman of Johnsons of Whixley, Britain's largest nursery stock growers. 'The international perception is that England is the origin of gardening,' he says, 'but I'm terrified for the future. We are losing the stock of people who really know about plants. People do not want dirty-handed jobs anymore. The quality and standard of people being trained has dropped badly.'

Brian Donohue, who is Labour MP for Cunninghame South, Ayrshire, and works with the parliamentary horticulture and gardening group, says consumers need more protection and the burgeoning industry must have higher standards as the giant 'sheds' move into the market. 'They have no staff with any expertise to warn people or advise them. A huge industry is growing up that needs codes of conduct.' Gardening now, says John Turner, a Hampshire plantsman at Chelsea this week, is 'all style and no substance. People are spending fortunes on their gardens but are being ripped off rotten. Fancy architectural designers who don't have a clue how plants grow are telling them one thing, the public doesn't know where to get decent advice and nobody seems to know how to plant and nobody wants to maintain a garden. People are thinking plants are just another product. The whole idea that you must tend and care for them is going. I personally blame that Charlie Dimmock and all the makeover programmes. There are going to be a lot of disappointed people.'

Paul Evans, a broadcaster and former head of a major National Trust garden, says: 'The instant makeover garden has greater prestige today than the natural processes behind gardening. Gardening is being appropriated by stylists and big business. But what happens when the dog craps on the gravel or rats move in under the decking? Gardening always expresses the power shifts and obsessions of society. Right now it's going through a celebrity, instant gratification, technological stage. It's all based on very shallow, fleeting needs. But it will change again.'

This year, it seems everyone must have water, reflections and an animal – giant wild boar sculptures are popular – to signify the well-heeled gardener's ultimate taming of nature. It is, of course, all artifice. Behind the facade of a lovingly recreated, early 20th-century brick outhouse (a snip at about £75,000), high technology is working hard. That waterfall tumbling down a rainforest shipped in from Miami is plastic, that twinkling rock pool is made of ceramics and can be installed in a day.

One garden stands out. By far the cheapest of the many exhibits on show (about £10,000), it is a recreation of a small Forest of Dean family coal mine. With its home-made winding gear, a rotting old hut, bits of brick wall and a shaft entrance, it is called Time the Healer. Aptly, it has been designed and installed by prisoners from HM open prison Leyhill in Gloucestershire, where gardening is now extraordinarily popular. It stands opposed to everything at Chelsea, an anti-garden full of dock leaves, cow parsley and wild flowers. Yet it is the most real and the closest to nature of all the Chelsea gardens. And whereas all the other exhibits and gardens will be sold off at the end of the week, possibly by internet auction, the Leyhill garden will not. 'There's nothing here that anyone wants really, is there?' says one of the prison staff yesterday. 'I mean, who wants a lot of weeds?'

John Vidal

Diary
August 2 2000

In the midst of all the hype about Viking helmeted barbarians in Blackpool, there is shocking news of further holiday mayhem. I suppose it was inevitable, but the latest group to reveal the thuggish underbelly to British society is – yes, you guessed it – gardening fans. Last Thursday at the Lost Gardens of Heligan, near St Austell in

Cornwall ('Not to be missed,' *Daily Telegraph*), some 500 plant watchers were inspecting the delightfully restored walled flower gardens when an enormous rain storm burst. Quickly, management opened the greenhouses and the tourists took shelter alongside a prized crop of several hundred delicious peaches ripening on the branch. You know the rest. Locusts, they were, these Heligan hooligans, and they stripped the branches clean. 'The trees were heaving with fruit all ready for picking,' says co-owner Candy Smit. 'It was the most amazing crop we've ever had – and it went in minutes. It's incredible how the most well-heeled customer can resort to taking things.' Indeed. How long now, I wonder, before outbreaks of lawlessness at *Gardeners' Question Time* imperil the life of Bob Flowerdew?

Matthew Norman

Books: the Chart
August 12 2000

This list of gardening books from WH Smith is dominated by two unstoppable forces utterly different in social character: the first is a variety of weighty reference tomes from the Royal Horticultural Society, the second is that hypnotic but cringe-making soap-opera of the herbaceous border, BBC1's *Ground Force*. Fronted by Alan Titchmarsh, backed up by Charlie Dimmock – or should that be the other way round? – it has afforded both opportunities to produce spin-off books of one kind or another (the beefy deck-builder Tommy Walsh adds another to the roster). The RHS volumes are heavy on detail – *nomina latina*, etc – and if they don't have the vertiginous cheerfulness of Charlie and Alan, they can always provide chapter and verse on elusive vegetation. Together with the Hessayon *Expert* books, these two streams of material make up large chunks of a massively profitable sector of publishing.

Country Diary: Northumberland
February 2 2001

With two graves to look after in our churchyard, I frequently enjoy wandering on God's acre. Too often churchyards are tidied and pruned and mown too frequently; burial grounds should not resemble gardens. Lichen grows on my parents' tombstones and I leave it. Of nearly 1,800 species of lichens in Britain, 300 of these are only found in churchyards, and some cemeteries boast yew trees which are centuries old. An overgrown churchyard is not disrespectful; the idea is to keep it tidy and enjoy the natives, the birds and wild creatures, the trees and wild flowers – should you have any left. Trees are of greatest value, particularly oak, ash, birch, holly, rowan, yew, field maple and wild cherry. A church yard is often the last refuge for cowslips and early purple orchids in the parish. Moles have to be discouraged, but even those can be tolerated within reason. Several churches I visited have introduced bird boxes to tempt avian residents. The parish church is the heart of a community, the true cathedral of locality – or it should be. Sadly, this year to date we have only two weddings booked in our lovely Norman church of St Mary Magdalene in Whalton and both of those are churchwardens' children. Our churches have been, for hundreds of years, our Christian stately homes. Too many are under-occupied, overtaxed, vulnerable to decay and a strain on their custodians. As part of our millennium celebrations in the year 2000, every household in our village was given a disposable camera to record images of what this small community means to them. Sections of these photos have now been used by a graphic artist to produce a stunning montage of Jesus Christ.

Veronica Heath

Millennium Domes: Gardens of Eden Open to Public
March 17 2001

After the wobbly bridge and the dome fiasco, a millennium success story. The Eden Project, three huge domes of horticultural diversity housed in a disused clay pit, opens today on time and to near universal approval. The £86m project, partly funded by the Millennium commission, was conceived by the horticulturalist and former TV executive Tim Smith. The greenhouse, in St Austell, Cornwall, will house 12,000 plant species from all five continents in three 'biomes' with artificial climates. The largest biome, 55 metres tall and 100 metres wide, reproduces the 65 per cent humidity and temperatures of the tropics and features plants from west Africa and south America. Philip McMillan Browse, horticultural director, said: 'This is not a garden. We are creating a museum and the plants are a series of exhibits.'

It is hoped that the project will boost Cornwall's economy with 750,000 visitors expected annually. Around 500,000 people have already been to watch the huge domes being built.

Paul Kelso

Land and Freedom
August 31 2002

Who hasn't dreamt of completely changing their lives – of handing in their notice at work, perhaps, and, as they clear their desk, telling that hideous colleague what they really think of them? But then reality kicks in (the bills, lack of courage ...) and suddenly everything is forgotten in the rush to get the morning train. Kate Nicoll is an exception. Four years ago, she was a radio producer at the BBC, when all she really wanted to be was a gardener. 'Not a day went past when I didn't want to be outside,' she says. So, at the age of 41, she decided to hang up her microphone and train for a life outdoors with the organisation that set up the Women's Land Army.

The Women's Farm and Garden Association is still going strong. It was established in 1899, by women, to encourage training and employment opportunities for women on the land. Its greatest claim to fame was setting up the land girls movement, celebrated in the 1998 film starring Anna Friel. More than 6,000 women were placed on farms to keep agriculture going between and during the wars. An original land girl, Lisa Webster, aged 82, has fond memories of the 1940s, getting up at 4.30am to milk a herd of Friesian cows (by hand), and continuing work until nightfall. 'I have never worked so hard in all my life, but I enjoyed it so much I stayed on for several years after the war ended,' she says. 'There was a great sense of camaraderie.'

The organisation now runs a gardening apprenticeship (WRAGS, or the Women Returners to Amenity Gardening Scheme) to help women trying to change their career, or return to work after having brought up a child. Through WRAGS, women work with and train other women. 'At 41 and with two young children, I couldn't join a full-time course,' says Nicoll, 'and I wanted practice, not theory, so this suited me perfectly.' Trainees work for the minimum wage and spend two days a week in a garden throughout the year, supervised by a head gardener or garden owner. Nicoll worked in a garden in Oxfordshire, owned by Helen Matthias, who, with her partner Gill Bath, runs a herbaceous perennial nursery and garden design business. Matthias is herself a product of the scheme, and Nicoll was her second trainee. 'The training particularly fostered my fascination with propagation,' says Matthias. 'When Gill and I found we couldn't get hold of varieties we wanted for our designs, we had the confidence and knowledge to raise them ourselves.'

Many employers seek out women gardeners. 'Men still so often go for control,' reasons Nicoll, 'great on mowing, clipping and organising. But women are increasingly appreciated for a more delicate touch.' Lisa Webster, a veteran land girl, agrees: 'Our farmer used to say that we women were more patient, sensitive and reliable than the men. Men too often used to try everything else then go back to the land as a last resort, but women have always taken it as a positive option.' Life wasn't always easy. 'My friend and I left our first placement, where we were always hungry and the farmer gave us near impossible jobs such as spreading dung by hand over a 30-acre field,' says Webster. Today, though, trainees on the scheme's 50 gardens are closely monitored. 'I once heard of a trainee cleaning a swimming pool. I had to ring the garden owner,' says Patricia McHugh, who runs WRAGS. Unlike war-time farms, where placements were allocated according to need, training gardens are chosen for the range of experiences they can provide.

With the WRAGS apprenticeship behind her, Nicoll is now a professional gardener. She has just finished working at the National Trust's Greys Court, and is now restoring the garden of a manor house in Oxfordshire. 'I've done an Elizabethan parterre based on a stained-glass window in the chapel of the house,' she enthuses. Beats office work any day.

Charlie Ryrie

Guarding Eden
November 6 2002

For more than 40 years, Betty Bishop, 83, has watched her garden in the south coast town of Shoreham-by-Sea and logged the natural events that mark the turning of the seasons. In autumn, she records the tinting of leaves, the first frost, and the arrival of the winter migrant birds. In spring, she notes down the date when her snowdrops first flower, and when the trees finally burst into leaf. 'Birds, insects, butterflies, trees changing, blossoms coming out – anything of interest, it all goes down in the diary,' she says.

Scientists have tended to regard diaries like Bishop's as natural history's equivalent of the trainspotter's notebook, but the climate change debate has brought phenology – the study of the relationship between environmental changes and seasonal events – centre stage. Natural records compiled by thousands of ordinary people are making a vital contribution to research on global warming.

Bishop is a volunteer for the UK Phenology Network, set up by the Woodland Trust to monitor the changing rhythms of nature's calendar. Launched in 1998, the network now has about 18,000 volunteers – from the Scilly Isles to the Shetlands – and their observations have already yielded a mass of data. After four years, the study has thrown up worrying evidence that the seasons are increasingly muddled, with many natural events thrown out of sequence by the warmer climate. Mild weather has caused spring to arrive early, while many autumn events are occurring days or even weeks later than usual. On average, oak trees are now losing their leaves a week later than they did 30 years ago, while migrant birds such as the swallow and the reed warbler have delayed their departure from the UK. Some, such as the chiffchaff, have remained here throughout the mild winters.

'The network is probably one of the soundest ways of demonstrating that change is already happening, because of the volume of data behind it,' says Tim Sparks, an environmental scientist with the Centre for Ecology and Hydrology (CEH), Cambridge.

Phenology has existed in the form of folk sayings for as long as humans have watched the weather and harvested crops, but its modern form dates back to the 18th century, when amateur naturalists started to observe the natural world systematically. In the Victorian era, it was seen as a natural extension of meteorology, and the Royal Meteorological Society ran a network of recorders until 1947. But, after the second world war, the programme was stopped. In 1998, the UK Phenology Network was revived by the Woodland Trust and the CEH, with the help of 70 volunteers. Since then, the number of participants has roughly doubled each year, and now the scheme is the largest of its kind in the world, says the project manager Jill Attenborough. 'It's captured people's imagination,' she says. 'We are seeing more and more unusual weather. People want to know why these things are happening – why are my roses blooming in November, or why am I seeing a butterfly in December?'

Some recorders are keen bird-watchers, but others simply keep an eye on the trees they pass while driving to work. Several housebound volunteers do what they can by recording through their windows. Government departments, including the Department of the Environment, Food and Rural Affairs, are using the Phenology Network's findings in their study of global warming, and scientists in Cambridge are using the data to study the impact that climate change has on the relationships between different species. The Woodland Trust hopes to see the project grow, especially in the Scottish uplands, northern England, Northern Ireland and Wales, where coverage is thin. Next year, the trust is launching a programme to involve more schoolchildren.

Martin Hodgson

Bogus Cull of Garden Gnomes
December 17 2003

Households in Derbyshire with gnomes in their gardens have been sent bogus letters from Amber Valley borough council, warning the ornaments are against planning rules and threatening prosecution.

Letter: It's All Rosy
May 6 2003

It is intriguing that the rose came top of the likes and second in the dislikes when gardeners were polled about garden flowers (Survey adds to the fame of the rose, May 1). The fact is that old roses are much more beautiful than modern hybrid teas and floribundas, and discerning gardeners appreciate this.

'English roses', bred from the old roses, have all their charm and fragrance. It is quite possible to develop these further, but we must not repeat the mistake we made with hybrid teas and floribundas and make sure that we preserve that particular charm which is the essence of a beautiful rose. Unfortunately, breeders of garden flowers have a way of destroying the thing they love.

It should be pointed out that the old roses are mainly French and to call them 'English roses' is inaccurate.

David Austin
Wolverhampton

Anti-Social Behaviour: Mr Leyland's Legacy
October 18 2003

The English have traditionally lived in their castles since time began, but it is only in modern times that they have surrounded them with that endless source of trouble, the leyland cypress hedge. One of the most potent of all apparently humble discoveries took place when Mr CJ Leyland happened on six hybrid seedlings in his grounds at Leighton Hall near Welshpool in 1888. His Alaskan cedars had accidentally crossbred with his Monterey cypresses, a most unusual event among conifers. Today they have 55 million offspring in Britain, almost as many as there are people. The effects were containable when ornamental gardening was confined to the relatively few, but in the age of garden centres and instant horticultural effects, the Leylandii hedge has got to bow to effective regulation.

There may be plenty of highly entertaining legal actions in the modern history of hedge battles, but there have also been murders. There are few things as venomous as a quarrel over neighbours' boundaries; and something which creates 'darkness at noon' is a certain trigger for disputes. The title of Arthur Koestler's book was deployed yesterday to describe the Leylandii effect by Stephen Pound, the Labour backbencher who has hewn mightily at this issue but had his private member's bill blocked in the Commons last year. The government has now honoured its promise to take on the issue itself. A new law will at last give local councils the power to intervene and act as honest brokers over hedge quarrels.

Fittingly, the measure is an amendment to the anti-social behaviour bill, reminding us that anti-social behaviour orders should not be seen as the exclusive preserve of the feckless young. There are more ways of making community life a misery than smashing bus shelters or scrawling graffiti, and the unintended consequence of Mr Leyland's gardening is one of them. As for unwanted Leylandii: they present a marvellous export opportunity. In the southern states of the US the plant is by far the most popular choice for Christmas tree.

A Tale of Two Duchesses
April 6 2004

If Alice returned today, she might well ask what was the point of duchesses. And for all the welcome removal of hereditary peers from the House of Lords, she would get a less dusty answer than might come from the Mad Hatter or the Red Queen. For a long time, the Duchess of Devonshire has flown as welcoming a flag as any democrat could wish for at Chatsworth, that marvel of gardening, architecture and landscape design on the edge of the Derbyshire Peak. Now, remarkably, she is being out-duchessed from 150 miles further north, as reported in yesterday's *Guardian*.

Thanks to the Duchess of Northumberland, who actually lives and works in the county whose name she carries, an extraordinary garden is appearing between the walls of Alnwick Castle and the park designed by Capability Brown. Last year, its first as a paying attraction, it unveiled even larger fountains than Joseph Paxton's at Chatsworth. The autumn saw work start on a 'village' of children's tree houses, costing over £3m. And now we learn that a poison garden, whose plants need Home Office licences as well as watering, will be open – safely at arm's length – by September. This attraction is appropriate for the duchess, whose grand idea has been sprinkled with mild venom by the meaner-minded part of the horticultural world. It is only human to feel a stab of envy about a project with an eventual budget of £42m. But the Alnwick Garden Trust, independent of the Northumberlands' one, has the last laugh. It is putting bums on lawns by the hundreds of thousands. Last year, the north-east's development agency says, its incomplete flowerbeds brought the region £13m. The ghoulish pleasure of watching strychnine plants come into bud will add to that. Not something, any more than the duchess's licensed cannabis fronds and cocaine shrubs, that you can admire in your local park. Cockney men raided the ducal vocabulary to describe their wives affectionately as 'my old dutch.' It would be right to return the term and confer it on the remarkable women in charge of Alnwick and Chatsworth.

Watch Out for Flowerpots
May 3 2004

Flowerpots cause 5,300 accidents a year, second only to lawnmowers (6,500) in the top 10 of the most dangerous garden equipment, the Royal Society for the Prevention of Accidents revealed.

How Does Your Garden Grow?
May 26 2004

As the Chelsea Flower Show blossoms this week with the brightest and barmiest of British horticulture, gardeners will drool over the sheer eroticism of exquisite plants, stunning designs and all the tempting tack that goes with modern garden technology. Despite its genius for spectacle and theatre, Chelsea – along with other flower shows – has also been moving slowly along the path to environmental awareness and social responsibility. But are gardeners really as green as their fingers?

Take the use of peat. For 15 years now, conservationists and leading horticulturists have been campaigning and advising gardeners not to use peat, to stem the tragic loss of peat bogs. The National Trust has banned peat from its own gardens, and the Royal Horticultural Society is encouraging rehab from the peat addiction. Yet, according to a report by World Wildlife Fund last year, 2,000 hectares of bog – an area 20 times the size of Monaco – is destroyed in Ireland each year, and 66 per cent of all imported peat in Britain is used by amateur gardeners. Some aspects of gardening are stubbornly conservative; painfully slow it may be, but change is coming.

As a backlash to the instant garden makeover, there is a trend towards 'proper' gardening, and taste in garden plants is becoming more sophisticated. With the fantastic choice on offer from nurseries and garden centres, we have a wider range of plants to choose from than ever before. However, choice and sophistication are not necessarily ethically driven. 'Proper' gardening does not distinguish between the value of plants that are decorative commodities, to be consumed and then discarded, and plants as living beings with ecological and cultural significance. In the dizzily rarefied atmosphere of shows such as Chelsea, aesthetics are paramount. Over the garden wall, where the inspired creations of gardeners stop and the turbulent dynamics of the real world begin, plants have a serious effect.

Take bluebells, for example. 'There is a clear problem,' explains Jane Smart, executive director of Plantlife, the wild plant charity. 'The hybridisation of the garden Spanish bluebell with our native wild bluebell is causing serious genetic pollution. In the spaces between the town and the woods, the hybrid is taking over. A similar thing is happening to our wild daffodils. Roadside and garden varieties are hybridising with the wild species. If we don't stop it, the true wild bluebells and daffodils could be wiped out in 10 years. We are in danger of getting rid of our heritage by accepting facsimiles.' Smart also sees gardens as a refuge for some wild flowers. 'Growing native primroses and cowslips in gardens increases the populations of these species. Cornflowers, only found in a handful of their original habitats, and corncockle, now officially extinct in Britain, can be sustained in gardens if the seed mix is genetically right.'

Gardens have a potential role in conserving plants threatened by global warming. Phil Gates, senior lecturer in botany at Durham University, believes that 'plants such as Scottish primrose and other wild alpine plants will be out-competed through climate change and will need horticultural skills to preserve them.' 'As in all things, there is a tendency to ignore the native,' says Matthew Wilson, curator of the RHS garden at Harlow Carr, Yorkshire. 'We don't get as excited about a field of meadow buttercup as we might, and this engenders complacency about our native flora.'

Celebrating its bicentenary this year at the Chelsea Flower Show, the RHS will be showing off its vast collection of plants, many of which are the legacy of plant collectors who scoured the world in search of beauty and benefit. Wilson points to an example where a globally endangered species is being saved by this tradition: 'The monkey puzzle tree, introduced from Chile to British parks and gardens by Archibald Menzies in 1795, and again by William Lobb in 1844, is so threatened in its native environment that seeds and plants are now being exported from Britain back to Chile.' For Wilson, the theatre of the Chelsea Flower Show is a way of getting people interested in wonderful plants and appreciating them in a less consumerist way, but he is also interested in the social impact of horticulture.

So, too, is Christian Aid. Aiming at the burgeoning trend in organic vegetables, herbs and allotment gardens, Christian Aid is creating a garden for the forthcoming Hampton Court Palace flower show that reveals the plight of people such as one woman from Senegal, whose market garden of onions and peanuts has fallen foul of trade tariffs, cheap European imports and World Trade Organisation policies. Claire Whitehouse, who is designing this 'Trading Places' garden, says: 'I want people to see a beautiful garden and to start thinking about the price of trade rules for growers in very poor countries. My role is to tell a story that is educational and entertaining without being "worthy". There will always be a place for the perfect, big-budget gardens at flower shows such as Chelsea, allowing people to see excellence in planting and design. They do, however, need to be seen for what they are – beautiful show pieces. Side by side with these, there should be gardens that discuss serious social and environmental themes, both within and outside the gardening world.'

All our garden plants originate from the wild. They all have an environmental and social value. They have the power to feed and heal us, physically and spiritually. So what will you plant this weekend, and why?

Paul Evans

The Battle for Little Sparta
August 8 2005

Ian Hamilton Finlay's Little Sparta, a unique artist's garden slung on the sinuous Pentland hills southwest of Edinburgh, has been described as the greatest Scottish work of art of any period, and one of the greatest contemporary pieces of art anywhere. Now the ownership of this unique artwork has legally passed from the artist, who will be 80 in October, to a charitable trust, effectively safeguarding it for the nation – assuming that sufficient funds can be raised to protect this most fragile and exposed of environments. The trustees of Little Sparta include Sir Nicholas Serota, the director of the Tate, Victoria Miro, a London dealer and long-time supporter of Finlay, and Richard Ingleby, whose gallery is showing one of three exhibitions devoted to Finlay at this year's inaugural Edinburgh art festival.

'The purpose is to safeguard the future of the gardens,' said Mr Ingleby. 'There is a realisation that Little Sparta is of national importance and it has effectively been given to the nation through the auspices of the Little Sparta Trust.'

Little Sparta is more than a garden: it is a complete artwork that uses the landscape, trees, plants, paths and pools as its materials; employing sculpture, inscriptions and poems to create something that combines intellectual rigour, philosophical profundity and imaginative allusiveness. It is infused with references to Finlay's preoccupations of classical myth and poetry, the French Revolution, and the second world war. It has its pastoralism – bucolic quotations from Virgil's Eclogues abound – but also a steely combativeness and revolutionary purity. The trust hopes to raise £1m for a maintenance fund and establish an endowment fund to safeguard Little Sparta's long-term future. Paul Nesbitt, director of exhibitions at Inverleith House, Edinburgh, which is displaying an exhibition of Finlay's work, said: 'It will be a wonderful 80th birthday present for Ian if he knows that steps towards fundraising have been made.'

Finlay – born to Scottish parents in the Bahamas who ran bootleg rum into prohibition America, and who still lives in the isolated farm cottage at Little Sparta – has long been an outsider in Scottish culture. That took actual and violent form in 1983 in the so-called first battle of Little Sparta, in which Finlay's supporters successfully prevented the removal of works from the garden's temple by the Strathclyde Regional Council in a dispute over rates. 'He probably hasn't ever received proper recognition here in Scotland,' said Mr Nesbitt. 'He is better recognised abroad, and he is an artist's artist, who has influenced generations of artists working today. He is not a household name – and he should be.'

As the inscriptions on rocks and pillars begin to weather and fade, or become overgrown with lichen or moss, Finlay and the Little Sparta trustees have to decide the extent to which the garden and its contents, which Finlay and his collaborators began to create in the 1960s, should be preserved and conserved. According to Mr Ingleby: 'Some of the works have been here for over 30 years and are beginning to fade away. Ian's view has been that each artwork has its natural life.' But, he said, Finlay and the trustees are currently discussing how they might gently intervene to prolong the life of the sculptures and other elements. 'The climate is extreme. It's so damp and cold; it's as bad as it gets for stone carving,' said Mr Ingleby. There are also issues of public access to settle. The garden can be reached only via a rocky, unmade lane, and there are no public facilities. On the other hand, until Finlay's death it remains the private home of a private individual – and even after that time, risks damage if overrun by visitors.

Charlotte Higgins

The Expert Gardener
December 17 2005

Does a garden die with its owner? It's a question that is often asked. Don't worry, I'm not thinking of dying, and it's not necessarily a gloomy question at all. A garden is bound to change when its creator is no longer there. If they are simply moving house, they may want to take plants with them, perhaps in the knowledge that their successor isn't in the least interested, anyway. Or maybe they want to make a new start. I, of course, wonder what is likely to happen at Dixter. I want it to continue to be dynamic, and most certainly not to be set in aspic, as can all too easily happen. I want it to be, 'That's the way he always liked to have it' – that sort of thing. Fergus Garrett, my head gardener and closest friend, wants the same dynamism. All being well, he will remain here, and there will be no fossilisation with him around. He is a brilliant teacher, for one thing, and people long for the opportunity to learn from him. He knows how to get the best out of people, which is where I sometimes fail. If he is to be interviewed, for example, he asks the interviewers about themselves and how they came to be interviewing in the first place. This breaks the ice and a relationship is established. When I was once interviewed at the same time, I terrified my interviewers by pointing out when they said something stupid or repeated a question.

Between the two of us, we're a pretty dynamic couple. Gardening should be a partnership, and we are both interested in how to keep ours dynamic. Sometimes we like things to stay as they are, while at others change seems to beckon. I don't much care for the question, 'What changes are you planning for this year?' because it pins me down, but changes there will be, you may be sure. Dynamism is in our bloodstream. We want this spirit to carry on, and have set up a trust to work with our management team to run the place. The people who are involved are well aware of what Dixter represents and what its aims should be. The trust is appealing for financial help to secure its future. Its members understand what it's all about, so the future is bright – insofar as we can look into it at all. We have always been optimists.

Christopher Lloyd

Christopher Lloyd Dies at 84
January 30 2006

Christopher Lloyd, who was one of Britain's greatest and most entertaining modern gardeners, has died from a stroke after a leg operation at the age of 84. He inherited a passion for plants from his mother, who was appropriately called Daisy Field and also bequeathed him a vigour and determination which she claimed to have inherited from Oliver Cromwell, a distant ancestor.

Lloyd was more of a cavalier than a roundhead, running a magnificent garden at Great Dixter in East Sussex, which his father expanded from a building whose earliest parts date from 1464 with the help of the architect Sir Edwin Lutyens. The resulting warren of a mansion, where overnight gardening friends sometimes got lost, was reflected in the complex and imaginative borders which Lloyd created, and regularly recreated, in the grounds.

One of six children, he learned to persist in getting his point across at a young age, if necessary by shouting, and thus prepared for the role which made him famous – as a writer and broadcaster about gardening. Never married, he cultivated a personality as characterful as his plants. The most fundamental of his many mottos was that gardening should be fun.

Always known as Christo, he began his journalism in 1963 on *Country Life*, whose 'girls with pearls' were part of the country set whose company his family had always shared. His 40-year career with the magazine was then supplemented by his column in the *Guardian*, where his often radical planting ideas won him new friends, his contribution on Saturday, published a day after his death, characteristically damning 'thuggish and stupid' leylandii cypresses. His great-nephew, also Christopher Lloyd, said: 'Over the past 50 years he built and developed Dixter into the country's premier plantsman's garden. He devoted his lifetime to creating one of the most experimental, exciting and constantly changing gardens of our time.'

Lloyd wrote 25 gardening books as well as miles of newspaper columns, and was awarded the OBE in 1998 for his services to horticulture. The award which gave him greatest satisfaction was the Victoria Medal of the Royal Horticultural Society, the highest formal honour a gardener in Britain can receive. The medal recognised not just his talents in gardening and writing, but the zeal he showed in passing on his knowledge to the young. He particularly like taking students round the 57 acres at Great Dixter, including frequent parties from Wye College in Kent, where he taught before taking up writing and the running of his estate full-time. More than 50,000 visitors toured the grounds annually, many encountering Lloyd pottering around in old clothes which regularly had him mistaken for one of the staff. He enjoyed this, and was generous with his time.

He was also a natural collaborator in his writing; some of his best books were co-authored with other gardeners. Lloyd was a celebrated host, even though guests were sometimes fazed by his habit of turning out all the lights, which made difficult navigation of the passages and corridors all but impossible. His cooking was celebrated and he enjoyed its results. After a heart bypass some years ago, he made few concessions to medical caution and continued to enjoy meals as generous and convivial as the way he ran his estate.

Martin Wainwright

Bone Dry and Beautiful
April 22 2006

It is probably as hard to change one's way of gardening as it is to change one's eating habits – both are a great source of pleasure, not to be denied. But even if you have no idea of your local rainfall figures, you cannot avoid the warnings. Sports people and holidaymakers revel in good weather – even weathermen speak of the 'threat' of rain – while we gardeners and farmers watch in vain for those threatening clouds to soak the baked soil with a good, steady rain. Preferably at night, of course.

For me, coping with a dry garden is no new phenomenon but a way of life. I began more than 60 years ago with a chalky boulder clay deposited by the Ice Age. Much of the country will have similar conditions – soil that slices neatly, like liver, with a spade when wet, or that sets like concrete in periods of drought, opening up cracks down which you can put your hand. My present garden, begun 46 years ago, consists largely of free-draining gravel and sand many feet deep. This, combined with the lowest rainfall in the country (an average 20 inches, falling equally in summer and winter), obliged me to consider carefully what plants, trees or shrubs would survive our reliable East Anglian summer droughts.

In 1991, I began an experiment on approximately three-quarters of an acre of rather tatty grass that had served as a car park for 25 years. In place of grass, I hoped to grow decorative plants adapted by nature to these difficult conditions. But before planting anything, it is vital – especially with water shortages in mind – to improve the texture of whatever type of soil you have. In large schemes such as mine, we used a tractor with a subsoiler on the back – a long, curved spike that drops down about 2ft, breaking up the compacted soil. In the average garden, a strong fork and spade are required. Whether you're replanting a border, making a good hole for a tree or shrub, or preparing for the vegetable season, try to dig two spits deep – that is, twice the depth of the spade. You will find yourself going through the hard pan that has resulted from digging to the same depth, or from years when little or no digging was done. Deep digging enables roots to go deeper into cooler soil.

But more is needed. In heavy, close-textured soil, we incorporate spadesful of the same gravel we lay down for paths (9mm) – it allows rain to enter more freely – together with any moisture-retentive material available. To improve the gravel soil, we use mushroom compost, well-rotted farmyard manure, or compost from local councils. And we make as much as we can ourselves, though there is never enough. Conserve any- and everything that will rot down; even newspapers and letters can be layered between kitchen waste and grass cuttings, which need some drier material to aerate the heap – use straw, if available, then cut down remains from herbaceous plants, even dry pea and bean haulms. Buckets of weeds, with some soil attached, help build up a healthy fermentation. Noxious weeds, such as bindweed or running grasses, should be burned.

Returning to the gravel garden: it was to be an experiment, to teach ourselves and with luck help other gardeners to see which plants could survive without hosepipe. Fifteen years on, it is furnished with a combination of drought-resistant trees, shrubs, plants and bulbs that ebb and flow with the seasons. It has not been irrigated during that time. Only when new plantings are made do we use the watering cans until the plants are established.

Now what else can we do to keep our gardens alive and attractive throughout a dry summer? To begin with, I fear, we should give up the idea of growing show-quality delphiniums, dahlias, cannas, even annual bedding – all need regular moisture. Concentrate on permanent plantings of drought-tolerant plants. Many are already familiar, such as small-leafed thymes, lavender and artemisias – they are protected from excessive evaporation by aromatic oils. Other plants, such as salvia, santolina, ballota and lamb's ears (Stachys byzantina) have leaves that are heavily felted in silky or woolly white hairs, which becomes denser as the drought bites, so the plants gradually appear even whiter. Whether planted singly or in groups, the contrast of shapes, textures and shades of green or silvery-grey makes a living pattern throughout the year. And in their season, they all produce flowers – white or pink carpets of thymes, crowds of yellow, button-like flowers on santolina, while helianthemums open fresh, silky-petalled flowers each day, in all shades from white, through pink to orange and red. A few dominant plants, verticals in particular, are needed among mound-forming plants to prevent the garden looking like a tray of buns. Verbascums are ideal. I especially value the tall candelabras of V. bombyciferum , while the smaller V. chaixii is good near the border edge. A few decorative grasses soften the scene, as they bend and bow in the slightest breeze. One of the earliest and longest-lasting is Stipa gigantea from Spain. From a neat base of narrow leaves spring many tall stems (2m) that carry a shower of oat-like flowerheads, looking as if made of beaten gold, acting as a standard lamp, illuminating the garden.

Dominant plants that I use to create shelter or a framework include cistus, ceanothus and the tree brooms Cytisus aetnensis and Genista hispanica. In spring and autumn, there is usually enough moisture in the soil to allow bulbs to flower and plump up for another year. In spring, my gravel garden is carpeted with seeding blue scillas and chionadoxas, scarlet Anemone fulgens contrasting with lime-green heads of euphorbia, followed by wild tulips, including Tulipa sprengeri , alliums and cammassias. Autumn favours the frosty-pink heads of nerines, colchicums and the autumn crocus.

Beth Chatto

This Blessed Plot
May 20 2006

May. The gardens are getting lush. Chelsea Flower Show is here again, and tickets are going for £50 on eBay. Supermarkets are offering three clematis plants for £10, and in a summer of hosepipe bans, sales of water butts have soared. Someone is planting red and white annuals in the shape of the English flag for the World Cup. What is this British obsession with gardens?

It certainly isn't a new bug, although it has now reached epidemic status. When the rows of red brick terraces spread out from the cities in the late 19th century, the great joy for clerks and counting-house men was to come home in the evening to a small plot, all their own. In *The Diary of a Nobody*, Mr Pooter summed up this delight, when he and his wife moved into The Laurels, Brickfield Terrace, Holloway, with 'a nice little back garden which runs down to the railway.' Soon Pooter had bought a book, planted annuals and 'discovered a beautiful spot for growing mustard and cress and radishes.' Then he waited, recording anxiously two days later: 'Mustard-and-cress and radishes not come up yet.'

Comic though this is, it contains elements that all gardeners know: the thrill of having a private place, imposing yourself on a small plot, the suspense of waiting, the dream of pleasure and produce, regardless of slugs and smog. This strand has echoed through English writing ever since Chaucer – a clerk himself – expressed the joy of rushing home from work to rest on a newly turfed bench in a small arbour and see the daisies spreading on the grass. Shakespeare knew that he spoke in terms that even the groundlings could understand in Richard II, when he translated politics into gardening, with courtiers like rampant weeds choking the good plants, and England itself a garden, encircled by the sea. Chaucer and Pooter shared the town dweller's pastoral dream, and gardens have special piquancy in an urban society today. Country people were more practical, but from the 17th century, cottagers as well as landed gentry took immense pride in their plants. In Goody Cantrey's garden in Northamptonshire on July 28 1658, a neighbour recorded double and single larkspurs, sweet Williams, three kinds of spiderwort, four colours of lupin, 'the great blue, the little blue, the yellow and the white,' purple and white scabious, marigold, London pride and hollyhocks. Among the herbs were fennel, for weak eyes, camomile for headaches, white lilies for 'bile' and feverfew, against the shaking fever.

But in other countries too workers flooded to the cities and villagers tilled rich soil. So what makes this garden addiction peculiarly British? Partly it is because we are lucky: the temperate island climate, with its varying seasons, allows most plants to grow, and adapting to the different terrain and conditions is part of the challenge. But British gardening also reflects an inveterate acquisitiveness: even Goody Cantrey's garden is a map of trade and colonisation, with spiderwort brought back from Virginia by the Tradescant family, and many earlier plants, such as the marigolds and lupins, reaching our shores from Africa and the Mediterranean.

The lure of the new plant, the chance to impress your friends, is intense. Even potatoes were once glamorous newcomers. But the key, I think, lies not in the soil or the plants themselves, but in politics. The ownership of land has been the nub of popular discontent in Britain since the Normans, when much of England and Wales – and large slices of Scotland and Ireland – was handed out piecemeal to henchmen. To own a piece of land gave you a stake in society. And if the garden could be cultivated in the current fashion, it gave you a stake in the culture too, proving you a person of status and taste.

A crucial turning point was the first half of the 18th century, and this was the time when the 'English garden' came into being. The Act of Union of 1707 created the British nation and the accession of George I in 1714 sealed the Protestant succession. Although the king was German, the leaders of taste were determined that the culture of the new nation would be distinctively 'British,' taking the best from the continent and the classical past but rejecting autocracy and formality, just as we had rejected absolute kingship. The ideal was 'politeness,' conversation, and easy interchange. In art, informal groups or 'conversation pieces,' often set in gardens, were preferred to grand court portraits. In gardening, designers turned their backs on Italianate fountains and grottoes and on the stiff French parterres, long vistas and avenues beloved of Stuart kings. 'Is there Any Thing more shocking than a stiff regular garden,' cried Batty Langley in 1720.

This was the era of the *Spectator*, which suggested that it was culture and benevolence, not breeding, that made a gentleman, and suggested too, in Addison's words, that 'a Man might make a pretty Landskip of his own Possessions.' A triple movement followed: first the softening of formality and opening of the garden to the country; then the pictorial, classical, allusive style, fusing the charm of the landscape paintings of Poussin and Claude Lorraine with our misty native contours; and finally the sweeping parkland of Capability Brown and his followers.

This was also the age that saw 'God save the King' and 'Rule Britannia' and the radical cry of 'Liberty and Property!' An Englishman's home was his castle, and 'liberty' meant owning the plot and forming it as he liked. A century later, Charles Dickens (who was very proud of his own garden and was vice-president of his local horticultural and floricultural society for many years) mocked this stance gently in *Great Expectations*, where the clerk Mr Wemmick shows Pip his Walworth home with its Gothic windows, drawbridge and gun. At the back 'so as not to impede the idea of fortifications,' there is a tiny garden, complete with bower, serpentine walk and minuscule ornamental lake, with 'an island in the middle that might have been our salad for supper.'

But in Britain, when folk like Wemmick start having ornamental lakes, it is time for men of taste to move on. Snobbery winds like bindweed through British gardening. In 1625, Francis Bacon, whose famous essay opens 'God first planted a garden: it is the greatest of human pleasures,' dismissed popular knot gardens and topiary with a sneer. 'They be but toys,' he wrote, 'you may see as good sights many times in tarts.' We find such sneers in every age. Yet the followers of fashion met with put-downs too, one of the best coming from Dr Johnson, when a Lincolnshire lady showed him a grotto she had been making: 'Would it not be a pretty cool habitation in summer, Mr Johnson?' she asked. 'I think it would, Madam,' replied he, 'for a toad.'

Popularity spells doom. When Sir Charles Isham brought some

fashionable *gnomen-figuren* from German to decorate his rockery at Lamport Hall in 1867, he thought them tremendously chic. A hundred years later gnomes were banned from Chelsea Flower Show, along with 'fairies or any similar creatures, actual or mythical for use as garden ornaments.' Similarly, as soon as hoi polloi copied the brilliant annuals that adorned the terraces of Victorian mansions, they were dropped in disdain by the rich. When hybrid roses and floribundas became the staple of suburban front gardens, there was a rush to find authentic 'old' roses to replace them. It takes courage to defy such trends. Only someone of the standing of the late Christopher Lloyd could be brave enough to dig up damask and bourbon roses and replace them with fiery, vulgar dahlias and cannas. Lloyd met with gasps, mutterings and dismay – but there was nothing wrong with colour, he declared stoutly. And now we all have 'hot' beds and are planting dahlias again.

Class and competition, the bones of British society, root quickly in the garden. There has always been a terrific amount of keeping up with the Joneses. And if we have to have the new, we may only pretend to knowledge, a pose caught by AP Herbert in *Punch* in 1932:

' "The anaemias are wonderful," I said.

'My companion gave me a doubtful glance, but said nothing. We walked on beside a herbaceous border. "And those arthritis," I said, pointing to a clutch of scarlet blooms. "Always so divine at this time of the year."

'Again the dubious glance, and again no utterance except an appreciative "um".'

Now, it seems, we are all gardeners. The sheer increase in numbers since the first garden centres opened in the 1970s has been dramatic, particularly after the arrival of container plants, which make it so much easier to grow things successfully. Garden centres have now outrun home improvement superstores in popularity: it's easier to get your shelves from Ikea than make them yourself, and anyway the garden can be an 'outside room' complete with lighting, heating and barbecue. But in one way, home improvement and gardens are now synonymous: estate agents reckon a good garden can add up to 10 per cent to the value of a house.

Garden visiting is also on the increase. Gardens top the National Trust's list of most-visited sites, while the Eden Project has drawn millions of people to Cornwall, encouraging an interest in bio-diversity that links gardening to our deep concern about ecology. At the other end of the scale, the National Garden Scheme has been opening private gardens for charity since 1927. This year their famous Yellow Book lists 3,500 gardens, county by county: castles and cottages, Japanese gravel, Victorian kitchen gardens, allotments and schoolyards. More than 500 will be open for the first time and I don't think the increase is due to the success of the large schemes like the Eden Project, but simply to the owners' excited realisation that everyone may enjoy a garden on which care has been lavished, however small, and that if others can do it, so can they. For a hundred years, gardening magazines have flourished, but now no weekend paper is complete without a garden page. On television, gardening programmes take up more and more space in the schedules, from history to makeovers, and presenters such as Alan Titchmarsh and Monty Don are household names. The best programmes are enabling, but the down side can be that a garden lovingly tended for years may suddenly feel shabby, or that viewers feel that instead of fostering small plants, growing slowly, year by year, they should rush out, buy huge shrubs and get it all done in an instant.

Chelsea is the perfect place to take the measure of our attitude to gardening, a blend of sentiment, horticultural passion and big business, where every kind of outside space is represented, from the wildlife habitat to shimmering steel and concrete water features. The constant exposure and talk of new plants, new designs and new products inevitably fuels that old British tendency to one-upmanship and snobbery, seen nowhere more strongly than in a big garden centre on a Saturday, where everyone peers suspiciously into each other's trolleys.

Yet although gardening is competitive it is also immensely sociable:

like football, it opens conversations everywhere. Friends swap seeds and cuttings, old allotment holders give advice and warnings to new hands, pensioners take coach tours to Wisley. Horticultural societies and shows, which began 200 years ago, still display prize marrows, giant leeks and perfect chrysanthemums. And the Royal Horticultural Society – born at a meeting in Hatchards bookshop, Piccadilly, in 1804 – still rules the clubs, while Chelsea is the queen of all shows. Rather disconcertingly, a recent article by the editor of the new *Oxford Companion to Gardens* revealed that foreign garden designers consider British gardening conservative, with no new styles emerging for a hundred years. Nonsense. Go to Chelsea and ask any gardener and they will say, with the certainty of fans for their home team, that British gardening reigns supreme.

Jenny Uglow

The Year in Gardens
December 30 2006

Some gardening years are identified with a particular colour – the year of purple, perhaps – others with a style: decking, say, or prairie planting. But this year was dominated by the climate, and in particular the drought. The long-standing hose pipe ban, experienced most extremely in the south, was at the forefront of horticultural discussion. And once we began to ponder its significance, climate change and its effect on gardening was bound to follow.

The implications are huge. The viability of gardening as we know it has been brought into question. Will we be able to continue with the same practices and plants we have come to know and love? How should we adapt?

The drought focused attention on conserving our most vital resource – water. Grey-water schemes, storage of rainwater in private reservoirs, and even sinking boreholes began entering the mainstream. There were record sales of water butts. Sales of hose pipes were down:

in the most of the country, by 25 per cent; in the south-east, by 76 per cent. Everyone became more water conscious. Well, almost everyone. At the Chelsea Flower Show, the RHS sank a borehole so that exhibitors could irrigate their stands and gardens, yet water still gushed and gurgled in more exhibits than ever. The marked exception to this conspicuous consumption was Cleve West's exciting garden designed with drought in mind, a tour de force of Mediterranean planting: think lavender, rosemary and santolina.

Especially in the drier counties of the south-east, planting habits have been changing. The Big Plant Nursery in West Sussex imported more and more olive trees to go with its big palms and bananas, huge old specimens 'salvaged' from Spain, Portugal and Italy. Instant Provence-on-Thames. For some retailers, plant sales verged on the dire. Last winter was long, Easter – prime time for business – was a wash-out, and the run-up to the Chelsea Flower Show in May was wet and cold. By the time many of us got round to seriously contemplating planting, we were put off by fears of the impending drought.

But is survival of a home counties maquis assured for those who plant the Mediterranean way? Not necessarily. This year, for a few days, the Atlantic conveyor that drives the Gulf Stream shut down. Warm sea water from the Caribbean that moderates our climate was halted by melting polar ice far in excess of 'normal.' With the Gulf Stream turned off like this, Britain could become a very different, much colder place. We are on the same latitude as Hudson Bay and Moscow. Could our once temperate islands become more like them, with short, intense summers and long, freezing winters? Could it be lichens rather than lavenders that dominate the gardening scene?

Luckily, gardeners can change their practices and plants. It's not so easy in the wild. Wild plants can't move, and can adapt only gradually to changes in climate. It is surely no coincidence that in 2006, Plantlife , the charity that works for the conservation of wild plants, intensified its 'Back from the Brink' campaign, which seeks to protect species most at risk. This year, more of us began to realise the importance of gardens as nature reserves. Sales of wildflower seed and bird food increased exponentially. Fewer of us used peat or chemicals. The gardening media had to beef up its organic credentials. BBC's *Gardeners' World* has long politely advocated organic gardening, but nowadays the organic debate is more commonplace. In supermarkets, sales of organic veg went up by 30 per cent despite price premiums, and more gardeners grew their own. Allotments became more popular than ever, but with a significant change in the demographic: young women were the major new applicants for a plot. Meanwhile, front gardens continued to disappear under concrete because there were too many cars and not enough parking spaces. It's worth noting that off-road parking can increase a property's value – provided at least 60 per cent of the rest of the street still has a garden out front. The back garden wasn't safe, either. In his haste to encourage housing development, John Prescott downgraded gardens to 'brownfield sites' with more relaxed planning regulations.

In 2006, then, the future of private gardens was thrown into question. This year was less about trends, more about what gardens are for. They have become more than just a private sanctuary for our personal indulgence. A lot of environmental and social issues have come in through the garden gate.

Carol Klein

Messy Gardens are a Bee's Best Friend
July 24 2007

A naturalist friend recently described my Somerset garden as unkempt – which I took to be a polite way of calling it messy. Fortunately this was meant as a compliment rather than an insult. For, as the latest research shows, messy gardens are undoubtedly better for wildlife. This year's National Bumblebee Nest Survey has revealed that leaving patches of your garden to run wild creates a rich habitat for nesting bumblebees and could help reverse the rapid decline in their population over the past 50 years.

Letting my own garden go to seed certainly seems to be working. In just over a year since we moved here we have recorded more than 65 species of bird and 17 different butterflies. Not to mention a whole host of mini-beasts, bugs and plants that I haven't even got round to identifying, let alone counting. And even though mine is a large rural garden, the same applies wherever you live; despite being hardly bigger than a pocket handkerchief, my previous garden in west London supported a wide range of creatures too. Size and location really don't matter – what's important is the level of messiness your garden can provide. By cutting the grass less often you will turn your neat, green lawn into the domestic equivalent of a hay meadow – good not just for bumblebees, but also for butterflies, whose caterpillars can feed on the weeds that grow there. A patch of brambles or stinging nettles in the corner of your garden will also act as a butterfly magnet; and in autumn blackberries are a vital food source for migrant birds about to head south to Africa, such as whitethroats and willow warblers. Log piles don't just lend your garden a rustic air, but also provide a safe place for slow worms; while your compost heap – or even just a pile of rotting grass cuttings – gives a home to the grass snake.

So if you feel like a break from gardening, take heart from the Wildlife Gardening Manifesto launched last week by Natural England. And of all its 'top tips,' I'm pretty keen on this one: 'Relax! Don't feel you have to be too tidy.'

Stephen Moss

The Exuberance of Tresco
April 5 2008

One unexpected thing you learn from the unique exotic garden at Tresco is that a straight path can never be too long and straight, nor an axial view too axial, for a garden's own good. And this feels especially true of a garden built on a steep slope. A winding path can be a charming thing, as can a gradual ascent; but a straight path, like a tough ski slope, showing off a gradient at its most severe, and flanked by something tall, creating a vista of the kind which so transfixed the artists who went to worship at Tivoli in the 18th and 19th centuries – that would be something to have achieved. If a garden has length, it should flaunt it. If it has height, it should revel in it.

This showing off of natural advantages – so unwelcome in a human – is in part an obligation laid upon the larger garden by the hopes and expectations of the visitors. It is true that discretion has its allure, and that a sequences of surprises can be very gratifying. Secrecy in the garden can be, well, cute. But a grand gesture – made, of course, in the right place – is inimitable. It is the way the garden inscribes its signature on the memory. Tresco is inimitable anyway, just as it is: a frost-free Scilly island where plants once only glimpsed in pots, behind lace curtains, or desiccated in hot offices, suddenly seem to explain themselves. This is what I was put on earth to do, they seem to say. To step off the Penzance helicopter is to remember that, oh yes, this is where the agapanthus will seed itself around as a kerbside incident. This is where the aeonium, with its great rosettes of succulent leaves, will colonise a wall, and not just a wall either – it will attach itself all the way up a tree-trunk.

And these walls, surprising traditional constructions of vertically arranged rocks, which look at first like illustrations of how not to build a wall, seen in Cornwall as turf-topped dividers of fields – these 'stone hedges' turn out to be ideal hosts for a bromeliad, a pineapple relative called fascicularia, whose leaves later in the year will turn red at the centre, where the blue flowers are formed. 'Baboon-arsed blue,' said my companion accurately.

There are succulents everywhere. The pesky mesembryanthemum that has rioted along the Cornish cliffs (as the triqetrous or three-cornered leek, *Allium triquetrum*, has infested the hedgerows) is here in plenty. The aloes, puyas and agaves, which elsewhere in Britain have to live in pots, and be taken indoors in winter, here have their moments of surprising grace, posing in the landscape like bodybuilders. There are African flowers in plenty. The osteospermums used Tresco as a bridgehead before launching their invasion of the gardens of Britain. The whole thing lives under great risk: a few days below zero (as happened in 1987) will knock all the garden plantings back to square one. The crucial trees providing the shelterbelt proved vulnerable, three years later, to a single hurricane. They had done sterling service for 130 years. Ninety per cent of them were knocked down at a stroke. 'Everything had grown together,' as Mike Nelhams, the garden's curator, put it, 'and everything fell together.' One is still conscious of some of these enormous casualties, just as in the great Cornish gardens (planted at roughly the same period in the 19th century) one is aware of the problems created when trees and hedges are left to their own devices, and a generation passes before any radical decisions are made. For decades, perhaps for a century, a kind of enchantment prevails.

A whole school of French painters in the 1730s were inspired by a garden of this kind, at Arcueil. It was the ruin of a 17th-century property belonging to the Prince de Guise, and, when you see dim alleyways and immensely tall hedges in French paintings and drawings, the chances are that they draw their inspiration from this particular garden, or, slightly earlier, the estate at Montmorency which Watteau frequented and adored: another case of benign neglect. One sees just a little of this at Tresco, ghostly, tall hedges that have almost lost their structure, but which seem to have been left because, though they will never again be neat, they are remarkable. One sees a similar effect at the Cornish garden of Tregrehan (the subject of a laudatory article by Roy Lancaster in the April issue of *Gardens Illustrated*), where a yew walk, planted in 1845, has practically lost its foliage but remains a living, venerable object – a sort of ancient monument in the green.

A garden is not a jungle, even though we like to use the word to indicate a wild tangle of neglect. In a jungle there is a continual process of growth and destruction: dead wood keeps falling from the canopy, and one is well advised, during any high wind in the rainforest, to make for open ground, to seek safety on the river bank. There is continual destruction and continual renewal.

The traumas of the great gardens and arboretums in the major storms of recent decades are rather more radical than what happens in the jungle as a matter of course, and they invite the visitor to consider this conundrum: would I prefer the landscape to offer a well-tended appearance, so that tree-surgeons are continually at work and there is nothing excessively old or dangerous or outgrown? Or would I prefer to go for the look of benign neglect, knowing that, years hence, catastrophe will eventually follow? Considered on this scale, the conundrum is not one which many people would actually have to face, but, writ small, it is the problem with which all owners of gardens are familiar: that tree, that plant, is far too large, but can I bear to get rid of it? How long will I have to wait before the replacement fills the gap?

Be radical, be merciless, says one voice. Leave well alone, show some respect, says another. The first voice is classical, and loves a landscape tended by man. The second voice is romantic – it is the call of the wilderness. The third voice is the voice of the hurricane that makes the decision for us.

James Fenton

Country Diary: Cornwall
April 9 2008

The 18th-century obelisk, 123 feet high, was erected in 'gratitude and affection to the memory of Sir Richard Lyttelton,' a benefactor to a one-time owner of Boconnoc. It protrudes above trees hiding the secluded house and park – the venue for the 111th spring flower show of the Cornwall garden society. Between verges sprinkled with primroses and violets, woodland drives lead through towering thickets of flowering laurel towards parkland – sheltered grazing for sheep and lambs, and a temporary car park. Competitive classes include hundreds of camellias – the pink, red, white, stripy, double, single, frilly, big and small blooms displayed in individual green vases lined up on black draped shelves and judged this year by visitors from New Zealand, in the county for a camellia convention.

Despite early mild weather gardeners have submitted late magnolias ranging from purple to pale yellow. There are collections of flowering shrub branches arranged in galvanised containers, with exotic lobster claw, dainty cream myrtle and bright blue ceanothus. Singles and triples of daffodil stems stand in moss-topped pots and large trusses of hybrid rhododendron are perfect and dewy. Crowds converge on marquees of specialist plant displays, food and floral arrangements. Alternately soothed and stirred by music from the Mount Charles band, people wander between stalls, admire scarecrows made by children, and deposit purchases in the plant creche, all backed by the afternoon sun glistening on the lake and lighting up leafing oaks in woods opposite. The next day wintry winds sweep across the spring landscape. Home, in the Tamar Valley, blossoming cherries, slopes of pheasant eye narcissi, swathes of primroses, uncurling ferns with early bluebells and wood anemones appear incongruous through flurries of swirling snow.

Virginia Spiers

Guerrilla Gardening
May 10 2008

To the list of nefarious urban activities that includes poster defacement and graffiti we must add a new pursuit – gardening. The idea is a simple one: to arrive at night with tools and plants to transform scrappy, forgotten corners of the inner city, from traffic islands burned out in the Camden fire to neglected lawns outside tower blocks. Written by the author of the book with the same title, this site brings news from 'the horticultural frontline' with 'before' and 'after' shots of their work and various run-ins with the authorities.

Attempting to plant some nasturtium (Tropaeolum majus for Latin readers) at a roundabout in Elephant & Castle can, it seems, land you in serious bother with the Metropolitan Police.

Johnny Dee

National Trust Tracks Down its Plants
May 13 2008

Experts and volunteers armed with satellite positioning systems and digital cameras yesterday began what is billed as Britain's biggest plant count.

Over the next three years the flora at 80 properties owned or managed by the National Trust, from manicured grand gardens to more functional vegetable plots, will be hunted out and recorded. A photograph will be taken of each plant or clump surveyed and its position marked using a global navigation satellite tracking system. Information from the survey will be entered into a database, and the results will be analysed and used to decide which plants are becoming rare and ought to be preserved and propagated.

Mike Calnan, head of parks and gardens at the trust, said: 'This is the biggest and most comprehensive plant survey undertaken in the UK. At the moment we have records for around 5 per cent of plants in National Trust gardens and this survey will take that figure to beyond 75 per cent in the next three years. Hundreds of staff and volunteers will help us catalogue the plants found in our gardens, something that we haven't had the resource to carry out before. We will be able to map out the thousands of rare species of plant in the care of the National Trust which have been bred by passionate plant collectors or gathered by plant hunters on expeditions during the last 400 years or so. We might even discover plants that we didn't know we had.'

Phase one of the project will see gardens in Devon and Cornwall, Wales, Yorkshire and the north-east surveyed. As well as professional gardeners, volunteers, students and members will be asked if they want to participate. The hunt began yesterday in blazing sun at Killerton, near Exeter, which is celebrated for its rhododendrons, magnolias and herbaceous borders. It is an appropriate place to begin as this year is the 200th anniversary of the laying out of the gardens by John Veitch. The Veitch family became a famous dynasty of nurserymen and landscape gardeners famed for their plant hunting expeditions, most notably to South America. In the coming months the trust will survey some of Europe's famous gardens, including Sissinghurst in Kent, the creation of Vita Sackville-West and her husband, Sir Harold Nicolson, and the 18th century Stourhead landscape garden in Wiltshire. Rare plants will be highlighted and, when possible, propagated at the trust's new plant centre at Knightshayes Court at Tiverton, Devon. Many of the trust's 20 working kitchen gardens will also be taking part in the survey, to help identify threatened varieties of vegetables, and which of them need to be preserved and propagated for wider use.

Franklyn Tancock, plants collection curator for the trust, said the idea was to target as many of the properties as possible. 'We have many gardens that I consider small treasures, such as The Courts in Wiltshire, a hidden gem. There are quite a few places like that, but they are as important to us as the famous ones.'

Steven Morris

The Garden of Cosmic Speculation
June 28 2008

The formal garden of the six senses is one of the highlights of Charles Jencks' Garden Of Cosmic Speculation. It is filled with sculptures and the paths are engraved with genetic code. Formerly the old kitchen garden, the traditional culinary herbs and rows of vegetables have been replaced with six plots. The garden for touch includes nettles and thistles. Each sense is represented by some scientific folly and Jencks has added the 'sixth sense' of intuition to the usual five.

The double helix of DNA is a common theme. The earth mound bordering the paisley-shaped lakes beyond the double-helix sculpture features two spiralling paths that don't meet until the summit. Aromatic plants from the Mediterranean are planted near the aluminium sculpture of a nose that represents the sense of smell. As landscaping concepts go, it doesn't get much grander – or eccentric – than this. The architectural writer and critic Charles Jencks created the Garden Of Cosmic Speculation with his late wife Maggie Keswick, a garden landscaper and an expert on Chinese gardens. The 30-acre site at Portrack House, near Dumfries, takes the creation of the universe and renders it in landscape form: black holes and the big bang to DNA and string theory, this garden attempts to express complex scientific theory without recourse to the physics lab. The innovative design uses twists and waves, optical illusions and sudden surprises. It is a stimulating, intellectual garden that's just to be interpreted and understood, yet simultaneously works as a feast for the eyes – it's a magical experience akin to visiting the 18th-century landscape at Stowe. Particularly striking are the black hole terrace, a twisted chequerboard of AstroTurf and aluminium that plays tricks on the eye, and the universe cascade, a zigzagging stairway sunk into a hillside that traces the history of the universe from its beginnings to the present day. 'There are obvious parallels between gardening and creating a cosmos,' Jencks once said. Just don't try this at home.

Andy Sturgeon

Growing Awareness
July 9 2008

The Royal Horticultural Society's Tatton Show in two weeks' time will be a glitzy affair, with the fashionable 'gardenistas' of Cheshire and Manchester out in force, admiring the plants and exchanging ideas about conservatories and lawnmowers. But anyone interested in the idea of gardens working to connect people with nature, to grow food and to develop self-sufficiency should head for the garden called Ladies Who Lunch.

It has been built by service users of Nacro, the crime reduction charity, in Manchester. 'The "ladies" are chickens, and it's a garden that combines supporting healthy eating with supporting people who literally have nothing,' says Louise Campbell, service user involvement worker for Nacro. 'Gardening is a great leveller, whoever you are, whatever scale you work on. It can bring people together, can be therapeutic, and can provide hope.'

Jacqui, a service user with Nacro in Manchester, says: 'Two years ago, I was homeless and addicted to drugs. I was persuaded to join in and it was amazing, seeing something grow from nothing, something so beautiful. It was such a buzz, everyone working together, and we won a silver medal. That was a turning point for me. I'd never experienced anything like it and it gave me the space to reflect. Today, I'm building bridges with my children and working with networks of other service users and getting qualified. I'm never going back to where I've been.'

Gardening has the power to transform lives and landscapes, but gardeners are nowhere near as green as they might like to think. A recent report, Plant for Life, produced for the Horticultural Trades Association (HTA), suggested that 65 per cent of gardeners polled were worried about climate change, and just under half worried about the use of garden chemicals, the loss of green-belt land, trees and hedgerows, and noise pollution. But it implied that nearly half of Britain's millions of gardeners were not bothered.

Depressingly for environmentalists, 69 per cent of those polled recognised the aesthetic importance of plants, but only nine per cent recognised their environmental benefits.

Nevertheless, gardens play a crucial role in the environment debate. They account for 15-25 per cent of the land area in Britain's towns and cities, and their importance in offsetting some of the effects of climate change – through plants absorbing CO_2, cooling urban micro-climates and supporting wildlife, and soils absorbing rainwater run-off and reducing flooding – is a message that is beginning to create trends in gardening.

But the big changes in gardening in recent years have more to do with a return to traditional values. Andrew Maxted, commercial director for HTA, says: 'Society has been through a substantial materialistic expansion in the last 10 to 15 years, but consumers now are more discriminating. In the same way that more people are looking to experience new cultures and taste real food when they go on holiday, rather than going on package holidays, this search for the authentic is feeding into lifestyles at home and transforming gardens. Having fresh fruit and vegetables, tasting the difference, and growing them yourself has financial benefits, but it's [also] authentic, and gardening for the table is producing a massive demand.'

Last year, the sales of fruit trees and plants went up by 43 per cent, seeds of edible plants were up 13 per cent, and herbs up 6 per cent, while the average spend by gardeners was £291 per household. There is also a massive rise in allotment gardening. 'The demand for allotments has risen logarithmically over the last few years,' says Bryn Pugh, legal adviser to the National Society of Allotment and Leisure Gardeners. 'The decline in allotment gardening between the 1950s and 1990s has reversed, and we now represent a third of a million allotment holders. The average size allotment is the 10 pole plot – 300 sq yards.'

But the traditional image of the granddad with his string bags of vegetables slung over his bike handlebars has been replaced by young professionals who want to grow vegetables free from chemicals.

So is this search for the authentic and self-sufficiency driven by economics and the credit crunch? Not according to Maxted. 'The current fashion is a reaction against conspicuous waste and towards recycling and back-to-nature,' he says. 'Economics is a factor, but I'm not convinced it's a major one. We are finding that consumers are polarised, between those families who are committed to debt such as mortgages and who feel the pressure, and traditional gardeners who are older and less cash-pressured.'

Perhaps this has something to do with gardening trends revisiting old traditions such as herb and kitchen gardens, old-fashioned fruit and vegetable varieties and antique seed swapping, cottage garden colours, and wildlife gardening. 'Wanting wildlife such as birds and butterflies, which we see less of now than in the past in our busy, urbanised lives, is a very important part of the garden experience,' Maxted says.

Ken Thompson, wildlife gardening author and senior lecturer in animal and plant sciences at Sheffield University, argues: 'In the great scheme of things, garden wildlife is not that important. Urban areas make up seven to eight per cent of the country, and only about a quarter of that is garden. It's a tiny fraction, and the impact of gardeners on wildlife is very small compared with that of farmers.

'The real importance of gardens is that they hold wildlife where people are. Although it's not realised, the potential for getting people interested in the wildlife where they live is enormous. Sadly, the huge majority of garden owners don't give a toss. They don't know about wildlife and don't care.'

So if gardeners don't need acres of wildflower meadow or wetland to be good for wildlife, they can with all conscience rekindle their love affair with their favourite garden plant, the rose. Michael Marriott, technical manager for the rose-breeder and grower David Austin Roses, says: 'It's about beauty and charm. What other plant can produce such flowers and fragrance for five to six months of the year?

'In parts of Australia suffering drought, there was a movement to grow drought-resistant succulents, but gardeners got fed up and wanted to indulge a bit, so went back to roses. Horticulture is expanding around the world, and in 20 years of designing rose gardens I have seen a huge increase in public, rather than private, gardens in Europe, the US and Japan. The flower show in Japan this year had 250,000 visitors in five days – compared with Chelsea, which has only 130,000.

'There are enormous levels of enthusiasm for gardening among people who don't even have gardens, who survive in apartments divorced from green and flowers, from connecting with something natural. This craving for association with plants and gardens is fundamentally human.'

Paul Evans

Garden Gnome Returns After Trip of a Lifetime
August 12 2008

A woman's stolen garden gnome has been returned to her doorstep seven months later – along with a photo album picturing him in the 12 countries he visited with his abductor. Eve Stuart-Kelso was stunned to see her gnome, Murphy, outside her Gloucester home, with a note in which he puts his world tour down to 'itchy feet'. The album shows Murphy abseiling down a mountain, swimming in the sea and riding a motorbike. Also with him were immigration stamps for all the countries he had been taken to visit. Murphy said in his letter that he attracted unwanted attention from custom officials.

AP

When I'm 84
August 13 2008

I met Garuth Chalfont at the UK Dementia Congress last year. He was coming off the lecturing podium, bubbling with joy and eagerness. He specialises in gardens, and particularly gardens for people with dementia. He is fanatical about them, in fact, and is brought close to tears by the contemplation of institutional gardens, with their 'Tesco parking lot shrubs,' and the ignorance of a care establishment that does not take gardens seriously. Chalfont was quite right, of course. When I was managing a specialist home for people with dementia and behavioural problems, I looked after a very difficult individual for a while, a beefy ex-farmer, big enough to hurt people badly when he was angry. And he was angry practically all the time. It took us longer than it ought to have done to work out how much he missed the outdoor life. We built in a circuit of the garden, showed him how to find it – and it worked wonders. Rain or shine, he was out there, and easier in his mind.

I was impressed by the Dutch attitude to gardens when I spent time over there looking at services for older people. They think of nature as integral to residential care and sheltered housing, and ensure that older people have access to them. I saw a terrific butterfly garden, for example, which drew people with dementia into it, fascinated and happy. I also very much liked the fact that residents kept chickens, and even sheep, enjoying caring for them, with occasional help. People who couldn't walk any more were also catered for with picture windows offering garden views, and water features, it seems, were de rigeur.

Chalfont works on a very similar basic set of assumptions about the healing effect of nature and its necessity to our spirit, but has taken the philosophy to a logical conclusion. The new slant he brings is to insist not just that gardens should be sensorily stimulating but also that they must be integral to the life of a home. What this means in practice is that he makes sure that living spaces open on to gardens, and that the gardens contain elements that engage people – he's keen on garden sheds for residents, for example, giving people a focus and a retreat. He builds in gates to open, and places where people sit, eat and drink. He puts together yards designed to draw people into activities, a simple-but-important familiar space where people can, for example, help hang up washing.

Chalfont also redesigns resident days with residents, staff and relatives, so that people often go out into the garden with a specific purpose, something that gives a focus to their day. Successful design, he says, stimulates people's interests and engages them with their surroundings. A garden is a failure if it isn't integral to people's lives.

And he hates that grim institutional vacancy – nothing to do all day, nowhere to go. He wants people to have a meaningful daily life, enabled by space, weather, pleasure and work. The theory works for carers at home, too. Hell, if we haven't got gardens, if we're living on the fourth floor, for example, we should be colonising allotments. Squat them if necessary.

Chalfont is hand-in-glove with those fierce conspirators for change, the Bradford Dementia Group, and is passionately involved in research and lobbying. He helps design new schemes and does consultancy work with homes and sheltered housing schemes, redesigning gardens and routines, bringing the garden into people's lives. He has even written a book, *Design for Nature in Dementia Care*, which sets out his principles very readably.

Christopher Manthorp

Cliff-Face Gardeners Spark Coastguard Alarm
September 29 2008

Two gardeners sparked a coastguard rescue operation after abseiling down a treacherous cliff face to plant flowers. The men had been working in the garden of a large house when the owner asked them to lower themselves over the edge and plant flowers and shrubs in an attempt to stabilise the crumbling cliff face. Despite their precarious position, neither gardener seemed worried by the work on a rocky outcrop in Branksome, Dorset, on Saturday. A coastguard spokesman said: 'We arrived and offered them some advice along the lines of 'don't do this' which I think they took.'

Matthew Taylor

Gems From the Jodhpur Court
December 5 2008

In the bleak midwinter, the British Museum yesterday announced a blaze of colour and perfume to come: an Indian garden blooming in paint on its exhibition walls, and in reality in a scented garden around a fountain and lotus pool which will be created in its rather grim Bloomsbury forecourt.

'In some magical way I can't quite get my head around, the garden will also cover a geographical spread from the foothills of the Himalayas to the lushness of the rainforest,' curator Richard Blurton promised. The task of creating the perfumed garden in the pigeon-haunted surroundings of the museum 's front doorstep, plagued by the eternal reek of frying onions from the burger stalls outside the gate, falls to the Royal Botanic Gardens at Kew, which will be celebrating its own 250th anniversary.

Maev Kennedy

Index

plantsmen 230–2
plant survey, National Trust 299–300
plant talk competition 173–4
poisons 129–31
political correctness 241–5
post-war house spring cleaning 67–9
Preston prison 202–3
prison gardens 78–9, 202–3
private gardens, opening of 84–5
publications, horticultural 14–16

rainfall 283–5, 291–2
resolutions 138–40, 148–50
Richmond Park 9–10
robberies, garden 20–1, 146–7
Rosenberg, Kristin 175
roses 83–4, 244–5, 272–3
Royal Horticultural Society gardens
  inauguration 19–20
Royal National Rose Society 175

Sackville-West, Vita 226–8, 231
Sanderson's Gardens 8–9
school gardens 40–3
seeds 64–6, 80–2
sensory gardens 245–7
settlements 200–2
shows 50–2, 121–3, 140–3, 218–22,
  275–8, 301–2
slugs 143–4
snobbery 140–3
software, garden design 252–3
Spitalfields 8–9
spring cleaning 67–9
stamps, postage 175
strange gardens 248–9
strangers in the garden 97–8
Strong, Sir Roy 228–30
students 163–7, 188
summer bedding 104–5
sundries 72–4, 156–9
Sydney Gardens, Bath 108–11

talking to plants 173–4
tap water for gardens 92
Tatton show 301–2

television programmes 240–1, 290,
  293
Thrower, Percy 174–5, 213–14, 240
tight trousers 151
town planning, parks and 47–9
trees 68–9, 152–4, 205–7
Tresco 294–7

UK Phenology Network 270–2
underground gardens 63

vegetable adoption 250–1
vegetable gardens 95–7, 171–3, 303
Victoria and Albert Museum Garden
  182–4
Victorian gardening 210–12
village school gardens 40–3
visually-impaired children 245–7

walled gardens 85, 86–7
war-time expenditure 55–6
water features 265
water for gardens 92
weather 283–5
weavers 8–9
wild flowers 194–7, 242, 292–3
wildlife gardens 254–7, 293–4, 304
Wisley 171
women
  gardeners 44–6
  horticulture for 28
  prison gardens 78–9
  vs. men as gardeners 185–8
Women Returners to Amenity
  Gardening Scheme (WRAGS)
  269–70
Women's Farm and Garden
  Association 268–70
Wood and Garden 30–2
working class gardens, Nottingham
  10–13

year in gardens 291–3